Shakespeare
Attacks Bigotry

Also by Elaine L. Robinson

Gulliver as Slave Trader: Racism Reviled by Jonathan Swift (McFarland, 2006)

Shakespeare Attacks Bigotry

A Close Reading of Six Plays

ELAINE L. ROBINSON

McFarland & Company, Inc., Publishers
Jefferson, North Carolina, and London

Library of Congress Cataloguing-in-Publication Data

Robinson, Elaine L., 1935–
Shakespeare attacks bigotry : a close reading of six plays / Elaine L. Robinson.
p. cm.
Includes bibliographical references and index.

ISBN 978-0-7864-4039-9
softcover : 50# alkaline paper ∞

1. Shakespeare, William, 1564–1616 — Criticism and interpretation. 2. Race in literature. 3. Toleration in literature. I. Title.
PR3069.R33R63 2009
822.3'3 — dc22 2009006682

British Library cataloguing data are available

Manufactured in the United States of America

McFarland & Company, Inc., Publishers
Box 611, Jefferson, North Carolina 28640
www.mcfarlandpub.com

To my children and grandchildren

Acknowledgment

To Ariel Kleinsmith, who volunteered the precious hours of her glorious youth to type my manuscript on her computer, not only with magnanimity, but with sweetness and eagerness. I am deeply grateful to her for making this publication possible.

Table of Contents

Preface

Speaking as a lifetime lover of Shakespeare, from a child growing up listening to her father recite Portia's mercy speech and Mark Antony's "Friends, Romans, Countrymen" speech by heart; to becoming a student; to acting in Shakespeare's plays in college and once professionally; to becoming a teacher and a scholar; and as a victim of the bigotry Shakespeare attacks; I am appalled at what is *not* taught, and at the misinformation that *is* taught about Shakespeare and the plays; and at the failure or negligence of scholars or critics to seriously consider Shakespeare's genius for satire and irony as reflected in his plays. This book seeks to call attention to such failure and/or negligence, to consider what is not taught and the misinformation that *is* taught. To that end, it seemed fundamentally crucial to project Shakespeare's "ultimate concern": "real Christianity" and Shakespeare's attacks on bigotry, which he treats as "heresies that come in like locusts, to devour the harvests of the Gospel."[1] Ironically, that to which this book calls attention validates and justifies Shakespeare's attack on bigotry.

There is irony in the fact that, although "Renaissance studies has only recently come to explore blackness,"[2] Shakespeare explored blackness some 400 years ago, *during* the Renaissance. That fact argues for the importance of my book. It's important because to really understand Shakespeare and the Renaissance is important; it's important because truth and justice are important; and protesting and eliminating bigotry are important, as, obviously, Shakespeare himself believed.

The realization that Shakespeare was protesting the African slave trade and racism in defense of "real Christianity" initially came to me by way of intuition while I was working on the manuscript for my book, *Gulliver as Slave Trader: Racism Reviled by Jonathan Swift.*

When I realized that Swift, in *Gulliver's Travels*, a masterpiece of satire and irony, was influenced by Shakespeare, and by the same saint who influenced Shakespeare, Bernard of Clairvaux, I was intensely driven to discover how and where. I figured if Swift used Shakespeare to support his protest of the African slave trade and racism, I wanted to understand the depths of that support. I was elated when, in the process of my research, I came across a work by Martin Orkin, a South African professor, titled: *Shakespeare Against Apartheid.* (The original title for my Gulliver book had been

Swift Against Apartheid.) My intuition was substantiated in at least five of Shakespeare's plays: *Titus Andronicus, The Merchant of Venice, Othello, King Lear,* and *The Tempest.*

For the most part, to prove my point, I was satisfied to let Shakespeare speak for me, finding few critics to support me but many racists, time-honored and recent, having studied both. The underlying basis of Shakespeare's attacks on bigotry and on the Renaissance is "real Christianity," Shakespeare's "ultimate concern," as I point out. I was drawn to this aspect of the connection between exegesis and bigotry by my long-held disbelief in the general consensus of opinion among scholars, critics, and teachers that Shakespeare was not religious. In my opinion, religion is pivotal in his attacks on bigotry and the Renaissance. What better argument against bigotry can there be than "real Christianity"? What better reason is there for attacking the Renaissance than that by it man was made the center of the universe, usurping the place of God? Aristotle provides another reason: his system of knowledge can be seen as the source of bigotry.

Harold Bloom, considered "the preeminent literary critic of our time,"[3] has said that if Shakespeare was religious he didn't let us know it. Bloom says "*Lear* is the least Christian of all Shakespeare's plays."[4] Most critics say it is the most Christian of all Shakespeare's plays. In his *New York Times* bestseller, *Shakespeare: The Invention of the Human*, Bloom says:

> No vision — neither Montaigne's skepticism nor Christian redemption — is appropriate to this surging on of superior vitality into copious suffering and meaningless death. You can deny the pragmatic nihilism of *King Lear* or of *Hamlet* if you are a firm enough theist, but you will be rather beside the point, for Shakespeare neither challenges nor endorses your hopes for a personal resurrection. Suffering achieves its full reality of representation in *King Lear,* hope receives none. Hope is named Cordelia, and she is hanged at Edmund's command; Edgar survives to battle wolves, and to endure a heroic hopelessness. And that, rather than ripeness, is all.[5]

This seems to bespeak Bloom's nihilism rather than Shakespeare's in either *King Lear* or *Hamlet.* The very fact that Cordelia is the Christ figure in the play, and symbolizes the Pieta, would seem Shakespeare's challenge to Bloom's point, and an endorsement of personal resurrection. The same can be said for *Hamlet,* given all of its allusions to Christ. Bloom tells us that "G. K. Chesterton, a wonderful literary critic, insisted that Shakespeare was a Catholic dramatist, and that *Hamlet* was more orthodox than skeptical." "Both assertions" seem to [Bloom] "quite unlikely."[6] But to me they seem quite likely, and would account for Shakespeare's copious allusions to Bernard.

On the subject of Bloom's statement that "Shakespeare neither challenges nor endorses your hopes for a personal resurrection," another scholar/critic,

Marjorie Garber, has this to say: "the play moves inexorably toward the contemplation of a Christian solution."[7] Placed in context, this conclusion becomes even more meaningful given what precedes it. In reference to *King Lear* she says:

> In 1606 Parliament passed "An Act to Restrain Abuses of Players"; it stipulated that "no person or persons ... in any stage play, interlude, show, maygame, or pageant" might "jestingly or profanely speak or use the holy name of God or Christ Jesus, or of the Holy Ghost or of the Trinity." Thus, swearing by the name of the Christian God on the stage was forbidden by law. Nonetheless, the play moves inexorably toward the contemplation of a Christian solution.[8]

Garber mentions also: "The play presents two different paradigms of biblical suffering, juxtaposed and paralleled...." In addition: "The latter part of *King Lear* places an increasingly heavy emphasis on this emblematic Christian theme in language. Cordelia is arguably the real "Christ figure" in the play, speaking of her "father's business" and making her final appearance in a gender-reversed Pieta, held in the arms of a grieving Lear."[9] Garber adds the following, but we part company at the very end:

> Yet as with all Shakespearean evocations of allegory, whether religious, mythological, or political, the Christian undertones and overtones in *Lear* work best when they are allowed to augment the dramatic action rather than displace it. The power of *King Lear* and its place in our cultural imaginary depend above all, at least for a modern audience, upon its depiction of a human story of love, suffering, and loss.[10]

But Shakespeare's meaning does not change with the weather, or with the times, or with fashion. His meaning is what it is; the Christian elements are integral and inseparable and function holistically with other elements so that the whole meaning cannot be understood without them, especially not when it comes to satire and irony. Without the Christian elements the satire and irony are ineffectual, losing their frame of reference. Take away the satire and irony and you take away the whole meaning. The power of *King Lear* depends upon much more than "a human story of love, suffering, and loss." And to eliminate or downplay the Christian elements is tantamount to bigotry.

Anyone, whether Christian or atheist, who studies Jesus Christ and Bernard of Clairvaux with an open mind should be able to see what Shakespeare is saying through them, and the validity of it. Anyone who has done this would know for certain that Shakespeare is no nihilist, nor any of his plays nihilistic. Anyone who does not want to study Jesus Christ and Bernard of Clairvaux with an open mind does not really want to understand Shakespeare, does not want to grasp his meaning. It stands to reason that the greatest influences on an author would have an effect on the author's work, especially when the author alludes to them in his work. Three of the greatest influences on Shakespeare have obviously been the Bible, Jesus Christ, and Bernard, just judging by his copious allusions to them.

This book does not offer religious interpretations of Shakespeare's major tragedies. It offers interpretations of the religiousness of these tragedies. It is not to be assigned to the separate category created for religious interpretations of literature, separate from mainstream criticism. Such an assignment would — in fact, such a creation does — smack of bigotry.

Introduction

There are alarming correspondences linking the dehumanizing Christian apologetics for the African slave trade; the Nazi Christian Holocaust of the Jews; and the Catholic Christian and the Christian Right antipathy toward gays. In all of these perversions, Shakespeare, himself gay and a real Christian, would have seen the AntiChrist, and the irony. But that black churches preach against gays and gay marriage would be too outrageous even for Shakespeare's genius for irony. Forgetting the Scripture, "Envy not the oppressor and choose none of his ways," the churches of former African slaves, who even when freed would have been criminalized and/or lynched for the "unnatural" act of marrying a white person, are now preaching against gay marriage as "unnatural." The black churches that protest the Hate Crimes Law, making gay-bashing a criminal offense, are just like the white people who protested the Anti-Lynching Law. The persecuted persecuting! The same can be said of the Jews who were intractably mired in the African slave trade at a time of the monstrous persecution of the Jews at the hands of the Christian English, who, "in their practical way, and their genius for large-scale undertakings, probably inflicted more suffering on the Negroes than any other nation."[1]

The alarming correspondences (and the Christian white supremacist capacity for hatred that links them), the irony, and Shakespeare's depiction of Aaron the Moor, the merchant of Venice, Othello the Moor, and Caliban speak directly to the playwright's dramatic revelations of the need for "real Christianity," his "ultimate concern."

"Ultimate concern" is borrowed from the distinguished theologian, Paul Tillich, who said, "Faith is the state of being ultimately concerned,"[2] and who uses the words of Jesus to Martha as symbolic. Jesus tells Martha that she is concerned about many things ("all of them finite, preliminary, transitory,"[3] but that Mary, who sits at the feet of Jesus, listening to his word, is concerned about one thing, the one needful thing: concern for the spiritual life, which "is infinite, ultimate, lasting."[4] Like Mary, Shakespeare "hath chosen that good part," the one thing that is needful. In other words, the spiritual claims ultimacy in Shakespeare — the effect of faith on behavior, on the goodness or wickedness of our lives. The kind of faith implicit in Shakespeare is preached by Jonathan Swift who was, in *Gulliver's Travels*, profoundly influenced by Shakespeare:

> Let no man think, that he can lead as good a moral life without faith as with it; for this reason, because he who hath no faith, cannot by the strength of his own reason or endeavours so easily resist temptations, as the other, who depends upon God's assistance in the overcoming of his frailties, and is sure to be rewarded for ever in Heaven for his victory over them.[5]

Humanists would not agree that man cannot lead as good a moral life without faith as with it, which is why Shakespeare attacks the humanism of his day, the philosophy that the moral philosophies of ancient Greece and Rome possessed the ability "to make man a fully realized human creature, elevated and distinct from the lower animals, and would be of value in teaching the modern Christian how to attain the perfections of life."[6] Renaissance humanism meant a revival of antiquity. "The classical myths were well known through readings of Ovid—a basic text in grammar school education...."[7] It may be said that this kind of learning provides role models for monsters, such as Lady Macbeth, through whom Shakespeare satirizes such a basic education. Shakespeare also satirized such humanistic ideas as "Man, not God, is the center of the universe" and "Man is the measure of all things."

As to the classical myths teaching the modern Christian how to attain the perfections of life, further proof from *Hamlet* of Shakespeare's satire of Renaissance humanism as a foundation for unnatural evil, compared to the goodness and holiness of Christ, can be found in the remarks of Marcellus in the opening scene of the play:

> Some say that ever 'gainst that season comes
> Wherein Our Saviour's birth is celebrated,
> The bird of dawning singeth all night long.
> And then, they say, no spirit dare stir abroad,
> The nights are wholesome, then no planets strike,
> No fairy takes nor witch hath power to charm,
> So hallowed and so gracious is the time [I, i, 158–164].

We are reminded of the irony in a similar scene in *Macbeth*, similar *only* because the gracious, Christ-like Duncan is present, standing before Macbeth's castle of hell and doom, in extremely high relief.

The irony deepens ominously when the first to greet Duncan is his contrary opposite, Lady Macbeth, intensifying Shakespeare's condemnation of humanism by holding forth as the combined personification of her role models from classical myth: "Here was the figure of Medusa, the Amazon, Omphale, Medea...."[8] Medusa had "the petrifying power to turn to stone anything that met its gaze. The Amazons were women warriors. The name means 'breastless' and it was said that they removed their right breasts in order to better handle the bow. Heracles was sold as a slave to Omphale, queen of Lydia. There he was set to women's work, while Omphale assumed his lion's skin and club. Medea was a witch, whose 'magic arts' helped Jason and the Argonauts recover the golden fleece. She falls in love with Jason, and when he deserts her for the daughter of Creon, the king of Corinth, she kills her own children by Jason to avenge herself on him, having found where he was most vulnerable."[9]

It's not at all difficult to see the combination of these role models in the character of Lady Macbeth. Implicit in this attack on humanism is the doctrine of Saint Bernard of Clairvaux, the foundation of Shakespeare's "ultimate concern." "Each of us holds forth in the style of the master he has learned from."[10] Perhaps the best example of Shakespeare's attack on classical myths is *Titus Andronicus*, in which Aaron the Moor is projected as symbolic of Bernard's doctrine. Aaron is Shakespeare's ironic tour de force in protest of the African slave trade. Aaron's depiction is unequivocal proof that Shakespeare "tweaked the conscience of his time,"[11] in the midst of the African slave trade.

Although I do not agree with Marjorie Garber that "Shakespeare is the defining figure of the English Renaissance,"[12] inasmuch as he condemns much of what defines the English Renaissance, nor do I agree with her that "there is no Shakespearean point of view,"[13] I do agree that *Titus Andronicus* "may serve as the root or radical form of all Shakespearean tragedy."[14] It demonstrates the closest causal relationship between classical myth and the capacity for unnatural evil in white people, of which Aaron is the epitome as symbolic of Shakespeare's protest of the African slave trade, also in *The Merchant of Venice*, *Othello*, *King Lear*, and *The Tempest*. In the years 1575 to 1591 (*Titus* was written in 1590), 52,000 slaves were shipped from Angola alone, with the shipments rising to an average of more than 5000 a year by the end of this period (*Black Cargoes*, 32). They continued to rise, and, by 1617, a year after Shakespeare's death, 28,000 slaves were being shipped annually from Angola to the Congo.[15] One who sees the goal of "playing" to be "to hold as 'twere the mirror up to Nature — to show Virtue her own feature, scorn her own image, and the very age and body of the time his form and pressure [imprint]," would certainly have reflected "the supplying, shipping and disposing of the vast number of human chattels which became a gigantic international operation..."[16] known as the African slave trade. "During the era of the High Renaissance in Europe, the pattern for the entire history of the Atlantic slave trade was set."[17]

Seminal in Shakespeare's background for tragedy and satire, then, was his education in the classical myths. Equally seminal was his background in religion.

> Without William Tyndale and Thomas Cranmer, without the great English translation of the New Testament and the sonorous, deeply resonant Book of Common prayer, it is difficult to imagine William Shakespeare.[18]

Shakespeare was a closet Catholic at a time of unbelievable persecutions of Catholics and Protestants. Tyndale, who translated the Bible into English, "was driven in the 1520s to the Continent, where eventually he was captured and garroted to death by Catholic authorities."[19] Cranmer, who encouraged the circulation of the Bible in English, "was burned at the stake at Oxford in 1556."[20] John Cottam, "whom Shakespeare certainly came to know, had strong Catholic connections."[21] His younger brother, Thomas, had gone abroad after graduating from Oxford, and taken orders as a Catholic priest. In 1580 he secretly returned to England. He was arrested as soon as he disembarked at Dover and was tortured with the horrific "scavenger's daughter" by officials in the Tower. The scavenger's daughter was a device that compressed the body to bend it almost in two. Cottam, arraigned as a traitor, was executed on May 30, 1582. He was dragged through London's muddy streets past jeering crowds, hanged, cut down while still alive, and castrated. "His stomach was then slit open and his intestines pulled out to be burned before his dying eyes, whereupon he was beheaded and his body cut in quarters, the pieces displayed as a warning."[22]

A Protestant named Henry Walpole was present at the execution of Catholic scholar Edmund Campion. As Campion's body was being quartered and the pieces were being thrown into a vat of boiling water, "a drop of the water mixed with blood splashed out upon his clothes, and Walpole felt at once, he said, that he had to convert to Catholicism. He left for the Continent, became a Jesuit, and was sent back to England, where he too was arrested and executed as a traitor."[23]

It is significant that Shakespeare was a closet Catholic, in that his ultimate concern is based primarily on the teachings of Saint Bernard of Clairvaux, in opposition to the orthodox Saint Thomas Aquinas who restructured Christianity according to Aristotle's system of knowledge. (Shakespeare also did not follow Aristotle's rules for tragedy.) We can see the influence of Bernard, and Shakespeare's use of Bernard ironically, in the midst of the most grotesquely irreligious of tragedies, *Titus Andronicus*. It is interesting to note Stephen Greenblatt's observations comparing this play with real life. "Whether or not Shakespeare went out of his way to witness the gory rituals of law and order ... they figure repeatedly in his plays."[24]

Actors of this time would have easily depicted Lavinia's fate realistically in *Titus Andronicus*— hands cut off, tongue cut out — because they would have seen it in real life. Audiences as well were exposed to these horrors, and could compare the display of the severed heads of Richard III or Macbeth with the real thing.

This justifies the point of Shakespeare's satire of classical myths, as they have been the basic education of both his actors and his audiences, thus causal in their loss of human sensibilities. So it is absurd to think that such an education would make man a fully realized human creature, let alone teach a Christian how to attain the perfections of life. Shakespeare demonstrates this absurdity by cause and effect. There is, in *Titus*, a precedence in classical myths for every horror performed, except for the egregious racism to which Aaron and his newborn baby are subjected. Of course, if we trace the origins of Aaron to the Old Testament, "Aaron," which means "enlightened," was the first high priest of the Jews. "A Mohammedan mosque marks the supposed grave of Aaron, on one of the tops of Mount Hor...."[25] Moreover, Aaron the Moor's plans for his son identify the child with the Biblical Ishmael, the son of Abraham and his African slave, Hagar. "In general, the name Ishmael, which means, 'whom God hears,' refers to any outcast from society because of the prophecy: 'And he will be a wild man; his hand will be against every man, and every man's hand against him.'" (Gen. 16:12). Ishmael was cast out of Abraham's household. "Ishmael is the spiritual father of the Mohammedans."[26] What Aaron the Moor says to his son is suggestive of Ishmael:

> I'll make you feed on berries and on roots,
> And fat on curds and whey, and suck the goat,
> And cabin in a cave, and bring you up
> To be a warrior and command a camp [IV, ii, 76–79].

Aaron is considered "irreligious," presumably because, Garber notes, he's non–Christian (86). The Biblical Aaron made a golden calf for the Israelites to worship (Exo, 32:4), which Shakespeare might be alluding to when he has Aaron "bury so much gold under a tree ... to coin a stratagem" (II, iii, 2, 5).

The subject of religion is aired with an urgency when Aaron makes an insistent emotional appeal to save the life of his son. When Lucius gives the order to hang the child, a newborn baby, Aaron cries: "Lucius, save the child.... If thou do this, I'll show thee wondrous things/That highly may advantage thee to hear...." The exchange continues:

> LUCIUS: Say on, and if it please me which thou speak'st
> Thy child shall live, and I will see it nourished.
> AARON: And if it please thee? Why, assure thee, Lucius,
> 'Twill vex thy soul to hear what I shall speak;
> * * *
> And this shall all be buried in my death
> Unless thou swear to me my child shall live.
> LUCIUS: Tell on thy mind. I say the child shall live.
> AARON: Swear that he shall, and then I will begin.
> LUCIUS: Who should I swear by? Thou believest no god.
> That granted, how canst thou believe in oath?
> AARON: What if I do not?—as indeed I do not—
> Yet for I know thou are religious
> And hast a thing within thee called conscience,

With twenty popish tricks and ceremonies
Which I have seen thee careful to observe,
Therefore I urge thy oath; for that I know
An idiot holds his bauble for a god,
And keeps the oath which by that god he swears,
To that I'll urge him, therefore thou shall vow
By that same god, what god soe'er it be,
That thou adorest and hast in reverence,
To save my boy, to nurse and bring him up,
Or else I will discover naught to thee.
LUCIUS: Even by my god I swear to thee I will [V, i, 53–86].

One wonders why the god Lucius speaks of is not spelled with a capital "G," and would have allowed him to hang a newborn baby. Aaron thus becomes the only parent in the play who does not either kill his own child or order it killed.

As previously mentioned, "Ovid was a basic text in grammar school education."[27] We are reminded of this historical and cultural fact when the young Lucius carries a book of which Titus asks the title. "Grandsire, 'tis Ovid's *Metamorphoses*, / My mother gave it to me," young Lucius answers (IV, I, 42–43). It's Lavinia's knowledge of the book that is significant, for she runs after young Lucius, who drops the book, enabling her to find in its tragic tale of Philomel the means of revealing her own tragedy and its perpetrators.

Relative to his ultimate concern, with the profusion of allusions to classical myths, Shakespeare proves Bernard's statement, that "Each of us hold forth in the style of the master he has learned from."[28] The truth of this is most vividly and ironically dramatized in Aaron, who holds forth in the style of the slave masters he has learned from, except when it comes to his son. If we compare the way the white characters hold forth, with the classical masters they have learned from, we will find they exceed the cruelty of their mythical role models and that the worst cruelty is in the African slave trade and racism/white supremacy of which Aaron bears the brunt. He is the hate that hate produced. Not only is he victimized by the unnatural evil his slave masters learned from classical myths, but also from their attempts to increase and improve upon those evils. For example, not only was Lavinia's tongue cut out, like Philomel, but, unlike Philomel, her hands were also cut off, so she couldn't, like Philomel, reveal her ravagers. So, with Aaron blamed for everything, we are tempted to ask, "Since when did the slave tell his master what to do?" Or, as Lavinia, hopelessly begging for mercy from the mother of her ravagers, puts it: "[Since] when did the tiger's young ones teach the dam?" (II, iii, 142). We can make the case, then, that, in this play about sons, Aaron ironically stands out as the most naturally human and humane, as Shakespeare's telling attack on the outrageously bigoted myth of white superiority/black inferiority.

Titus Andronicus

The whole revenge cycle starts and ends about "sons," with Titus, to begin with, failing to measure up to the humaneness demonstrated in the classical myth he alludes to. In the midst of Shakespeare's condemnation of the glorification of war, especially as glorified by the number of sons killed, Titus compares himself to King Priam. We are reminded of the pathetic figure of Priam lamenting the death of many sons killed in the Trojan War. Achilles killed Hector, Priam's favorite son, and treated Hector's body with "gross outrage." Priam "nerves himself to the perilous undertaking of entering the Greek camp alone to beg from Achilles the dead body of Hector, and save it from the threatened fate of being thrown to the dogs. Achilles' passion has now spent itself: he feels pity for the old man, and returns the body to Priam."[1]

Titus knows well from his own experience and from Priam's experience, what it's like to lose a son, but this knowledge does not teach him empathy for a mother begging him not to kill her son and subject his body to "gross outrage." The revenge cycle starts with Titus's demonstrative ignorance of the Second Step of Truth, following the command given by his son, Lucius: "Give us the proudest prisoner of the Goths,"

> That we may hew his limbs and on a pile
> "Ad manes fratrum" sacrifice his flesh
> Before this earthly prison of their bones,
> That so the shadows be not unappeased,
> Nor we disturbed with prodigies on earth [I, i, 96–101].

Titus answers:

> I give him you, the noblest that survives,
> The eldest son of this distressed Queen.

The mother begs Titus on her knees:

> Stay, Roman brethren! Gracious conqueror,
> Victorious Titus, rue the tears I shed —
> A mother's tears in passion for her son —
> And if thy sons were ever dear to thee,
> O, think of my son to be as dear to me!
> Sufficeth not that we are brought to Rome
> To beautify thy triumphs, and return
> Captive to thee and to thy Roman yoke;

> But must my sons be slaughtered in the streets
> For valiant doings in their country's cause?
> O, if to fight for king and commonweal
> Were piety in thine, it is in these.
> Andronicus, stain not thy tomb with blood.
> Wilt thou draw near the nature of the gods?
> Draw near them then in being merciful.
> Sweet mercy is nobility's true badge.
> Thrice-noble Titus, spare my first-born son [I, i, 104–120].

One would be hard put to come up with a more reasonable, legitimate, moving, sincere, and profoundly valid argument covering all bases in full knowledge of Bernard's Second Step of Truth, in which ["sweet"] mercy is the key element. "Blessed are the merciful, for they shall obtain mercy." "And this is the second step of truth, when they seek it in their neighbors, when they know from their own miseries how to commiserate with others who are miserable."[2] This prefigures the end: Titus is not merciful now in saving this mother's son, and he will not obtain mercy when he begs the powers that be to spare his two sons. The second step of truth is the very basis of Tamora's argument, in that she expects Titus to know from his own miseries how to commiserate with her being miserable: "And if thy sons were ever dear to thee, / O, think of my son to be as dear to me!" Isn't it enough you've beaten us and taken us prisoner, do you also have to slaughter my son for doing for his country what you and your sons have done for your country? She even begs him to "draw near" to "sweet mercy," Shakespeare's allusion to Jesus Christ, but her plea for mercy falls on deaf ears, for Titus either doesn't know Christ or has withdrawn from him. But he at least had a role model in Achilles, who, for understandable personal reasons could have chosen to refuse Priam, for Priam's son killed his best friend. After which, Achilles is described as "maddened with grief,"[3] and in revenge kills Priam's son. And, forgetting his chivalry, treats Hector's dead body with "gross outrage."[4] If Achilles under the circumstances could take pity on an old man Titus identifies with begging for the dead body of his son, it doesn't seem a lot to expect for old man Titus to take pity on a *mother* trying to prevent what happened to Hector from happening to her son.

In his rejection to the mother's second step of truth plea, Titus proves he not only is ignorant of the second step of truth, but also of the first step of truth — Knowing Yourself — and the third step of truth — Knowing God. In the first step, Bernard says to "observe what you are, that you are wretched indeed, and so learn to be merciful, a thing you cannot know in any other way."

> For if you regard your neighbor's faults but do not observe your own, you are likely to be moved not to ruth but to wrath, not to condole but

> to condemn, not to restore in the spirit of meekness but to destroy in the spirit of anger.[5]

Titus does the latter: he destroys in the spirit of anger, unmindful of his own grief, just expressed, over his own son, and of the grief of Priam, with whose grief he has just identified. He says, for example, to the grieving mother:

> Patient yourself, madam and pardon me.
> These are their brethren whom your Goths beheld
> Alive and dead, and for their brethren slain
> Religiously they ask a sacrifice.
> To this your son is marked, and die he must
> T' appease their groaning shadows that are gone [I, i, 121–126].

Titus's son, Lucius, just as mercilessly puts an end to the contention over the mother's son, although the same horrific fate could have been his own:

> Away with him, and make a fire straight
> And with our swords upon a pile of wood
> Let's hew his limbs till they be clean consumed [I, i, 127–129].

The mother's reaction is efficaciously accurate:

> O cruel irreligious piety! [I, i, 130].

After the sacrifice of Alarbus, the son for whom his mother, Tamora, begged, beseeched, and implored on her knees for his life to be spared, Titus's son, Lucius, reports back to him happily:

> See, lord and father, how we have performed
> Our Roman rites. Alarbus' limbs are lopped
> And entrails feed the sacrificing fire,
> Whose smoke like incense doth perfume the sky.
> Remaineth naught but to inter our brethren
> And with loud 'larums welcome them to Rome [I, i, 142–147].

Wasn't there enough killing and maiming and loss of limbs during the war? As crude a choice of words as "lopped" is, it accurately reflects the absence or destruction of human sensibilities Shakespeare is exposing as associated with the love of war and the "pomp and circumstance" of war. What could be more perverse than the association of the smoke of human entrails burning with "perfume"? "Roman rites" and "pomp and circumstance" are far more important than the dead and the killing they're designed to honor. Shakespeare's allusion to the "Queen of Troy" (I, i, 136) calls attention to *Helen*, a drama by Euripides; "The poet does not fail to point out the grim humour of the situation: the ten years' siege of Troy has been all for naught; and the lore of seers is not worth much, for Calchas and Helenus gave no inkling of the deception."[6] Shakespeare seems to take the view of Euripides, who "did not accept unquestioningly the traditional religion and morality, but displayed vigorous independent thought, frequently scandalizing public opinion. Allusions here and there show him a keen critic of contemporary society."[7] "He attacked, above all, the glory of war. He found no glory in war, but only needless suffering and inhumanity."[8] This is Shakespeare's position exactly. The war-caused inhumanity is demonstrated not only in Titus's loss of humanity in the blatant refusal to spare the life of a grieving mother's son, but the impulsive, arrogant killing of his own son, Mutius, for taking a rightful stand against him. Ironically, however, that stand did later prove disastrous. Titus wanted his daughter, Lavinia, to marry the emperor, who asked for her hand (that hand would have been saved), but she is already betrothed to and in love with the emperor's brother, Bassianus. When Mutius bars the door to keep Titus from going after Lavinia, Titus, the ultimate patriarch, kills him, and shows no remorse when Lucius says:

> My lord, you are unjust; and more than so,
> In wrongful quarrel you have slain your son [I, i, 288–289].

Titus answers: "Nor thou nor he are any sons of mine. / My sons would never so dishonour me. / Traitor, restore Lavinia to the Emperor." It seems the honor had lain in his daughter's being the Empress. The Emperor had said to Titus: "...Titus, to advance"

> Thy name and thy honourable family,
> Lavinia will I make my empress,
> Rome's royal mistress, mistress of my heart,
> And in the sacred Pantheon her espouse.
> Tell me, Andronicus, doth this motion please thee? [I, i, 239–243].

Titus answers:

> It doth, my worthy lord, and in this match
> I hold me highly honoured of your grace... [I, i, 244–245].

In ancient times honor was considered the reward of virtue, but in Titus, it is the reward of vainglory. He subordinates the lives of his own son and daughter to the ostentatious style of military men and persons with titles who pretend to birth and quality. One would expect him to have on his conscience the cold-blooded murder of his own son, but he has no conscience, only the "false principles of honour," which he sets up in place of conscience.[9] Obviously, honor does not produce virtue and is no substitute for a religious conscience, Shakespeare is saying, satirizing humanism.

He is soon to show us just how false this principle of honor is, in the Emperor's turn-coat displeasure when Titus promises to bring back Lavinia, which will mean taking her from the Emperor's brother to whom she was already betrothed when the Emperor asked for her. The Emperor's unconscionable response to Titus's promise after so recently overwhelming him with accolades, underscores the absurdity of any justification for the concept of the emperor as a divine monarch.

> No, Titus, no. The Emperor needs her not,
> Nor her, nor thee, nor any of thy stock.
> I'll trust by leisure him that mocks me once,
> Thee never, nor thy traitorous haughty sons,
> Confederates all thus to dishonour me.
> Was none in Rome to make a stale
> But Saturninus? Full well, Andronicus,
> Agree these deeds with that proud brag of thine
> That saidst I begged the empire at thy hands [I, i, 296–304].

Titus's first reaction is correct, but he is soon to misdirect its effects by taking his anger out on his sons rather than on the Emperor: "O monstrous, what reproachful words are these?" The Emperor responds to Titus, berating his own brother. Titus's next reaction is shocking. We're shocked to learn he has a heart, howbeit a mechanical, superficial, sycophantic heart, in that being out of favor with the Emperor wounds him more than the death and unhappiness of his own children, which is unnaturally unfeeling. Titus says, "These words are razors to my wounded heart." The Emperor announces his plans to marry one of the prisoners Titus, in his victory over the Goths, brought back to Rome. She is Tamora, Queen of the Goths, the mother to whom Titus refused mercy when she implored him to spare the life of her son. Titus is not invited to the wedding ("I am not bid to wait upon this bride").

Even when the body of his son, Mutius, is brought in by his brother, Marcus, and his three other sons, Titus is still so hung up on the pride of his military and humanistic code of honor that he vehemently protests the burial of his son in the family tomb, even when "nature" is appealed to. Marcus and Titus's other sons have been kneeling in their pleading. Finally, Titus says:

> Rise, Marcus, rise.
> The dismall'st day is this that e'er I saw.
> To be dishonoured by my sons in Rome.
> Well, bury him, and bury me next [I, i, 383–386].

Shakespeare's allusions to Ajax and Odysseus provide further insight into Titus's character and to his acquiescence. Ajax is depicted by Homer "as a man obstinate in his bravery to the point of stupidity. After the death of Achilles, Ajax and Odysseus contended for the hero's arms. When these were awarded to Odysseus, Ajax, maddened with resentment, slaughtered a flock of sheep in the belief that they were his enemies, and afterwards from shame took his own life." According to Sophocles, "Ajax angered the gods by his arrogance. Menelaus forbids his burial, as an enemy to the Greeks, and Agamemnon confirms the edict, but is persuaded by Odysseus to relent, and Ajax is carried to his grave."[10]

Act I ends with Shakespeare's descriptions of white people as heartless, unscrupulous, cruel, treacherous, arrogant, deceitful, vengeful, cunning, malicious, vicious, unconscionable, and unnaturally evil. We have seen unnatural father against innocent sons. We've next to see unnatural brother against innocent brother, in the Emperor's unjust pronouncement and malice against his brother, Bassianus, who has married Lavinia, to whom he was betrothed before the Emperor presumptuously asked for her. For example, the Emperor says to Bassianus:

> Traitor, if Rome have law or we have power,
> Thou and thy faction shall repent this rape [I, i, 403–404].

In truth, Bassianus answers:

> "Rape" call you it, my lord, to seize my own—
> My true betrothed love, and now my wife?
> But let the laws of Rome determine all;
> Meanwhile am I possessed of that is mine [I, i, 405–408].

The emperor threatens in response:

> 'Tis good, sir; you are very short with us.
> But if we live we'll be as sharp with you [I, i, 409–410].

Bassianus answers his brother's threat and, in Titus's behalf, tries to square things with the Emperor. Even though the offered proof of Titus's zeal for the Emperor is unspeakable, it nonetheless moves no one. In fact, the response it elicits is almost as abominable as the proof. Titus rejects the efforts of Bassianus, attacking him as one of the ones who dishonored him. Bassianus addresses the Emperor:

> My lord, what I have done, as best I may
> Answer I must, and shall do with my life.
> Only this much I give your grace to know
> By all the duties that I owe to Rome,
> This noble gentleman, Lord Titus here,
> Is in opinion and in honour wronged,
> That, in the rescue of Lavinia,
> With his own hand did slay his youngest son
> In zeal to you, and highly moved to wrath
> To be controlled in that he frankly gave.
> Receive him then to favour, Saturnine,
> That hath expressed himself in all his deeds
> A father and a friend to thee and Rome [I, i, 411–423].

That Titus killed his own son out of zeal for the Emperor, is, to the heartless, arrogant Emperor, insufficient evidence, and he nonetheless seeks revenge.

But, with deceptive conciliatory gestures, Tamora, with malicious and vicious treachery, changes the dynamics of the situation. With "superior cunning," she persuades her husband to "pardon what is past," to "look graciously" on Titus, and to

> Lose not so noble a friend on vain suppose,
> Nor with sour looks afflict his gentle heart [I, i, 440–441].

In an aside to Saturninus, almost simultaneously, she says: "Dissemble all your griefs and discontents... / Yield at entreats; and then let me alone":

> I'll find a day to massacre them all,
> And raze their faction and their family,
> The cruel father and his traitorous sons
> To whom I sued for my dear son's life,
> And make them know what 'tis to let a queen
> Kneel in the streets and beg for grace in vain [I, i, 443–448].

In the foregoing, Shakespeare holds up a mirror to the execrable for the purpose of introducing the character the execrable call "the villain," who, ironically, holds forth in the style of the execrable, the slave masters he has learned from. It's important to note he makes virtually the last statement of the play.

Act II opens with Aaron the Moor. He enters alone. The first indication he holds forth in the style of the masters he has learned from is his allusions to classical mythology, with which it seems unlikely he would have otherwise been familiar. In this, his first, soliloquy, he deifies Tamora, placing her atop Mount Olympus, in Greek mythology, the residence of the gods, and compares her with the sun. He then, in adoration, tells us of her diabolical power,

> Upon her wit doth earthly honor wait,
> And virtue stoops and trembles at her frown [II, i, 10–11],

to emphasize his power over her. That is, in their lust relationship, she is the slave and he is the master who "in triumph long"

> Hast prisoner held [Tamora] fettered in amorous chains,
> And faster bound to Aaron's charming eyes
> Than is Prometheus tied to Caucasus [II, i, 15–17].

We also learn this from his putting an end to the subject: "Away with slavish weeds and servile thoughts," but adds his place is not "to wait upon" her but "to wanton with this queen, this goddess, this Semiramis, this nymph...." Through Aaron's allusions to classical myths, we learn a great deal more about the character of Tamora from her role models. For example, Semiramis is a mythical queen of Assyria:

> She married Onnes, an Assyrian general, and accompanied him to the siege of Bactra, where her prudent advice hastened the fall of the city.

> She subsequently married Ninus, king of Assyria, the reputed founder of Ninevah, and succeeded him on the throne (having contrived his death).[11]

Prefigurative of the "shipwreck" that the "charms" of "this siren" will make of "Rome's Saturnine and his commonweal's," Aaron's allusion to Prometheus is provocatively suggestive of Tamora, like an eagle, daily feeding on Saturnine's liver, and of her similarity to Pandora:

> Athene breathed life into Pandora, and the other gods endowed her with every charm ... but Hermes taught her flattery and guile. This woman was sent, not to Prometheus ... but to his brother.... She brought with her a box from which when opened there issued all the evils and distempers that have since afflicted the human race. Hope alone remained at the bottom of the box to assuage the lot of man.[12]

The hope Shakespeare has in mind is Christ. ("Hope thou in Christ.") Tamora is also referred to as a "siren." In Greek mythology, the Sirens are "fabulous creatures that had the power of drawing men to destruction by their song."[13] They were often represented as birds with the head of women (monsters). Birds are also involved in identifying Tamora with Semiramis: "Various legends claimed that Semiramis was fed as a child by doves (which fact later identified her with Ishtar)." Ishtar was the Babylonian goddess of love and war. "Though the goddess of erotic love, she was often warlike and, at best, had a remarkably irritable disposition."[14] There is an irony in the mythological association of Tamora with birds. In the very last words of the play, when funerals are planned for the many dead, Lucius says:

> As for the ravenous tiger, Tamora,
> No funeral rite nor man in mourning weed,
> No mournful bell shall ring her burial;
> But throw her forth to beasts and birds to prey.
> Her life was beastly and devoid of pity,
> And being dead, let birds on her take pity [V, iii, 194–199].

Tamora, it can well be said, is true to her role models from classical myths, and we have it on the best authority.

Immediately following Aaron's soliloquy, Tamora's two sons enter, arguing with much bravado, and Aaron prevents them from killing each other over a natural emotion for which neither has the capacity: love. They each claim to love Lavinia. The younger brother, Chiron, says, "I love Lavinia more than all the world." To which Demetrius states, "Youngling, learn thou to make some meaner choice. / Lavinia is thine older brother's hope." It's amazing how quickly, with a mere suggestion, love turns to rape. Not that the masters are bound or likely to follow the advice of a slave, but, with a reference to Lucrece, who, after being raped, told her husband, and then committed suicide, Aaron suggests the brothers rape Lavinia ("strike her home by force, if not by words, / This way or not at all stand you in hope"). He adds:

> The woods are ruthless, dreadful, deaf, and dull.
> There speak and strike, brave boys, and take your turns.
> There serve your lust, shadowed from heaven's eye,
> And revel in Lavinia's treasury [II, ii, 128–132].

Then later, once hounds and horns announce the royal hunt, Demetrius says to Chiron:

> Chiron, we hunt not, we, with horse nor hound,
> But hope to pluck a dainty doe to ground [II, ii, 25–26].

All exit.

Scene Three opens with Aaron with gold, which he buries under a tree, saying:

> Know that this gold must coin a stratagem
> Which, cunningly effected, will beget
> A very excellent piece of villainy [II, iii, 5–7].

Soon after, Tamora enters clandestinely to rendezvous with the Moor, whom she addresses: "My lovely Aaron," suggesting—

> We may, each wreathed in the other's arms,
> Our pastimes done, possess a golden slumber
> Whiles hounds and horns and sweet melodious birds
> Be unto us as is a nurse's song
> Of lullaby to bring her babe asleep [II, iii, 9, 25–29].

But lust is not what Aaron has in mind:

> Vengeance is in my heart, death in my hand,
> Blood and revenge are hammering in my head.
> Hark, Tamora, the empress of my soul,
> Which never hopes more heaven than rests in thee,
> This is the day of doom for Bassianus.
> His Philomel must lose her tongue today,
> Thy sons make pillage of her chastity
> And wash their hands in Bassianus' blood.
> Seest thou this letter? Take it up, I pray thee,
> And give the King this fatal-plotted scroll.
> Now question me no more. We are espied.
> Here comes a parcel of our hopeful booty,
> Which dreads not yet their lives' destruction [II, iii, 38–50].

Tamora's response (aside to Aaron): "Ah, my sweet Moor, sweeter to me than life!" Aaron (aside to Tamora):

No more, great Empress; Bassianus comes.
Be cross with him, and I'll go fetch thy sons
To back thy quarrels, whatsoe'er they be [II, iii, 52–54].

As a reflection of Tamora, cunning, malicious, vengeful, murderous, but without provocation or cause, Aaron obviously holds forth in the style of the slave master/mistress he has learned from, especially according to his description of her character by way of allusions to role models from classical mythology.

Bassianus and Lavinia come upon Tamora and Aaron in the forest, and are surprised to find them secluded. With a subtle tinge of racism, introduced into the play for the first time, Bassianus addresses Tamora as Diana, "the Latin goddess associated with the plebian class and with slaves. She was originally a spirit of the woods and of wild nature":

Who have we here? Rome's royal empress
Unfurnished of her well-beseeming troop?
Or is it Dian, habited like her
Who hath abandoned her holy groves
To see the general hunting in the forest?[15]

Tamora's retort is anything but subtle, or original:

Saucy controller of my private steps,
Had I the power that some say Dian had,
Thy temples should be planted presently
With horns, as was Actaeon's, and the hounds
Should drive upon thy new-transformed limbs,
Unmannerly intruder as thou art! [II, iii, 60–65].

Actaeon, (in Greek mythology), "having accidentally observed Dian in her bath, while hunting on Mount Cithaeron, was changed by the goddess into a stag and torn to pieces by his own hounds."[16] The "sweet" Lavinia counters with vulgar innuendos:

Under your patience, gentle Empress,
'Tis thought you have a goodly gift in horning,
And to be doubted that your Moor and you
Are singled forth to try experiments.
Jove shield your husband from his hounds today—
'Tis pity they should take him for a stag [II, iii, 66–71].

Bassianus follows with blatant racist attacks:

Believe me, Queen, your swart Cimmerian
Doth make your honour of his body's hue,
Spotted, detested, and abominable.
Why are you sequestered from all your train,
Dismounted from your snow-white goodly steed,

> And wandered hither to an obscure plot,
> Accompanied but with a barbarous Moor,
> If foul desire had not conducted you? [II, iii, 72–79].

"The Cimmerians were a legendary tribe which Homer placed beyond Oceanus in a land of never-ending gloom on which the sun never shone. Immediately beyond was Hades. The phrase 'Cimmerian darkness' signifies intense darkness."[17] "Swart" means black, swarthy, baneful, malignant. "Swart Cimmerian," then, means that Aaron is of intense darkness or black, baneful and malignant, although, at this point, Bassianus has no cause to speak of Aaron as baneful and malignant, no cause, that is, except racism. Nor has Lavinia, at this point, cause to chime in,

> And being intercepted in your sport,
> Great reason that my noble lord be rated
> For sauciness. (To Bassianus) I pray you, let us hence,
> And let her joy her raven-coloured love.
> This valley fits the purpose passing well [II, iii, 80–84],

and to speak of Saturninus as "Good King, to be so mightily abused!" especially since it was Saturninus who called Bassianus "traitor," and his marriage to Lavinia "rape." Nor has Lavinia, at this point, cause to berate Tamora, since it was Tamora, as Empress, who talked, howbeit disingenuously (unbeknownst to Lavinia), Saturninus into forgiving her, her whole family, and Bassianus.

Tamora's two sons enter and, seeing their mother, wonder why she "looks so pale and wan." She tells them, describing the place she's in in terms of Bassianus' racist reference to Aaron as "swart Cimmerian." She tells them that Bassianus and Lavinia "have 'ticed me hither to this place. / A barren detested vale you see it is"; and that, "Here never shines the sun," and that, "they told me that would bind me here / Unto the body of a dismal yew / And leave me to this miserable death."

> And then they called me foul adulteress,
> Lascivious Goth, and all the bitterest terms
> That ever ear did hear to such effect.
> And had you not by wondrous fortune come,
> This vengeance on me had they executed.
> Revenge it as you love your mother's life,
> Or be ye not henceforward called my children [II, iii, 91–115].

Her sons respond, killing Bassianus on the spot, without hesitation.

In response, and almost immediately after she insulted and condemned Tamora and her "raven-coloured love," Lavinia has the amazing temerity to provoke and again insult the woman she is just about to beg for mercy:

Ay, come, Semiramis— nay, barbarous Tamora
For no name fits thy nature but thy own [II, iii, 118–119].

Tamora, surfeited, starts to right off kill her for those remarks, but Tamora's sons, who have so recently professed to love Lavinia more than life, have other plans for her. Their idea is to "drag hence her husband to some secret hole, / and make his dead trunk pillow to our lust." Lavinia appeals to Tamora's womanhood for mercy, to which Demetrius responds, saying to Tamora:

Listen, fair madam, let it be your glory
To see her tears, but be your heart to them
As unrelenting flint to drops of rain [II, ii, 139–141].

Lavinia's reply is significant, in that it will be similarly applicable to Aaron. Instead of "When did the tiger's young ones teach the dam"— it will be "Since when did the slave tell the master what to do?"

In Lavinia's attempt to move Tamora to empathy and sympathy based on their both being women, Shakespeare is alluding to Bernard's Second Step of Truth, Knowing Your Neighbor. However, since "we can know our neighbor only by love,"[18] Lavinia, who is appealing by hatred and arrogance, is, ironically, taking the opposite approach. Also ironically, she seems void of sensitivity, instinct, intuition, insight —characteristics usually associated with or attributed to woman. In addition, in using her father to justify her second-step-of-truth appeal, she couldn't have hit a more raw nerve in Tamora, and simply talks herself right out of even the remotest possibility of pity, if there were ever any possibility to begin with, when she offers to teach Tamora pity:

O, let me teach thee for my father's sake,
That gave thee life when well he might have slain thee.
Be not obdurate, open thy deaf ears [II, iii, 158–160].

As one might expect her to, Tamora answers:

Hadst thou in person ne'er offended me
Even for his sake am I pitiless.
Remember, boys, I poured forth tears in vain
To save your brother from the sacrifice,
But fierce Andronicus would not relent.
Therefore away with her, and use as you will—
The worse to her, the better loved of me [II, iii, 161–167].

We are reminded of Lavinia's role model, Philomel, who, after being raped, and her tongue cut out so she can't tell who ravaged her, was hidden in a lonely place, but who ultimately enables Lavinia to reveal her similar outrage and who caused it. Lavinia tells Tamora: "'tis not life that I have begged so long; / Poor I was slain when Bassianus died" (II, iii, 170–171). "What begg'st thou then," says Tamora (II, iii, 172). To which Lavinia replies:

'Tis present death I beg, and one thing more
That womanhood denies my tongue to tell.
O, keep me from their worse-than-killing lust,
And tumble me into some loathsome pit
Where never man's eye may behold my body.
Do this, and be a charitable murderer [II, iii, 173–176].

Ironically, Lavinia gets what she asks for, but also what she does not ask for: her hands chopped off so she cannot imitate Philomel and reveal her outrage in needlework. The "one thing more" she asks for she gets first—"That womanhood denies my tongue to tell." What she wants most: death, believing that rape is worse than death, she gets last, at the hands of her own father. Her very last words ever to be spoken again, begin with a statement Shakespeare makes throughout the play as a whole. In other words, Lavinia is correct in saying: "No grace!" Her complete statement is not true in its entirety:

No grace, no womanhood—ah, beastly creature,
The blot and enemy to our general name,
Confusion fall [II, iii, 182–184].

There is "no grace" because the will to do good is completely lacking. "In order that our willing, derived from our free choice, may be perfect," says Bernard, "we need the twofold gift of grace: namely true wisdom, which means the turning of the will to good, and full power, which means its confirmation in good." Such is the restoration promised by Malcolm at the end of *Macbeth*:

... and what needful else
That calls upon us, by the grace of grace
We will perform in measure, time, and place [V, xi, 37–39].[19]

Lavinia, of course, is right: "No grace," and that speaks for the play as a whole, needless to say. There is also no restoration in the end, just genocidal racism as usual. "The end is in the beginning," as Ralph Ellison's invisible black man states. Chiron says to her:

Nay then, I'll stop your mouth. (To Demetrius)
Bring thou her husband.
This is the hole where Aaron bid us hide him [II, iii, 184–186].

Since when does the master do the bidding of a slave? The two brothers, who were going to kill each other for love of Lavinia, now drag her off to take turns raping her, and then cut out her tongue and chop off her hands.

In the meantime, Aaron enters with Quintas and Martius, two of Titus's sons. Aaron leads them to the pit covered with branches, where the body of Bassianus has been thrown. Martius falls into the pit and discovers the bloody body of Bassianus. Quintas falls in while trying to pull Martius out. Aaron says (aside):

> Now will I fetch the King to find them here,
> That he thereby may have a likely guess
> How these were they that made away his brother [II, iii, 206–208].

Aaron returns with Saturninus the Emperor, and Tamora enters with Titus Andronicus and Lucius. And, as plotted, Quintas and Martius are declared guilty of the murder of Bassianus and carried away to prison amidst threats such as:

> There let him bide until we have devised
> Some never-heard-of torturing pain for them [II, iii, 284–285].
>
> For by my soul, were there worse end than death
> That end upon them should be executed [II, iii, 302–303].

Ironically, these threats by Saturninus recall the threats he so recently made against Bassianus. He seems to have gotten what he threatened when he called Bassianus traitor and said he would "repent this rape" (Bassianus' marriage to Lavinia), adding to his brother:

> 'Tis good, sir, you are very short with us.
> But if we live we'll be as sharp with you [I, i, 406–407].

Titus begs for mercy on behalf of his sons, in front of Tamora, who earlier begged Titus for mercy on behalf of her son. She now, with malicious, cunning revenge, lies to Titus:

> Andronicus, I will entreat the King.
> Fear not thy sons, they shall do well enough [II, iii, 304–305].

The next to enter are the Empress Tamora's vile sons, Chiron and Demetrius, with terrifyingly afflicted and outrageously pathetic and forlorn Lavinia, her hands cut off and her tongue cut out, and ravished. Is there anything more unspeakably monstrous, more cruelly merciless, more diabolically insensitive, more grossly inhuman, more heinously execrable, more horrifically villainous, than Tamora's two sons, Chiron and Demetrius, not only because of their atrocities against Lavinia, but also because they waxed derisive concerning them?

> DEMETRIUS: So, now go tell, and if thy tongue can speak,
> Who 'twas that cut thy tongue and ravished thee.
> CHIRON: Write down thy mind, bewray thy meaning so,
> An [if] thy stumps will let thee play the scribe.

DEMETRIUS:	See how with sighs and tokens she can scrawl.
CHIRON:	(to Lavinia) Go home, call for sweet water, wash thy hands.
DEMETRIUS:	She hath no tongue to call nor hands to wash, And so let's leave her to her silent walks.
CHIRON:	An 'twere my cause I should go hang myself.
DEMETRIUS:	If thou hadst hands to help thee knit the cord [II, iv, 1–10].

In his anguish, Marcus, coming upon his niece, Lavinia, alludes to the appalling precedence of Philemon and Tereus in Greek mythology. He says to her:

> But sure some Tereus hath deflowered thee
> And, lest thou shouldst detect him, cut thy tongue....
> Fair Philemon, why she but lost her tongue
> And in a tedious sampler sewed her mind.
> But, lovely niece, that mean is cut from thee.
> A craftier Tereus, cousin, hast thou met,
> And he hath cut those pretty fingers off,
> That could have better sewed than Philomel [II, iv, 26–27, 38–43].

"Philomel managed to depict her misfortunes on a piece of needlework and send it to Procne, her sister, the wife of Tereus, the ravager of Philomel. Procne, to revenge her sister, killed her own son Itys and served up his flesh to her husband, Tereus, the father of Itys."[20] Procne is, perhaps, the role model for Titus, who chops up Chiron and Demetrius and serves them in a pie to their mother, Tamora. This is another example of Renaissance humanism's belief in the ability of classical mythology "to make a man a fully realized human creature, elevated and distinct from the lower animals."[21]

Act III opens with Titus pleading before the judges, tribunes, and senators for the life of his innocent sons, Quintas and Martius, who are bound and passing to the place of execution. Titus, blinded by weeping, continues to plead until Lucius enters and says:

> O noble father, you lament in vain.
> The Tribunes hear you not. No man is by.
> And you recount your sorrows to a stone [III, i, 27–29].

When Lavinia is brought on the scene, her condition seems more than Titus can bear: "But that which gives my soul the greatest spurn / Is dear Lavinia, dearer than my soul" (III, i, 101–102). In trying to decide what to do: ("What shall we do? Let us that have our tongues / Plot some device of further misery, / To make us wondered at in time to come" [III, i, 133–135].) Titus hits upon one of the main reasons for the horrors Shakespeare is exposing in this play: "To make [white people] wondered at in time to come."

A symbol of the plotted device of unspeakable misery (the African slave trade) "to make [white people] wondered at in time to come," enters. That symbol is the slave, Aaron the Moor, who enters alone, with a proposition:

> Titus Andronicus, my lord the Emperor
> Sends thee his word: that, if thou love thy sons,
> Let Marcus, Lucius or thyself, old Titus,
> Or any one of you, chop off your hand
> And send it to the King. He for the same
> Will send thee hither both thy sons alive,
> And that shall be the ransom for their fault [III, i, 150–156].

Titus, Marcus, and Lucius, each eager to sacrifice a hand to save the lives of Quintas and Martius, argue over whose hand it will be. While Marcus and Lucius go out to find an ax, Aaron cuts off Titus's hand at the latter's request, seeking to deceive Marcus and Lucius. Ironically, Titus is grossly deceived. Aaron says:

> I go, Andronicus; and for thy hand
> Look by and by to have thy sons with thee.
> (Aside) Their heads, I mean. O, how this villainy
> Doth fat me with the very thoughts of it!
> Let fools do good, and fair men call for grace.
> Aaron will have his soul black like his face [III, i, 199–204].

The implication is that white men, the "fair men," did not teach the slaves real Christianity, nor did white men practice "real Christianity," or, needless to say, there would have been no African slave trade, no Aaron the slave. Ironically juxtaposed to Aaron's ignorance of "real Christianity" is Titus's ignorance of real Christianity, which means his soul is as black as Aaron's. Kneeling, Titus says:

> O, here I lift this one hand up to heaven
> And bow this feeble ruin to the earth.
> If any power pities wretched tears,
> To that I call [III, i, 205–208].

Aaron's ignorance is understandable, but not Titus's. Titus should have known that "The sacrifices of God are a broken spirit: a broken and contrite heart, O God, thou wilt not despise" (Ps.51:17).

The brief exchange that follows between Titus and Marcus suggests Shakespeare may be alluding to Bernard's allusion to Jeremiah in defining the purpose of the reason. Marcus cautions his brother, Titus, to "let reason govern thy lament." Titus answers:

> If there were reason for these miseries,
> Then into limits could I bind my woes [III, i, 218–219].

But there is reason, for "the sons of this world are wise in doing evil, but to do good they have no knowledge" (Jer.4:22). "Indeed," says Bernard, "prudence or wisdom cannot be present in a creature, even in wrongdoing, by any means other than reason."[22] Titus is correct in saying his sorrows are deep, "having no bottom," for the evil has no bottom, for there is more to come. A messenger enters with two heads and a hand:

> Worthy Andronicus, ill art thou repaid
> For that good hand thou sent'st the Emperor.
> Here are the heads of thy two noble sons,
> And here's thy hand in scorn to thee sent back—
> Thy grief their sports, thy resolution mocked,
> That woe is me to think upon thy woes
> More than remembrance of my father's death [III, i, 233–239].

The messenger sets down the heads and hand, and exits.

Marcus is the first to be devastated. Alluding to the Scripture Bernard alludes to in defining the Second Step of Truth, Shakespeare has Marcus say:

> These miseries are more than may be borne.
> To weep with them that weep doth ease some deal.
> But sorrow flouted at is double death [III, i, 242–244].

In other words, to be contemptuous or scornful of the sorrowful rather than compassionate and empathetic is to invite punishment the equivalent of a double death. The "double death" is also that of Marcus and Titus; the merciful and the neighbor in Bernard's definition:

> The merciful quickly grasp truth in their neighbors, extending their own feelings to them and conforming themselves to them through love, so that they feel "their" joys or troubles as their own. They are weak with the weak; they burn with the offended. They "rejoice with them that do rejoice, and weep with them that weep."[23]

Marcus also, as Bernard states, "burns with the offended":

> Now let hot Etna cool in Sicily,
> And be my heart an ever-burning hell [III, i, 240–241].

Titus's laugh: "Ha, ha, ha!" at this point does seem to indicate, as Garber says, that "the mocking return of the heads and the hand appears to drive Titus over the edge of madness."[24] I think the laugh serves as commentary on the absurdity of it all, in addition to absurdity's being a form of irony. Marcus asks Titus: "Why dost thou laugh? It fits not with this hour." Titus's answer is appropriate: "Why, I have not another tear to shed." It's too outrageous for grief. He seeks Revenge with a capital "R"; *arch*revenge; or, he seeks to be Revenge incarnate. On the decapitated heads of his sons, Titus "swears unto [his] soul to right their wrongs." The vow is made, with Marcus, Lucius and Lavinia kneeling with Titus in a circle.

Later, at dinner, in an oppressively morose atmosphere, Aaron the Moor is called to mind when Marcus kills a fly and is reprimanded by Titus. Titus's reprimand can be seen as Shakespeare's allusion to the message in the sermon by Bernard which reminds us that "the countless species of creatures [including flies] are rays emanating from the Godhead, showing that he from whom they came truly is.... Though not seeing God but what comes from him, you are made aware beyond all doubt that he exists, and that you must seek him."[25]

When Marcus strikes a dish with a knife, Titus asks him what he strikes at with his knife. Marcus answers: "At that I have killed, my lord—a fly." Titus exclaims:

> Out on thee, murderer! Thou kill'st my heart.
> Mine eyes are cloyed with view of tyranny.
> A deed of death done on the innocent
> Becomes not Titus's brother. Get thee gone.
> I see thou art not for my company.

Marcus answers: "Alas, my lord, I have but killed a fly" (III, ii, 54–58). Titus retorts:

> "But"? How if that fly had a father, brother?
> How would he had his slender gilded wings
> And buzz lamenting dirges in the air!
> Poor harmless fly,
> That with his pretty buzzing melody
> Came here to make us merry—and thou hast killed him! [III, ii, 60–65].

Titus' ridiculous attempt at mercy, humanizing a fly, one of the most detested by humans of all God's creatures, calls attention, by comparison to a fly, to how detested black people are by white people; not seen as "rays emanating from the Godhead, and far from making white people aware beyond all doubt that God exists and that they should seek him."[26] For example, Marcus goes on to say:

> Pardon me sir, it was a black ill-favored fly,
> Like to the Empress' Moor. Therefore I killed him [III, ii, 66–67].

This brings Titus to his racism, back to reality. He says:

> O, O, O!
> Then pardon me for reprehending thee,
> For thou hast done a charitable deed.
> Give me thy knife. I will insult on him,
> Flattering myself as if it were the Moor
> Come hither purposely to poison me.
> (He takes a knife and strikes.)
> There's for thyself, and that's for Tamora. Ah, sirrah!
> Yet I think we are not brought so low
> But that between us we can kill a fly
> That comes in likeness of a coal-black Moor [III, ii, 68–77].

We have to assume that here Shakespeare is exposing racism because thus far neither Titus nor Marcus is aware of Aaron's personal involvement in their grief and tragedies. Titus so recently embraced Aaron as a harbinger of hope for his sons, not knowing Aaron was a false harbinger. With Aaron's news of a ransom, Titus exclaims:

> O gracious emperor! O gentle Aaron,
> Did ever raven sing so like a lark
> That gives sweet tidings of the sun's uprise?
> With all my heart I'll send the Emperor my hand.
> Good Aaron, wilt thou help to chop it off? [III, i, 157–161].

So, the comparison of Aaron to a fly is a racist comparison Shakespeare is exposing.

Act IV opens with Lavinia running after young Lucius, who's carrying books under his arm. He drops them, and she discovers that one of them is Ovid's *Metamorphoses*, which contains the tragic tale of Philomel, with whom Lavinia can identify. Finding the tale in young Lucius' book enables her to begin to reveal her ravagers. Titus, Lavinia, young Lucius, and Marcus all kneel and vow "Mortal revenge upon these traitorous Goths, / And see their blood, or die with this reproach" (IV, i, 92–93). This should be viewed in the ironic context of Marcus' prayerful invocation that follows when he is left alone, and that ends with "Revenge the heavens for old Andronicus!" (IV, i, 128) The irony can be seen in terms of the Scripture Shakespeare alludes to:

> Dearly beloved, avenge not yourselves, but rather give place unto wrath: for it is written, Vengeance is mine; I will repay, saith the Lord [Rom.12:19].

With all of the horrors, atrocities, abominations, blood and gore in *Titus Andronicus*, Shakespeare creates an ironic context for projecting the nadir in unnatural evil, hatred, and arrogant inhumanity: white supremacy and the African slave trade. Soon after Marcus' prayerful invocation, Shakespeare again exposes white people's racism. Lavinia's having revealed her ravagers, Titus sends a message to them:

> "Integer vitae, scelerisque purus;
> Non eget Mauri iaculis, nec arcu" [IV, ii, 20–21].

which they recognize from their schoolboy "grammar" as a verse from Horace, although they miss the message. Translated the quote reads:

> The man of upright life and free from crime does not need the javelins or bows of the Moor.[27]

Having learned Horace from his masters, Aaron the slave can translate the message and understands it to mean that Titus is on to them. But the message is also to the reader. Anticipating the reader's racism as traditional, Shakespeare exposes the reader's racism and ignorance, and educates him through Bernard (insinuating the time-honored tradition of identifying the black man with the devil). Shakespeare also condemns his characters' racism in blaming all of the evil on Aaron. As Bernard says: "It is our own will that enslaves us to the devil, not his power." In other words, "free will makes us our own; bad will, the devil's; and good will, God's."

> As long as by bad will we belong to the devil, we are, in a certain sense, no longer God's; just as, when by good will we pass over to God, we cease to belong to the devil. "No one," in fact, "can serve two masters."[28]

Shakespeare makes it obvious that Chiron and Demetrius are men of bad will, and that it is their own bad will that enslaves them to the devil, but that Aaron is not the devil, except to racists.

Racism takes center stage very soon after Chiron, Demetrius, and Aaron receive the weapons and message brought by young Lucius from Titus. A nurse enters with a "blackamoor child." When Aaron asks her what she's carrying, she says: "O, that which I would hide from heaven's eye" (IV, ii, 59). When told the Empress has delivered, Aaron asks what hath God sent her? The nurse replies: "A devil" (IV, ii, 62). To describe an innocent newborn baby with such venomous racism is appalling. And telling, which Shakespeare exposes. To correct Aaron's calling the baby "A joyful issue!," the nurse describes him inhumanly as:

> A joyless, dismal, black, and sorrowful issue.
> Here is the babe, as loathsome as a toad
> Amongst the fair-faced breeders of our clime.
> The Empress sends it thee, thy stamp, thy seal,
> And bids thee christen it with thy dagger's point [IV, ii, 66–70].

Aaron retorts with human feeling, echoing Shakespeare: "Zounds, ye whore, is black so base a hue?" (IV, ii, 71). And to the baby: "Sweet blowze, you are a beauteous blossom, sure" (IV, ii, 72). These two ways of seeing the baby reflect Shakespeare's allusion to Bernard's teaching on seeing:

> Visible things are investigated by means of sense perception, which reveals corporal objects not as they are in themselves but as they appear to our sensitivity.[29]

Shakespeare also alludes to Robert Grossteste, a disciple of Bernard's who warns us that:

> the soul itself is a mirror, whose spiritual condition dictates the rectitude with which it records the figures of nature, and that only the soul/mirror which is able to subject itself to the will of Christ will be free of distortion. If distortions and lack of correspondence in the "speculum"

> of nature occur, it is not that there are distortions in creation, but rather in the attitude of the observer.[30]

Racism, of course, is an attitude, and it is not to be missed on Chiron and Demetrius, the scum of the earth, who refer to Aaron as their mother's "loathed choice," and to the baby as "Accursed the offspring of so foul a fiend" (IV, ii, 79). "Cursed" is one of the time-honored epithets hurled at black people, derived from the Old Testament. Demetrius savagely dehumanizes the baby with a nonhuman threat:

> I'll broach the tadpole on my rapier's point.
> Nurse, give it to me. My sword shall soon dispatch it [IV, ii, 84–85].

(We are reminded of the racist killing of the fly by Marcus and Titus, who say the fly resembles Aaron.)

In answer to that threat, Aaron threatens Demetrius, saying: "Sooner this sword shall plough thy bowels up," (IV, ii, 86) as he takes the baby and draws his sword, having more *human* nature than Titus, who killed his own son for the "honor" of the empire, a false and arrogant honor, and unnatural priority.

> Stay, murderous villains, will you kill your brother?
> Now, by the burning tapers of the sky
> That shone so brightly when this boy was got,
> He dies upon my scimitar's sharp point
> That touches my first-born and heir.
> I tell you, younglings, not Enceladas
> With all his threat'ning band of Typhon's brood,
> Nor great Alcides, nor the god of war
> Shall seize this prey out of his father's hands.
> What, what, ye sanguine, shallow-hearted boys,
> Ye whitelimed walls, ye alehouse painted signs,
> Coal-black is better than another hue
> In that it scorns to bear another hue;
> For all the water in the ocean
> Can never turn the swan's black legs to white,
> Although she lave them hourly in the flood.
> Tell the Empress from me I am of age
> To keep mine own, excuse it how she can [IV, ii, 86–104].

In this, Aaron reveals how fiercely protective he is of his son, to the extent he will kill anyone who tries to take him, including giants (Enceladas), Hercules (descendent of Alcides), Mars, and Typhon, "a terrible monster with a hundred serpents' heads, fiery eyes, and a tremendous voice."[31] The Greek mythology he learned from his masters. And to thusly allude to the myths demonstrates he holds forth in the style of the masters he has learned from. This is also true of his referring to his son as "prey," as he is regarded by white people, for the African slave trade; and when he says: "Look how the black slave smiles upon the father" (IV, ii, 119). But he also, perhaps schizophrenically, expresses pride in his blackness as a skin color superior to white; schizophrenia being one form of the deterioration of black people, caused by the African slave trade and racism. On the other hand, his priorities are natural and not misplaced. For example, in answer to Demetrius' question regarding Aaron's determination to protect and save his son, "Wilt thou betray thy noble mistress thus?" Aaron states: "My mistress is my mistress, this myself,"

> The figure and the picture of my youth.
> This before all the world do I prefer
> This maugre [in spite of] all the world will I keep safe.
> Or some of you shall smoke for it in Rome [IV, ii, 106–110].

Like his white masters, Aaron is capable of killing on the spot, without warning or expectation; the nurse, for example. Very Machiavellian. Also like his masters, "Vengeance is in [his] heart, death in [his] hand / Blood and revenge are hammering in his head," and justifiably so, given the African slave trade. But there is a contradiction in this regard when he speaks to his son thusly: "Come on, you thick-lipped slave, I'll bear you hence," (IV, ii, 174) as a white person would speak to him. This justifies the vengeance in Aaron's heart, but seems also indicative of schizophrenia. In alluding to Ishmael in the Old Testament, in Aaron's plans for his son, Shakespeare confirms the son's outcast status in the eyes of Aaron. It is prophesied of Ishmael that "he will be a wild man; his hand will be against every man, and every man's hand against him" (Gen.16:12). Aaron's plans for his son seem designed to fulfill this prophecy, or seem an acceptance of the prophecy as inevitable, and his son's status as "outcast" inevitable. For example, he says to his son:

> I'll make you feed on berries and on roots,
> And fat on the curds and whey, and suck the goat,
> And cabin in a cave, and bring you up
> To be a warrior and command a camp [IV, ii, 176–179].

After these words, Aaron exits with the baby.

Meanwhile, Titus' revenge plot begins to unfold, as exiled Lucius goes abroad and, like Coriolanus, raises an army of enemies recently defeated, the Goths, to march on Rome and depose the Emperor Saturninus, while Titus sends weapons and Horace to the ravagers of Lavinia, and has arrows with attached letters shot into the court of the Emperor. A messenger arrives at the court to warn the Emperor:

> Arm, my lords! Rome never had more cause.
> The Goths have gathered head, and with a power
> Of high-resolved men bent to the spoil
> They hither march amain under conduct
> Of Lucius, son to old Andronicus,

Who threats in course of this revenge to do
As much as ever Coriolanus did [IV, iiii, 62–68].

Saturninus is fearful, knowing that "the citizens favour Lucius / And will revolt from him to succour Lucius." The wily Tamora, true to her mythical role models— Pandora, with her "flattery and guile"; the Sirens, who "had the power of drawing men to destruction"; and Ishtar, "goddess of erotic love, who was often warlike"— devises a plot to entice Titus to entreat Lucius for the emperor. She says:

I will enchant the old Andronicus
With words more sweet and yet more dangerous
Than baits to fish [IV, iiii, 89–91].

Saturninus insists: "But Titus will not entreat his son for us." Tamora says:

If Tamora entreat him, then he will,
For I can smooth and fill his aged ears
With golden promises that, were his heart
Almost impregnable, his old ears deaf,
Yet should both ear and heart obey my tongue.
* * *
Now will I to that old Andronicus,
And temper him with all the art I have
To pluck proud Lucius from the warlike Goths.
And now, sweet Emperor, be blithe again,
And bury all thy fear in my devices [IV, iiii, 95–99, 108–112].

She fails, of course, and Titus' plot ends true to "pattern and precedent" (V, iii, 43). Like Virginius, Titus kills his own daughter, Lavinia. Having cut the throats of Chiron and Demetrius, Tamora's sons, he grinds their bones, makes two pasties of their heads, and bakes them in a pie which he serves to their mother; like Procne, who kills her son Itys and serves up his flesh to his father, Tereus, because he ravaged and cut out the tongue of Philomel, her sister. After Titus tells Tamora she has eaten her sons, he stabs her to death, after which, Saturninus kills him. Tamora's body is to be thrown out for beasts and birds of prey to devour. The African slave, Aaron, the prey of preys, is to be buried breast-deep in earth and famished: "There let him stand, and rave, and cry for food," says Lucius, adding:

If anyone relieves or pities him,
For the offence, he dies. This is our doom.
Some stay to see him fastened in the earth [V, iii, 178–182].

Lucius doesn't have to worry about the white people pitying Aaron, for obviously there's no capacity for pity among them. One glaring message of this play is the absurdity of the pattern and precedent of racism, and how it reveals white people's ignorance of themselves, ignorance of Bernard's First

Step of Truth, Knowing Yourself. After all of their hatred, gore, carnage, and degenerate violations of the laws of nature, they, ironically, call Aaron "this execrable wretch / That hath been breeder of these dire events" (V, iii, 176–177). It's ironic, since white people have been the breeder of Aaron. He holds forth in the purpose they gave him, as Prospero tells his slave, Caliban. And although Garber is troubled by the placement of Aaron's last speech—

> What is slightly unusual—and dramatically unsettling—is the placement of Aaron's speech of defiance "after" Marcus's and Lucius' remarks on the restoration of Roman governance[32]—

Aaron's tortured state symbolizes the restoration of business as usual for the African slave.

It is not without significance that Aaron is found hiding in a ruined monastery guardedly holding his baby son. The monastery may have been ruined by the outlawing of Catholicism by the Protestant government. Or Shakespeare may be saying what Swift later says, that Christianity was ruined by Thomas Aquinas' taking the church in the wrong direction by restructuring it according to Aristotle's system of knowledge. Shakespeare is most assuredly exposing Christianity, racism and the African slave trade as incompatible, which an African slave hiding in a ruined monastery and attacked by racism could symbolize. He and the baby are discovered by a Goth soldier and forcibly taken by Lucius, whose racist attack pointedly reveals Shakespeare's genius for irony. He first calls Aaron "the incarnate devil," then "wall-eyed slave." The irony is that Lucius is the "incarnate devil" based on Shakespeare's use of Bernard's doctrine of the will. Bernard states, "It is our own will that enslaves us to the devil, not his power."[33] But, in the case of the African slave trade, the slave, lacking a free will, is enslaved to the white devil by the latter's power. And the slave holds forth in the style of the white master he has learned from. Moreover, Bernard also asks the question: "On what basis, in fact, can one impute anything to a man, whether good or bad, if he is not known to have the free disposal of himself? Necessity excuses from both. For necessity's presence means freedom's absence; and where there is no freedom, neither is there merit, nor consequently judgment..." (Grace, 59). Whatever lacks this freedom of voluntary consent lacks also undoubtedly merit and judgment.[34] In other words, since slaves do not retain the use of their own will, nor consequently the judgment of freedom, they can't or shouldn't be held responsible for what they do. This is summed up in Aaron's last speech:

> Ah, why should wrath be mute and fury dumb?
> I am no baby, I, that with base prayers
> I should repent the evils I have done.
> Ten thousand worse than ever yet I did
> Would I perform if I might have my will [V, iii, 183–187].

This is to say that, blaming Aaron for everything, making him the villain, is consummately racist.

It goes without saying that Aaron is more human that the white people in the play, not only because he would otherwise not be their slave, but also because he goes to greater lengths to save the life of his son, including the sacrifice of his own life, which is more than they go to for theirs. Not only does Titus kill his own son and daughter, the most he sacrifices to save the life of his two sons is one hand. And, needless to say, it is horrifyingly inhuman of Lucius to even consider hanging a baby. Aaron begs Lucius to "save the child," promising to give him information that would be to his advantage, only demanding that Lucius "swear to him the child shall live." The "ruined monastery" is the perfect prelude to the conversation that follows, which is an irreligious discussion about religion. Aaron again commands Lucius to swear that his child shall live. Lucius answers:

> Who should I swear by? Thou believest no god.
> That granted, how canst thou believe an oath?

The irreligious Aaron, presuming Lucius is Catholic, makes a mockery of Lucius' Catholic religion, of which Lucius himself makes a mockery, and which, as practiced, makes a mockery of "real Christianity."

Lucius vows: "Even by my god I swear to thee I will." But we still don't know "what god soe'er it be." However, by all indications past and present, including the lower case "g" for god, it is a god from classical myths, not God, which means he is as irreligious as Aaron. What Aaron, to save his son, confesses to, is equally ironic. There is nothing in his confession for which there is pattern or precedence among his white masters and their mythical role models. In other words, he holds forth in the style of the white masters he has learned from, including the amazing absence of, except toward his son, human feeling which made him a slave and the African slave trade a reality. He is the hate that hate produced. Shakespeare repeats this irony in *The Tempest* when Prospero says to his slave, Caliban:

> When thou didst not, savage,
> Know thine own meaning, but wouldst gabble like
> A thing most brutish, I endowed thy purposes
> With words that made them known [I, ii, 355–357].

And Caliban appropriately answers:

> You taught me language, and my profit on't
> Is I know how to curse.[35]

In other words, in "endowing Caliban's purposes," Prospero has the supremacist arrogance to impersonate God, in the same way implied when Shakespeare has Aaron complain in his last speech of not having a will, not having "the free disposal of himself." And since that is the case, white slave masters making the black slave Aaron what he is, and, for example, Titus thinking Aaron more hateful than the fly he kills "That comes in the likeness of a coal-black Moor," Aaron, with causal transparency, confesses:

> I have done a thousand dreadful things
> As willingly as one would kill a fly... [V, i, 141–142].

So that, in addition to Aaron's carrying out the desire of his mistress, "to massacre them all" (I, i, 447), the vengeance in his heart, the death in his hand, and the blood and revenge hammering in his head (II, iii, 38–39) (all justifiable) were all put there by white people, who made him a slave, and reflect white people as a mirror held up to them.

With his genius for satire and irony, Shakespeare condemns the African slave trade and exposes the absurdity of white supremacy, racism, classism, humanism, imperialism, and war, in defense of "real Christianity," using this play to implant a "real Christian" conscience in white people, in addition to making them aware of the need of one, in the sense that "the play's the thing to catch the conscience...." Shakespeare gives us dramatically powerful evidence of this in his allusion to the Christ child through Marcus' racist, thus irreligious, speech at the end of the play:

> Now is my turn to speak. Behold the child.
> Of this was Tamora delivered,
> The issue of an irreligious Moor,
> Chief architect and plotter of these woes [V, iii, 118–121].

"Behold the child" is an allusion to the Christ child, spoken of as God's salvation for all people, by Simeon, who said unto Mary, the mother of Jesus: "Behold this child is set for the fall and rising again of many in Israel; and for a sign which shall be spoken against." The exegesis on this Scripture, from the *Interpreter's Bible*, reads as follows:

> God has ordained this child to separate the righteous from the unrighteous among many in Israel. Some are to reject him and fall (Isa.8 14–15); others are to accept him and rise. He is to be a sign that many will dispute. This is part of the purpose of God, for by their attitude to Christ, men will reveal their true nature.[36]

The same can be well said for the black child, Shakespeare, in so many words, is saying, which is his point. In other words, Shakespeare is saying, as he demonstrates with Aaron, Othello, and Caliban, that black people function to separate the righteous from the unrighteous among many, for by their attitude toward black people, white people reveal their true nature.

The Merchant of Venice

As we have seen in *Titus Andronicus*, Shakespeare protests the African slave trade and racism by projecting the black slave, Aaron the Moor, as reinvented by his white slave masters. In other words, as holding forth in the style of the masters he has learned from, forced to take on their definition of black people, buying into the myth of "black inferiority" and "white superiority," and acknowledging his own son in that light and regard. In *The Merchant of Venice*, this perverted, dehumanizing identity theft is depicted in invisibility (Ralph Ellison style). Kim Hall says: "It may be that this pregnant, unheard, unnamed, and unseen (at least by critics) black woman is a silent symbol for the economic and racial politics of *The Merchant of Venice*,"[1] is a silent symbol of the African slave trade and racism, I would say, which Shakespeare protests. The black woman is relegated to references in two lines of a debasing banter between Lorenzo and Launcelot. Speaking of "the getting up of the negro's belly," Lorenzo says: "the Moor is with child by you, Launcelot!" Launcelot answers: "It is much that the Moor should be more than reason, but if she be less than an honest woman she is indeed more than I took her for" (III, v, 32–36). The Norton glosses on these lines are as follows: 34–35. "It is much ... than reason: It makes sense that the Moor is unreasonably large (with pun on "more") since she is pregnant." This play is a scathing attack on racism, anti–Semitism, homophobia, nominal Christianity, and legalism, the basis of Judaism, and patriarchy.

Because of the obvious racism in *Titus Andronicus*, an earlier play, and because of the imprint of history, I cannot agree with Leah Marcus in her Preface to the *Norton Critical Edition of the Merchant of Venice* when she says:

> Of course, to apply the term "racism" to a work of the late sixteenth century is in one sense anachronistic: defenders of the play have pointed out that neither Moors nor Jews were sufficiently visible in the England of the 1590s, when the play was written and first performed, to constitute a distinct cultural category and to receive the systematic institutional discrimination that we now associate with the twentieth-century term "racism."[2]

To apply the term "racism" to work of the late sixteenth century is in *no* sense anachronistic, considering England's involvement in the African slave trade than which no more consummate definition of racism can be found:

> Captain John Hawkins knew the blackamoors would fetch a good price in Hispaniola or the Spanish Main. Alas, the slave trade was controlled by Portugal, backed by the power of imperial Spain. His first voyage to Guinea was in 1562, an illegal raid in which he "acquired three hundred Negroes..." when Queen Elizabeth heard of Hawkins' slaving venture, she said "It was detestable and would call down vengeance from heaven upon the undertakers." Hawkins went to see the queen and showed Her Majesty his profit sheet. Not only did she forgive him but she became a shareholder in his second slaving voyage. That was in 1564, and Hawkins then had four vessels.[3]

Moreover, "the systematic and institutional discrimination that we now associate with the twentieth century term "racism" *did*, it seems, exist in England in the 1590s:

> In 1596 [the year *Merchant of Venice* was written], despite her earlier support of English piracy in the slave trade, Queen Elizabeth expressed concern over the presence of blacks in the realm. She issued a proclamation to the Lord Mayor of London which states her "understanding that there are of late divers blackamoores brought into this realm, of which kinde of people there are already here to manie" and demands that blacks recently brought to the realm be rounded up and returned. This effort was evidently not very successful, as she followed up with another order of expulsion....
>
> ... whereas the Queen's Majesty, tendering the good and welfare of her own natural subjects greatly distressed in these hard times of dearth, is highly discontented to understand the great number of Negars and Blackamoors which (as she is informed) are crept into this realm since the troubles between her Highness and the King of Spain, who are fostered and relieved here to the great annoyance of her own liege people that want the relief which those people consume; as also for that the most of them are infidels, having no understanding of Christ or his Gospel, hath given especial commandment that the said kind of people should be with all speed avoided and discharged out of this Her Majesty's dominions.... And if there shall be any person or persons which are possessed of any such Blackamoors that refuse to deliver them in sort as aforesaid, then we require you to call them before you and to advise and persuade them by all good means to satisfy Her Majesty's pleasure therein; which if they shall eftsoons willfully and obstinately refuse, we pray you then to certify their names unto us, to the end Her Majesty may take such further course therein as it shall seem best in her princely wisdom.[4]

Obviously, Her Majesty herself had no understanding of Christ or his Gospel, or she could not have been involved in the African slave trade nor, indeed, have written such a racist proclamation. Her troubles with the King of Spain no doubt bordered on a fight over control of the African slave trade. Troubles with the King of Spain notwithstanding the Queen seems to have made the aim of the preceding King of Spain her aim. "Ferdinand II of Aragon [the home of one of Portia's suitors] sought to assure the racial and religious purity of Spain, which he achieved by the establishment of the Spanish Inquisition (1478) and by the conquest of Granada (1492), the last Moorish kingdom in Spain. In the same year the Jews of Spain were ordered to become Christians or face expulsion; the same alternatives were offered to the Moors of Castile in 1502."[5] The hatred of Jews, of course, goes farther back, which Shakespeare would have known and used to fuel his protest of anti–Semitism in *Merchant*, among other forms of anti–Christian bigotry.

> In 1290, during the reign of Edward I, all Jews were expelled from England with no explanation or apparent precipitating crisis. The Jewish community was forbidden from returning on pain of death. England was the first Christian nation to rid itself of all Jews by law.
>
> No jurist seems to have thought it necessary to justify the deportations; no chronicler bothered to record the official reasons. Perhaps no Jew or Christian thought reasons needed to be given. For decades the Jewish population of England had been in desperate trouble: accused of Host desecration and the ritual murder of Christian children, hated as moneylenders, reviled as Christ killers, beaten and lynched by mobs whipped into anti–Jewish frenzy by the incendiary sermons of itinerant friars.[6]

Although lynching is most infamously associated with black victims, there were many similarities between the victimization of Jews and of black people at the hands of the English. The signal difference, of course, is that, Jews, as merchants, were solidly entrenched in the African slave trade. Portia's question to Antonio and Shylock: "Which is the merchant?" is loaded with irony. But the devastation by the English upon blacks and Jews was similar in singularity; Just as England was the first nation to rid itself of its entire Jewish population; the English, "in their practical way, and their genius for large-scale undertakings, probably inflicted more suffering on the Negroes than any other nation" (in the African slave trade).[7] In the depiction of Aaron and Shylock, Shakespeare shows white people what they created. Apparently, and rightly so, Shakespeare considered the abominations visited upon black people to be the worst in human or inhuman history. Surely no one can deny the significance of the inclusion of black people in at least five of Shakespeare's plays during a time of major accelerations in the shipments of African slaves, a time when "the pattern for the entire history of the Atlantic slave trade was set!"[8] As one historian tells us, "Shakespeare tweaked the conscience of his time."[9]

And Venice, a "commercially adventurous city,"[10] was a significant setting for Shakespeare's protest of the African slave trade and merchant class, of which Antonio and Shylock are members:

> In the late fifteenth century, Venetians probably enjoyed the services of about three thousand slaves from North Africa or Tartary. Anxiety was

> sometimes expressed because there were too few slaves (for example, in a debate in the Senate in Venice in 1459); but there was also the fear lest slaves might become so numerous as to constitute a danger to the city, a familiar cry in later slave societies in the Americas.[11]

It is interesting to note the attitude of Pope Pius II toward slavery:

> evidence about Pius's acceptance of slavery in Italy shows that the pontiff was not censorious about slavery in general. He was, after all, a great Renaissance prince; the Renaissance implied the recovery of the practices and traditions of the "Golden Age," of antiquity; and antiquity ... never questioned slavery, nor the slave trade on humanitarian grounds.... The revival of the slave trade was to be an integral part of the recovery of the ideas of antiquity.[12]

As Shakespeare demonstrates, "The Renaissance in Europe had no humanitarian pretensions. Its "hard, gemlike flame" reburnished the ideas and practices of antiquity, the institution of slavery among them."[13]

Of course, no protest of the African slave trade would be complete that did not include the merchant class. As one historian put it: "The merchant on land and the fleet at sea were the key to empire, openly confessed."[14] John Ruskin, English writer and critic, the son of a wealthy merchant, "thought that Venice was corrupted in the Renaissance by the advent of mercantile rationalism.* He read Venetian history as an omen of England's doomed empire."[15] History confirms what Antonio, the merchant of Venice in Shakespeare's play, says to Salerio: "Investment partners of different ages and status binding them together, and any one merchant normally had a web of such engagements."[16] As Antonio says:

> My ventures are not in one bottom trusted,
> Nor to one place; nor is my whole estate
> Upon the fortune of this present year [I, i, 43–46].

The merchants of Venice were the key to the culture of Venice. Venice had a "single source of government — a compact patrician (nobili) class that had a secure monopoly on all the shifting positions."[17] It's interesting to note that the "nobili" were merchants (Wills, 112). Another elite group in the Venetian caste system, but lower than the patrician (nobili) class, which was "locked in" permanently, was the notables' class. "The main activity of the notables was as merchants. They had to be given the trading privileges of patricians (nobili) so that the latter could tap into their wealth for commercial projects. One of the joint trading forms in Venice was the "colleganza," in which a partner with smaller capital supplied something else — family connections, commercial information, or labor (like sailing with the ship carrying the part-

* The African slave trade

ner's merchandise and negotiating its foreign disposition)—to earn an equal share of the profit. Shakespeare picked up a vague awareness of such contracts in his source for *The Merchant of Venice.* In that play, Bassanio is a nobleman down on his luck who undertakes the trip to Belmont to woo an heiress with funds advanced him by Antonio. It is a colleganza, with Antonio as the merchant venturing capital and Bassanio as the impoverished noble undertaking the labor of travel and negotiation.[18] Kim Hall mentions "ships that contain Antonio's West Indian fortune,"[19] which leads one to believe that Antonio is involved in the African slave trade. So, in Venice, it seems, we have primarily a merchant-trade-profit-and-loss mentality or "mercantile rationalistic" culture. "Venice permitted Jews to reside relatively unmolested for extended periods of time, forbidding them, to be sure, to own land or practice most 'honest' trades but allowing, even encouraging, them to lend money at interest. Such fiscal liquidity was highly useful in a society where canon law prohibited Christians from taking interest, but it made the Jews predictable objects of popular loathing and upper-class exploitation," although "the realm's mercantile economy could not function without the possibility of moneylending" and "many individuals [including Shakespeare's father] devised clever means, legal and illegal, to get around the official constraints."[20]

The Merchant of Venice is a play of a thousand ironies exposing a thousand contradictions and hypocrisies, but not to "play" with, as Greenblatt states, rather, to expose the absurdity of and condemn presumptions of superiority and supremacy; whether white over black, straight over gay; male over female; Christian over Jew; mercantilist/mechanistic love over pure love. For example, to condemn gay-bashing and hatred of gays, Shakespeare has his main character, Antonio, who is gay, possess the purest love in the entire play, Antonio's love for Bassanio. But, at the same time, Antonio holds forth ironically as the persecuted (being gay) persecuting, for he is an African slave trade merchant persecuting blacks (to say the least), and he is anti–Semitic, persecuting Jews. The irony of ironies is that, while he claims to be a Christian, his persecuting of blacks and Jews proves him not to be a "real Christian" at all.

In spite of Shakespeare's use of irony to condemn, among others, anti–Semitism, racism, nominal Christianity, revenge, homophobia, the African slave trade, usury, patriarchy and legalism, the play is very much, if not essentially, about love, on which subject irony proves most revelatory of contradictions. For example, the causes of the aforementioned perversions are summed up in the context of love. As Bassanio attempts to determine where love is bred, he concludes (unlike Portia regarding the price of Morocco) it is not "engendered in the eyes" (III, ii, 75–82):

> So many the outward shows be least themselves.
> The world is still deceived with ornament.

In law, what plea so tainted and corrupt
But being seasoned with a gracious voice,
Obscures the show of evil? In religion,
What damned error but some sober brow
Will bless it and approve it with a text,
Hiding the grossness with fair ornament? [III, ii, 75–82].

In other words, when the tainted, corrupt and damned error of the African slave trade, racism, anti-Semitism, homophobia, are "seasoned with a gracious voice" by law, and "blessed and approved with a text" by religion, the evil of the African slave trade, racism, homophobia, etc., is obscured and hidden. Shakespeare reveals this by defining real love and having a gay man demonstrate real love, that love is sufficient unto itself, pure, unadulterated by racism, religion, homophobia, sexism, money, law, or patriarchy. The very debt that the play turns upon is Antonio's love for Bassanio, who needs money to compete for the love of Portia, in full knowledge of which Antonio puts himself in hock to Shylock. He remains true to his word when he says to Bassanio, "be assured / My purse, my person, my extremest means, / Lie all unlocked to your occasions" (I, i, 140–142):

You know me well, and herein spend but time
To wind about my love with circumstance.
And out of doubt you do me now more wrong
In making question of my uttermost
Than if you had made waste of all I have.
Then do but say to me what I should do
That in your knowledge may by me be done,
And I am pressed unto it. Therefore, speak [I, i, 156–160].

These lines confirm for us the meaning of the opening lines of the play, that is, Antonio's suffering the classic symptoms of being in love, as he describes them:

In sooth, I know not why I am so sad.
It wearies me, you say it wearies you,
But how I caught it, found it, or came by it,
What stuff 'tis made of, thereof it is born,
I am to learn;
And such a want-wit sadness makes of me
That I have much ado to know myself [I, i, 1–7].

Antonio is, in other words, by his own admission, ignorant of Bernard's First Step of Truth, Knowing Yourself. As both anti-Semitic and an African slave trade merchant, he is also ignorant of Bernard's Second and Third Steps of Truth, Knowing Your Neighbor ("We can know our neighbor only by love"), and Knowing God (Truth in its own nature).[21] Antonio's friend, Salerio, attributes Antonio's sadness to anxiety over his African slave ships. He says to Antonio:

> Your mind is tossing on the ocean,
> There where your argosies [great merchant ships] with portly sail,
> Like signors and rich burghers on the flood—
> Or as it were the pageants of the sea—
> Do overpeer the petty traffickers
> That curtsy to them, do them reverence,
> As they fly by them with their woven wings [I, i, 8–14].

Salerio and Solanio go on and on in a similar vein. But Antonio assures them that this vein is not the cause of his sadness. Salerio then unwittingly hits the mark: "Why then, you are in love." Antonio, not knowing himself, answers: "Fie, fie."

Once they've all left Antonio and Bassanio alone, the conversation changes to Portia, and Bassanio's need for money to compete for her. Love is cheapened and adulterated by this need for money, especially when compared to Antonio's love. Moreover, although Bassanio later contradicts himself, in this conversation, love is bred in the eyes, and accordingly can be seen as racist as Portia's revulsion for black skin, for example, as in the case of the Moroccan prince. It's a subtle reminder that "Man judges by appearance, but God judges the heart." Portia is "a lady richly left, / And she is fair, and fairer than that word, / Of wondrous virtues... / ...her sunny locks hang on her temples like a golden fleece...." In addition to the Scripture, Shakespeare may also have been thinking of something Augustine said: "beauty ... is not of much moment to the wise man, whose blessedness lies in spiritual and immortal blessings, in far better and more endearing gifts, in the good things that are the peculiar property of the good, and are not shared by good and bad alike."[22] In other words, Portia's attributes—beauty, fair skin, blond hair, and riches—are shared by good and bad alike, and thus are not of much moment to the wise man, nor to real love.

In answer to Bassanio's question, "Tell me where is fancy [love] bred: / Or in the heart or in the head," / Love is bred in the heart, not in the head, Shakespeare is saying, for passion is not subject to reason, according to Bernard ("Passion, one of the four natural emotions, is not subject to reason."[23] Shakespeare has Portia echo Bernard in this:

> The brain may devise laws for the blood, but a hot temper leaps o'er a cold decree. Such a hare is madness, the youth, to skip o'er the meshes of good counsel, the cripple [I, ii, 17–20],

as she bemoans being forced to abide by a patriarchal will that contradicts it,

> But this reasoning is not in the fashion to choose me a husband. O me, the word "choose"! I may neither choose who I would Nor refuse who I dislike; so is the will of a living Daughter curbed by the will of a dead father [I, ii, 18–25].

In other words, she is saying she does not "retain the use of her own will, nor consequently the judgment of freedom." She's a sort of slave. The last words of Aaron the slave are: "...if I might have my will" (V, iii, 183–187). "To act freely means to act willingly."[24]

She states emphatically: "If I live to be as old as Sibylla I will die as chaste as Diana unless I be obtained by the manner of my father's will" (I, ii, 103). Perhaps her maid's prophetic take on the written will, ironically, strengthened Portia's will. Says Nerissa:

> Your father was ever virtuous, and holy men at their death have good inspiration; therefore the lottery that he hath devised in these three chests of gold, silver, and lead, whereof who chooses his meaning chooses you, will no doubt never be chosen by any rightly but one who you shall rightly love [I, ii, 24–29].

Such an inspiration would seem to derive from a desire that Portia have "love in the strict sense." According to Bernard, "there are three kinds of love—that which is emotional but not spiritual, that which is spiritual but not emotional, and that which is both emotional and spiritual; only the last is love in the strict sense."[25] Antonio's love for Bassanio is love in the strict sense.

The scene comes to an end with Portia speaking fondly of Bassanio, whom she remembers seeing when her father was alive. These romantic thoughts are interrupted by the arrival of a suitor, the Prince of Morocco, of whom she has a racist opinion before even meeting him. She says to Nerissa: "If he have the condition of a saint and the complexion of a devil, I had rather he should shrive me than wive me." In other words, because of the color of his skin, Portia cannot give a black man even one of the three kinds of love, certainly not love in the strict sense. A similar kind of absence, denial, or rejection of all three kinds of love, opens the next scene: racial and religious hatred.

The scene begins with Bassanio and Shylock, the Jew, discussing the loan of three thousand ducats that will bind Antonio. The idea of Antonio being bound to him pleases Shylock very much. And all the more so when he considers the precariousness of Antonio's "ventures" at sea, the profits from which Antonio would be paying his debt to Shylock. Shylock recites all of the ports for which Antonio's merchant ships are bound. All of the ports are African slave trade ports of call: Tripoli; the East and West Indies; Mexico; England. And he eagerly anticipates the hazards of such voyages, agreeing to the loan, obviously based on the likelihood of the ships floundering and sinking. He asks to speak with Antonio. Bassanio asks Shylock to dine with him and Antonio. We are then immediately made privy to the barrage of anti–Christian emotions Shylock is harboring. He says (aside):

> Yes, to smell pork, to eat of the habitation which your prophet the Nazarite conjured the devil into! I will buy with you, sell with you, talk with you, walk with you, and so following, but I will not eat with you, drink with you, nor pray with you [I, iii, 29–33].

At the approach of Antonio, Shylock continues in the same vein and manner (aside):

> How like a fawning publican he looks.
> I hate him for he is a Christian;
> But more, for that in low simplicity
> He lends out money gratis, and brings down
> The rate of usance here with us in Venice.
> If I can catch him once upon the hip
> I will feed fat the ancient grudge I bear him.
> He hates our sacred nation, and he rails,
> Even there where merchants most do congregate,
> On me, my bargains, and my well-worn thrift—
> Which he calls interest. Cursed be my tribe
> If I forgive him [I, iii, 35–46].

For the character of Shylock in these asides, Shakespeare goes directly to the characterization of Jews in the Bible. For example, Shylock's reaction to pork is an allusion to Old Testament Jewish law (Deut. 14:8): "the swine is unclean unto you: you shall not eat of their flesh, nor touch their dead carcass." Shakespeare combines this law with Shylock's anti–Christ ridicule of Jesus casting devils into swine, which echoes the anti–Christ attitude of New Testament Jews (Matt. 8:28–32; 9:34):

> Jesus came into the country of the Gergesenes where he met two possessed with devils, coming out of the tombs, exceeding fierce, so that no man might pass that way.... And there was a good way off from them an herd of many swine feeding. So the devils besought him, saying, If thou cast us out, suffer us to go away into the heard of swine. And he said unto them, Go. And when they were come out, they went into the herd of swine and, behold, the whole herd of swine ran violently down a steep place into the sea, and perished in the waters.

But the Pharisees said, "He casteth out devils through the prince of the devils."

Also, there was a Jewish ceremonial law that would have prohibited Shylock's eating and drinking with Antonio, a Gentile. Of course, the same discrimination was observed by the early Christians, mainly right-wing conservatives who believed Christianity was a movement "within" Judaism, that you couldn't be a Christian unless you were a Jew first. Peter, the apostle, believed that Christianity was a movement "from" Judaism. There was a protest against him for eating and drinking with a Gentile. But Peter answered them, saying:

> Ye know how that it is an unlawful thing for a man that is a Jew to keep company, or come unto one of another nation; but God hath shewed me that I should not call any man common or unclean [Acts 10:28].

Earlier, Peter had fallen into a trance and had had the following vision:

> He saw heaven opened, and a certain vessel descending unto him, as it had been a great sheet knit at the four corners, and let down to the earth: Wherein were all manner of fourfooted beasts of the earth, and wild beasts, and creeping things, and fowls of the air. And there came a voice to him, Rise, Peter; kill, and eat. But Peter said, Not so, Lord; for I have never eaten any thing that is common or unclean. And the voice spake unto him again the second time, What God hath cleansed, that call not common [Acts 10:10–15].

In discussing with Shylock the amount and duration of the loan, Antonio lets his Christian position be known from the outset, which is also a measure of his love for Bassanio:

> Shylock, albeit I neither lend nor borrow
> By taking nor by giving of excess,
> Yet to supply the ripe wants of my friend
> I'll break a custom [I, iii, 59–62].

As the bond is set, three thousand ducats for three months, Shylock tries to justify or defend usury by the example of Jacob and Laban in Genesis 30:27–43, which is to identify usury with fraud, scheming, and expediency, while claiming God's blessing on the most cunning schemer, the implication being, that, "prosperity ought to be the concomitant of religion."[26] One Biblical scholar's gloss on the Jacob/Laban story suggests the purpose of Shakespeare's use of it: "The people of Israel were convinced that there is an intimate relationship between favor with heaven, and material well-being in this world." Similarly, John Calvin taught that "the Christian citizen would be more evidently a man of God if he was a success in business."[27] This explains the heavy involvement of Jews and Calvinists in the African slave trade, "which was so enormously profitable that nothing else could compete with it."[28]

Shylock's example of the Jacob/Laban story prompts a response from Antonio, attacking Shylock's defense:

> Mark you this, Bassanio—
> The devil can cite scripture for his purpose.
> An evil soul producing holy witness
> Is like a villain with a smiling cheek,
> A goodly apple rotten at the heart.
> O what a goodly outside falsehood hath! [I, iii, 95–100].

Shylock performs according to Antonio's description, especially given the fact that his true feelings are in "asides." But, although he may dissemble, Shylock, given his litany of abuses by Antonio, has just cause to harbor in his heart feelings of hatred and murder toward Antonio. The latter's anti–Semitic behavior toward Skylock is as un–Christian as Shylock's hatred of Christianity. For example:

> Signior Antonio, many a time and oft
> In the Rialto you have rated me
> About my moneys and my usances.
> Still have I borne it with a patient shrug.
> For sufferance is the badge of all our tribe.
> You call me misbeliever, cut-throat dog.
> And spit upon my Jewish gaberdine,
> And all for use of that which is mine own.
> Well then, it now appears you need my help.
> Go to, then — you come to me and you say,
> "Shylock, we should have moneys," you say so—
> You that did void your rheum upon my beard
> And foot me as you spurn a stranger cur
> Over your threshold. Moneys is your suit.
> What should I say to you? Should I not say
> "Hath a dog money? Is it possible
> A cur can lend three thousand ducats?" Or
> Shall I bend low and in bondman's key,
> With bated breath and whispering humbleness,
> Say this: "Fair sir, you spit on me on Wednesday last;
> You spurned me such a day; another time
> You called me dog, and for these courtesies
> I'll lend you this much moneys"? [I, iii, 104–126].

Surely the above is Shakespeare bringing white people face to face with their anti–Semitism. How anyone can deny Shakespeare's condemnation of anti–Semitism is inconceivable. And it seems pretty obvious that Shakespeare is here condemning Christopher Marlowe's anti–Semitism in *The Jew of Malta*, "which was probably first performed in 1589, near the beginning of Shakespeare's career as a playwright, and it was an immediate success."[29]

Antonio's anti–Semitism remains undisturbed at Shylock's pain:

> I am as like to call thee [dog] again —
> To spit on thee again, to spurn thee too.
> If thou wilt lend this money, lend it not
> As to thy friends, for when did friendship take
> A breed for barren metal of his friend?
> But lend it rather to thine enemy
> Who, if he break, thou mayst with better face
> Exact the penalty [I, iii, 127–134].

Antonio's obdurateness and unabashed anti–Semitism may well have been responsible for the severity of the terms of the bond. Shylock was certainly not unprovoked, and *had* offered kindness. He says:

This kindness will I show:
Go with me to a notary, seal me there
Your single bond, and in a merrysport
If you repay me not on such a day
In such a place, such sum or sums as are
Expressed in the condition, let the forfeit
Be nominated for an equal pound
Of your fair flesh, to be cut off and taken
In what part of your body pleaseth me [I, iii, 141–149].

Bassanio objects: "You shall not seal to such a bond for me," but Antonio assures him: "I will not forfeit it." Speaking of his African slave ships, he adds, "I do expect return / Of thrice three times the value of this bond.... My ships come home a month before the day." They all agree to meet at the notary's.

Shakespeare abruptly changes the subject. From exposing anti–Semitism he changes to exposing racism and the similarities between the two. As Act I closes with Antonio timing the arrival of his African slave ships, Act II opens with the statement: "Mislike me not for my complexion," by Portia's tawny North African suitor, the Prince of Morocco. In praise of his dark complexion, he says:

I tell thee, lady, this aspect of mine
Hath feared the valiant [brought fear to] by my love I swear
The best regarded virgins of our clime
Have loved it too. I would not change this hue
Except to steal your thoughts, my gentle queen [II, i, 8–12].

Portia lies when she tells him if she were not bound by the conditions of the lottery: "Yourself, renowned prince, then stood as fair / As any comer I have looked on yet / For my affection" (II, i, 20–22). He answers: "Even for that I thank you. Therefore I pray you lead me to the caskets / To try my fortune" (II, i, 23–24). Portia had seen him coming and had said then, "If he have the condition of a saint and the complexion of a devil, I had rather he would shrive me than wive me." When he chooses the wrong casket, she says:

A gentle riddance! Draw the curtains; go.
Let all of his complexion choose me so [II, vii, 79–80].

Ironically, Morocco's criticism of the lottery as a way of choosing a husband is also true of choosing a husband by racism (the white man may be the unworthier compared to the black):

But, alas the while,
If Hercules and Lychas play at dice
Which is the better man, the greater throw
May turn by fortune from the weaker hand—

> So is Alcides beaten by his rage.
> And so may I, blind Fortune leading me,
> Miss that which one unworthier may attain,
> And die with grieving [II, i, 32–39].

Shakespeare's protest of prejudice and discrimination continues even during the comic relief. The similarity between racism and anti–Semitism surfaces in Launcelot's calling Shylock the "devil," a debasement usually reserved for the black man. Launcelot the clown seems to have just cause for leaving the service of Shylock, but it need not have anything to do with Shylock's being a Jew, other than the prejudicial designating of his abuses as characteristically Jewish, which would be difficult to support since white slave masters are notorious for worse abuses to their black slaves. We are reminded that the wise man's blessedness lies "in the good things that are the peculiar property of the good, and are not shared by good and bad alike."[30] Launcelot's anti–Semitism is denounced as absurd in that it is his good angel that tells him to stay in the service of Shylock, while his bad angel, the devil himself, urges him to leave. It is the desperation caused by his anti–Semitism that makes him say, "I am a Jew if I serve the Jew any longer," and leave. But Shakespeare seems to identify or equate anti–Semitism with evil, with the devil, in Launcelot's proclaiming, "The fiend gives the more friendly counsel: I will run. Fiend, my heels are at your commandment."

As far as Jessica is concerned, motivations and machinations are more difficult to decipher. She admits to Launcelot, "Our house is hell." But it's more complex than that. She could just be rebelling against a patriarchal father rather than hating to be a Jew. Or, it could be that falling in love with a Christian has made her desire to be one with him in every way. In spite of one of the ten commandments—"Honour thy father and thy mother: that thy days may be long upon the land which the Lord thy God given thee" (Exodus 20:12)—she says to herself prior to her own exodus:

> Alack, what heinous sin is it in me
> To be ashamed to be my father's child
> But though I am a daughter to his blood
> I am not to his manners. O Lorenzo,
> If thou keep promise, I shall end this strife—
> Become a Christian and thy loving wife [II, iii, 15–20].

Most likely it's the horrifying effect of anti–Semitism that makes her hate being a Jew, just as it is the horrifying effect of racism that often makes black children hate being black. Moreover, it is most likely the effects of anti–Semitism that makes Shylock's "manners" a source of shame for his daughter. Did she steal from him, breaking another commandment, out of a lack of self-worth, feeling the need of money and jewels to win approval? The irony is that these two Jewish commandments she breaks are part of the Christian canon as well. Shakespeare could be equating canon law with bigotry.

One is simply blown away by the power of the play's indictment of anti–Semitism. This is sometimes demonstrated through its indictment of racism. For example, when Shylock says: "Why revenge! / The villainy you teach me I will execute, and it shall go hard but I will better the instruction," we are reminded of Aaron the Moor, and the villainy the same masters taught him:

> Vengeance is in my heart, death in my hand,
> Blood and revenge are hammering in my head[31]
> [*Titus Andronicus*, II, iii, 38–39].

Both Aaron and Shylock "hold forth in the style of the masters they have learned from."[32]

When Shylock adamantly declares he'd rather have his bond, a pound of Antonio's flesh, than any amount of money, the Duke asks him: "How shalt thou hope for mercy, rend'ring none?" There's irony in the question, in that, being a spat-upon Jew, he is rendering the hoped-for mercy *he* has received: none! That's just the point. Shylock's answer is profoundly telling:

> You have among you many a purchased slave,
> Which like your asses and your dogs and mules,
> You use in abject and in slavish parts
> Because you bought them. Shall I say to you,
> "Let them be free; marry them to your heirs!
> Why sweat they under burdens? Let their beds
> Be made as soft as yours, and let their palates
> Be seasoned with such viands"? You will answer,
> "The slaves are ours." So do I answer you.
> The pound of flesh which I demand of him
> Is dearly bought, as mine, and I will have it [IV, i, 91–101].

To this there is no rebuttal possible. "Venice was an important slave market during this period."[33] And slavery is worse than usury, Shylock reminds us.

Shylock is called some of the same names Aaron the Moor is called: For example, Aaron is called, "hellish dog"[34]; Shylock is called "damned inexecrable dog" (IV, i, 130). Aaron is called, "incarnate devil"[35]; of Shylock, it is said, "Certainly the Jew is the very devil incarnation" (II, ii, 22); and, "Let me say amen betimes lest the devil cross my prayer, for here he comes in the likeness of a Jew" (III, i, 17–18). And Aaron's justifiable rage in the end, verifying the hate that racism's hate produced, is echoed in Shylock's justifiable rage in the end, verifying the hate that anti–Semitism produced. What is said of Shylock in the following is implied of Aaron as well, and is consummate commentary on the effects of racism and anti–Semitism, that he is:

> A stony adversary, an inhuman wretch,
> Uncapable of pity, void and empty
> From any dram of mercy [IV, i, 4–6].

Ironically, in thus standing forth in the style of his oppressors, Aaron, after being informed of his punishment, is able to remain unbroken, head neither bloody nor bowed, inhumanly in the face of a most inhumanly atrocious punishment: to be set breast-deep in the earth and famished (V, iii, 78).

> Ah, why should wrath be mute and fury dumb?
> I am no baby, I, that with base prayers
> I should repent the evils I have done.
> Ten thousand worse than ever yet I did
> Would I perform if I might have my will.
> If one good deed in all my life I did
> I do repent it from my very soul.[36]

In other words, his wrath and fury against slavery and racism are given vent in evil acts performed. And more to come, if he might have his will. Being a slave, he does not have the use of a free will. "On what basis in fact can one impute anything to a man, whether good or bad, if he is not known to have the free disposal of himself?"[37]

In his rage against anti-Semitism, Shylock becomes a crucifier of Christ:

> These be the Christian husbands! I have a daughter—
> Would any of the stock of Barrabas
> Had been her husband rather than a Christian! [IV, i, 303–305].

(Barrabas was a thief whom the Jews wanted released from crucifixion instead of Christ.)

In the end, Shylock is broken. He leaves the court, alone, bereft, and unwell, the latter, no doubt, at the thought of becoming a Christian and thus anti-Semitic. Through irony too painful in its absurdity to ignore, Shakespeare demonstrates that both Aaron and Shylock are punished for what they've been turned into by those responsible for what they have become. So, just because the anti-Semites go away happy does not mean Shakespeare is saying anti-Semitism is right or good, any more than he would say racism is right or good because lynch mobs go away happy, leaving,

> Black bodies swinging in the southern breeze,
> Strange fruit hanging from the poplar trees.
> Pastoral scene of the gallant South,
> The bulging eyes and the twisted mouth,
> Scent of magnolia sweet and fresh,
> Then the sudden smell of burning flesh.[38]

Shakespeare's exquisitely poignant and powerful indictment of anti–Semitism can be fittingly applied to racism if one substitutes in turn, "a black man," for "a Jew," in the following:

> Hath not a Jew eyes? Hath not a Jew hands, organs, dimensions, senses, affections, passions—fed with the same food, hurt with the same weapons, subject to the same diseases, healed by the same means, warmed and cooled by the same winter and summer as a Christian is? If you prick us do we not bleed? If you tickle us do we not laugh? If you poison us do we not die, and if you wrong us shall we not revenge? If we are like you in the rest, we will resemble you in that. If a Jew wrong a Christian, what is his humility? Revenge! If a Christian wrong a Jew, what should his sufferance be by Christian example? Why revenge! The villainy you teach me I will execute, and it shall go hard but I will better the instruction [III, i, 48–60].

It's not revenge so much as it is what he and black people have been turned into by the villainy of white people, in particular, by so-called "Christians."

It is quite unlikely that Shakespeare would have had "Christian" so often mentioned in an unchristian context if he were not intending to call attention to the contradiction, in order to draw a distinction between the genuine and the counterfeit, like Irenaeus (ad 120–202) when he spoke "against the heresies that came in, like locusts, to devour the harvests of the Gospel"[39]:

> A clever imitation in glass casts contempt, as it were, on that precious jewel the emerald (which is most highly esteemed by some), unless it come under the eye of one able to test and expose the counterfeit.[40]

Shakespeare is one who is able to test and expose the counterfeit. The ultimate irony, which fuels the scathing indictment of anti–Semitism and racism in defense of "real Christianity," is that none of the Christians are "real Christians," their so-called Christianity is counterfeit. Essentially, in other words, the play is a powerful indictment of nominal Christianity. Antonio's love for Bassanio is that precious jewel, the emerald, but his Christianity is "a clever imitation in glass."[41]

No *real* Christian would be an African slave trade merchant, like Antonio. No *real* Christian would spit on a Jew, like Antonio spits on Shylock. No *real* Christian would look upon a Jew or a black human being as a "dog," like Antonio looks upon and calls Shylock. In addition, there is a hypocritical contradiction, to say the least, in Antonio's remark to Bassanio: "The Hebrew will turn Christian — he grows kind," when Antonio, the Christian, has been anything but kind to the Hebrew.

The subject of mercy, ironically introduced by the Duke's hypocritical allusion to the Beatitudes of Christ: "Blessed are the merciful for they shall receive mercy" (Matt. 5:7), brings into focus Bernard's three Steps of Truth, and the imitation Christianity practiced by the so-called Christians. When the Duke asks Shylock, "How shalt thou hope for mercy, rend'ring none?" the first part of Shylock's answer: "What judgment shall I dread, doing no wrong?" proves his ignorance of the First Step of Truth, Knowing Yourself, "For all have sinned, and come short of the glory of God" (Rom. 3:23). But as he continues his answer, Shylock proves the Duke doesn't know himself either, and that the same question can be asked of him that he asks Shylock: "How shalt thou hope for mercy, rend'ring none?" inasmuch as:

> You have among you many a purchased slave,
> Which like your asses and your dogs and mules,
> You use in abject and in slavish parts
> Because you bought them. Shall I say to you,
> "Let them be free; marry them to your heirs!
> Why sweat they under burdens? Let their beds
> Be made as soft as yours, and let their palates
> Be seasoned with such viands"? You will answer,
> "The slaves are ours." So do I answer you.
> The pound of flesh which I demand of him
> Is dearly bought, as mine, and I will have it [IV, i, 90–100].

In other words, the Duke is much more without mercy than is Shylock, by not knowing himself, and has the hypocritical audacity to accuse Shylock. Bernard speaks to them both: "Observe what you are, that you are wretched indeed, and so learn to be merciful, a thing you cannot know in any other way."[42]

In the last statement of Shylock's answer to the Duke, he says quite adamantly: "I stand for judgment." What Bernard says puts the whole courtroom scene in proper perspective as to judgment:

> Love, like hate, is a stranger to true judgment. Will you hear a true judgment? "As I hear, I judge;" not as I hate, not as I love, not as I fear. There is a judgment of hate, for example, "We have a law, and by our law he ought to die." (JHN, 19:7) (This is stated by the Jews in reference to crucifying Christ.) Also of fear, for example (again in reference to Christ), "If we let him thus alone, the Romans shall come and take away both our place and nation." And there is a judgment of love, as David's command concerning his parricide son, "Deal gently with the young man, even with Absalom." And I know it is a rule in human law observed in both ecclesiastical and secular cases that personal friends of the litigants cannot be admitted as judges, lest they either defraud or be defrauded by their love for their friends. Now if your love for a friend either lessens or completely conceals his guilt in your judgment, how much more will your love of yourself deceive you in judging yourself.[42]

According to Shakespeare's allusion to Bernard, then, Shylock will not have the judgment he stands for, a true judgment, but a judgment of hate, and therefore not a true judgment. Nor is Portia's a true judgment, but a judgment of love. She defrauds Shylock and the court by her love for her husband, and because of how dear a lover of her husband Antonio is. She speaks with insight on that score, which is later revealed:

> ...in companions
> That converse and waste the time together,
> Whose souls do bear an equal yoke of love,
> There must be needs a like proportion
> Of lineaments, of manners, and of spirit;
> Which makes me think that this Antonio,
> Being the bosom lover of my lord,
> Must needs be like my lord. If it be so,
> How little is the cost I have bestowed
> In purchasing the semblance of my soul
> From out the state of hellish cruelty! [III, iv, 11–21].

Portia is a liar, a forger, a charlatan, and as such, a felon, with no legal right to be in the courtroom and should not have been admitted. Shylock, on the other hand, has a legal claim which even his claim's victim submits to. The fact that charlatan Portia is to judge Shylock's suit is blatant proof, Shakespeare is saying, that a Jew can't get a fair trial because he is a Jew, no matter how legitimate his claim. And those who make it so take no responsibility for the hatred they create and cause.

Portia begins with a beautiful speech about mercy. Her giving it reminds us of something stated earlier:

> The world is still deceived with ornament
> In law, what plea so tainted and corrupt
> But being seasoned with a gracious voice,
> Obscures the show of evil? [III, ii, 76–79].

Portia preaches mercy but she does not practice mercy; she is not merciful to Shylock but legalistic, canceling out mercy, ironically, giving him what he asks for. The mercy speech is triggered by Shylock's pride, his believing he does not need mercy. In answering Portia's assertion, "Then must the Jew be merciful," he says: "On what compulsion must I? Tell me that" (IV, i, 186–187). One of the Scriptures that may have influenced Shakespeare's depiction of Portia's judgment of Shylock is James 2:13: "For he shall have judgment without mercy, that hath shewed no mercy; and mercy rejoiceth against judgment." The opening lines of Portia's mercy speech are to remind us that "God maketh his sun to rise on the evil and on the good, and sendeth rain on the just and on the unjust" (Matt. 5:45).

To paraphrase Bernard: we cannot know our neighbors by anti–Semitism or racism or homophobia. "We can know our neighbors only by love, and this purifies the mind's eye so as to make it able to contemplate Truth in itself. Knowledge of other men is, therefore, the path which leads from knowledge of yourself to knowledge of God."[43] Antonio, Shylock, Portia, and others "stand for law." Shakespeare's message is "Love is the fullness of the law and if you love your brother you have fulfilled the law."[44] "Greater love had not man than this, that a man lay down his life for his friend" (John 15:13). This is "real Christianity." Shakespeare's depiction also reveals a different, if not ironic, aspect of Bernard's definition of love; "A man's enemies, who do not love him, he cannot love: Bernard rejects as absurd a literal interpretation of the commandment to love your enemies."[45]

Bernard's definition of love pulls the whole play together significantly. Leah S. Marcus has said: "*The Merchant of Venice* is one of Shakespeare's most beautiful plays; it is arguably also one of his ugliest."[46] We've discussed the ugliness, the anti–Semitism and racism. I would say, without hesitation, that the beauty of *The Merchant of Venice* is the love of two men for each other, especially Antonio's love for Bassanio. It stands also as an example of "real Christian" love, in protest of homophobia, "tainted and corrupt law," and the "damned gross error of religion." In other words, in the face of the legal and religious prohibitions of Shakespeare's day, Shakespeare glorifies homosexual love. Greenblatt notes the following:

> Elizabethans acknowledged the existence of same-sex desire; indeed, it was in a certain sense easier for them to justify than heterosexual desire. That men were inherently superior to women was widely preached; why then wouldn't men naturally be drawn to love other men? Sodomy was strictly prohibited by religious teaching and the law, but that prohibition aside, it was perfectly understandable that men would love and desire men.[47]

Another scholar notes, "Sodomy was condemned almost universally in legal and religious discourses, and the penalty upon conviction was death."[48]

Shakespeare's glorification of homosexual love is made possible through his use of Bernard's definition of love, which, of all of the types of relationships in the play, the love between Antonio and Bassanio comes closest to exemplifying:

> Love is sympathy, a symmetrical relation; therefore it is always returned. It makes two souls one spirit just as marriage makes two bodies one flesh; you can no more love without being loved in return than you can marry without being married in return. Both parts of the mutual love must exist, although both need not be equal. The greatest love a man can have is willingness to lay down his life for his friends.[49]

In the case of Antonio and Bassanio, each is willing to lay down his life for the other. Antonio's willingness to lay down his life for Bassanio is indicated from the beginning, when he says to Bassanio: "My purse, my person, my extremest means / Lie all unlocked to your occasion" (I, i, 141–142). His willingness is obvious when laying down his life for Bassanio is required:

> Sweet Bassanio, my ships have all miscarried; my creditors grow cruel; my estate is very low; my bond to the Jew is forfeit; and since in paying it, it is impossible I should live, all debts are cleared between you and I if I might see you at my death. Notwithstanding, use your pleasure; if your love do not persuade you to come, let not my letter [III, ii, 324–330].

And later he says to the jailer: "Pray Bassanio come / To see me pay his debt, and then I care not" (III, iii, 38–39). Portia's love of Bassanio, in reflecting Bernard's definition of love, enables her to understand the love between Antonio and Bassanio, a love she does not fear, knowing it can go nowhere because of law and religion.

Bassanio first expresses his willingness to lay down his life for Antonio in saying to Antonio: "This Jew shall have my flesh, blood, bones, and all, / Ere thou shalt lose for me one drop of blood" (IV, i, 114–115). Antonio stresses his willingness again:

> I am armed and well prepared.
> Give me your hand, Bassanio, fare you well;
> Grieve not that I am fall'n to this for you,
> * * *
> Commend me to your honorable wife:
> Tell her the process of Antonio's end;
> Say how I loved you; speak me fair in death.
> And when the tale is told, bid her be judge
> Whether Bassanio had not once a love.
> Repent but you that you shall lose your friend
> And he repents not that he pays your debt;
> For if the Jew do cut but deep enough,
> I'll pay it instantly with all my heart [IV, i, 272–274, 280–289].

With equal intensity, echoing David to Jonathan ("Thy love to me was wonderful, passing the love of women" [II Samuel 1:26]), Bassanio answers, again with his willingness to lay down his life for Antonio:

> Antonio, I am married to a wife
> Which is as dear to me as life itself;
> But life itself, my wife, and all the world
> Are not with me esteemed above thy life.
> I would lose all — aye, sacrifice them all
> Here to this devil — to deliver you [IV, i, 290–295].

On the whole and throughout, Antonio, in his love for Bassanio, embodies other aspects of Bernard's definition of love. According to Bernard:

> Love is sufficient in itself, it is pleasing in itself and for its own sake. It is itself a merit, and is its own reward. Love seeks no reason or fruit beyond itself. Its use is its fruit. I love because I love; I love in order to love. It is a bond of affection, not of law; it neither acquires nor is acquired by contract. It moves freely, and makes us free. True love is content with itself. It has a reward, but it is the beloved object. For whatever you pretend to love for the sake of something else, you are obviously loving that which is the end of your love, not that which is its means. The true lover always does desire the real possession of the loved object, but in the sense of loving it.[50]

We can sense that desire in Antonio when he sees Bassanio off on his way to court Portia, which Antonio, in full knowledge, has made possible. Salerio describes Antonio at the parting, saying to Solanio:

> his eye being big with tears,
> Turning his face, he put his hand behind him
> And with affection wondrous sensible
> He wrung Bassanio's hand; and so they parted [II, viii, 46–49].

Solanio comments: "I think he only loves the world for [Bassanio]."

For the quintessential message of the play we have to examine Shakespeare's use of irony in the trial scene, especially the emanation from Portia's mercy speech. In a way the scene can be viewed as Old Testament vs. New Testament, legalism vs. love; Torah vs. Crucifix. The law, Shylock's only salvation, fails him in the end. But so does love, given the anti-Semitic environment. Legalism wins the day, but not for Shylock. For example, when Gratiano asks Shylock on Antonio's behalf: "Can no prayers pierce thee?" Shylock's answer—"No, none that thou hast wit enough to make"—is ironically apropos, given the anti-Semitic barrage it elicits, proof Gratiano has already wavered in his faith:

> Oh, be thou damned, inexecrable dog!
> And for thy life let justice be accused.
> Thou almost makest me waver in my faith,
> To hold opinion with Pythagoras
> That souls of animals infuse themselves
> Into the trunks of men. Thy currish spirit
> Governed a wolf who, hanged for human slaughter,
> Even from the gallows did his fell soul fleet [lose]
> And whilst thou lay'st in thy unhallowed dam
> Infused itself in thee, for thy desires
> Are wolvish, bloody, starved, and ravenous [IV, i, 128–138].

Shylock remains impervious:

> Till thou canst rail the seal from off my bond,
> Thou but offend'st thy lungs to speak so loud.
> Repair thy wit, good youth, or it will fall
> To cureless ruin. I stand here for law [IV, i, 139–142].

The law he stands for is a fraud and should not be admitted, according to Bernard: "I know it is a rule in human law observed in both ecclesiastical and secular cases that personal friends of the litigants cannot be admitted as judges, lest they either defraud or be defrauded by their love for their friends."[51] No fair trial for Shylock!

Ironically, it is Portia the fraud who gives an exquisite expression of "real Christianity" and the best reason so far presented as to why Shylock would be merciful. When Antonio answers, "I do," to her question "Do you confess the bond?" she says: "Then must the Jew be merciful." Shakespeare uses a significant word, "compulsion" for Shylock's protest, especially in keeping with Bernard's Second Step of Truth. Shylock says: "On what compulsion must I? Tell me that." She tells him:

> The quality of mercy is not strained [forced],
> It droppeth as the gentle rain from heaven
> Upon the place beneath. It is twice blest;
> It blesseth him that gives and him that takes.
> 'Tis mightiest in the mightiest. It becomes
> The throned monarch better than his crown.
> His scepter shows the force of temporal power,
> The attribute to awe and majesty
> Wherein doth sit the dread and fear of kings.
> But mercy is above this sceptered sway,
> It is enthroned in the hearts of kings,
> It is an attribute to God himself,
> And earthly power doth then show likest God's
> When mercy seasons justice. Therefore, Jew,
> Though justice be thy plea, consider this,
> That in the course of justice none of us
> Should see salvation. We do pray for mercy,
> And that same prayer doth teach us all to render
> The deeds of mercy [IV, i, 184–202].

She adds: "I have spoken thus much / To mitigate the justice of thy plea, / Which if thou follow, this strict court of Venice / Must needs give sentence 'gainst the merchant there." Shylock is adamant and obdurate:

> My deeds upon my head! I crave the law,
> The penalty and forfeit of my bond [IV, i, 201–202].

And soon after, he seals his own fate:

> By my soul I swear
> There is no power in the tongue of man
> To alter me. I stay here on my bond [IV, i, 235–237].

Shylock is motivated by being bound by his religious faith in the law, on which his religion is based, and his justifiable hatred of his enemy, Antonio, who hates him and has demonstrated it in cruel, perverse, and dehumanizing ways, which Shakespeare projects as historically symbolic. Regarding Shylock's hatred of Antonio, Shakespeare seems influenced by Bernard (as previously noted), who said: "Man's enemies, who do not love him, he cannot love." "Bernard rejects as absurd a literal interpretation of the commandment to love your enemies."[51]

Reflecting Bernard's teaching: "Love, like hate, is a stranger to true judgment,"[52] Bassanio beseeches Portia for a judgment of love and hate. Out of love of Antonio and hatred of Shylock, he asks Portia to do something illegal or unprecedented:

> And I beseech you
> Wrest once the law to your authority.
> To do a great right, do a little wrong,
> And curb this cruel devil of his will [IV, i, 214–217].

Portia responds hypocritically as if outraged, when she, by impersonating a judge, is an outrage:

> It must not be. There is no power in Venice
> Can alter a decree established.
> 'Twill be recorded for a precedent
> And many an error, by the same example,
> Will rush into the state. It cannot be [IV, i, 218–222].

Shylock applauds her with an ironic allusion to Daniel:

> A Daniel come to judgment! Yea, a Daniel!
> O wise young judge, how I do honor thee [IV, i, 233–234].

But he shouldn't honor her, for the allusion to Daniel is not meant to compare Portia to Daniel, but to the two corrupt judges in the story, who, like Portia, deliver judgments of hate. Daniel saves the life of a beautiful, condemned young woman who is falsely accused of adultery by two lecherous elder judges who lusted after her but were refused by her. Daniel discovered their lies by questioning them separately.

For all of the beauty of her mercy speech, we will find that in Portia's court "mercy does not season justice," and justice is anti–Semitic. She tries again to persuade Shylock to change his mind. After looking at the bond, she says:

> Why, this bond is forfeit,
> And lawfully by this the Jew may claim
> A pound of flesh, to be by him cut off
> Nearest the merchant's heart. Be merciful.
> Take thrice thy money, bid me tear the bond [IV, i, 230–234].

Shylock answers: "I charge you by the law... / Proceed to judgment." When she says to him: "Have by some surgeon, Shylock, on your charge, / To stop his wound, lest he do bleed to death." He asks: "Is it so nominated in the bond?" She answers: "It is not so expressed, but what of that? / 'Twere good you do so much for charity." He says: "I cannot find it. 'Tis not in the bond" (IV, i, 238–240, 260–265).

Portia makes a mockery of Shylock's obsession with the letter of the law, and will use that obsession against him. While hypocritically making Christian demands upon Shylock, howbeit she is certainly no "epistle of Christ," she alludes to Scripture that can be construed as anti-Semitic or as superseding the Old Testament, by which Shylock is bound:

> Forasmuch as ye are manifestly declared to be the epistle of Christ ministered by us, written not with ink, but with the Spirit of the living God; not in tables of stone, but in fleshly tables of the heart ... our sufficiency is of God; Who also hath made us able ministers of the new testament; not of the letter, but of the spirit: for the letter killeth, but the spirit giveth life [II.Cor.3:3–6].

Demonstrating that "the letter killeth," this is all building up to an anti-Semitic judgment based on legalistic technicalities arising out of anti-Semitic laws. Climaxing the setup, which this whole trial has been, Portia tells Shylock:

> A pound of that same merchant's flesh is thine.
> The court awards it, and the law doth give it.
> ...And you must cut this flesh from off his breast.
> The law allows it, and the court awards it [IV, i, 299–303].

Shylock, of course, is elated: "Most learned judge! A sentence! Come, prepare!" But then, Portia drops the first bomb, after having won his confidence:

> Tarry a little. There is something else.
> This bond doth give thee here no jot of blood.
> The words expressly are "a pound of flesh."
> Take then thy bond, take thou thy pound of flesh,
> But in the cutting it if thou dost shed
> One drop of Christian blood, thy lands and goods
> Are, by the laws of Venice, confiscate
> Unto the state of Venice [IV, i, 305–312].

Now we shall see how much mercy the Christian judge practices, whether she practices the mercy she preaches. Shylock asks, without proof: "Is that the law?" With cruel mockery, Portia answers:

> Thyself shalt see the act.
> For, as thou urgest justice, be assured
> Thou shalt have justice, more than thou desirest [IV, i, 314–316].

Knowing he's beaten, Shylock attempts to settle for an earlier offer he vehemently turned down: "I take this offer, then. Pay the bond thrice and let the Christian go." Bassanio says: "Here is the money" (IV, i, 318–320).

Unmercifully, Portia sticks the knife in Shylock, using the same obsession with the letter of the law as Shylock's, to punish him. But it's at the same time an anti–Christian and anti–Semitic attack:

> Soft!
> The Jew shall have all justice. Soft! No haste.
> He shall have nothing but the penalty....
> Therefore prepare thee to cut off the flesh.
> Shed thou no blood, nor cut thou less nor more
> But just a pound of flesh. If thou cut'st more
> Or less than a just pound, be it so much
> As make it light or heavy in the substance,
> Or the division of the twentieth part
> Of one poor scruple — nay, if the scale do turn
> But in the estimation of a hair —
> Thou diest and all the goods are confiscate [IV, i, 320–332].

Shylock, relinquishing the offer of three times the bond, states: "Give me my principal and let me go." But this judge is going for the jugular, even though it was Shylock's money that enabled Bassanio to court her. Even after Bassanio says: "I have it ready for thee. Here it is," Portia ruthlessly objects: "He hath refused it in open court. / He shall have merely justice and his bond." Shylock asks: "Shall I not have barely my principal?" Portia answers: "Thou shalt have nothing but the forfeiture, / To be so taken at thy peril, Jew" (IV, i, 336–339, 342–344).

This judge's obstruction of justice knows no limits. The end is in the beginning, Shylock is spat on again. The next bomb Portia drops is a blatant anti–Semitic law. It applies to Shylock because he is an alien. If he were not a Jew, he would not be an alien, and this law would not apply to him. When he tries to leave, Portia says:

> Tarry, Jew.
> The law hath yet another hold on you.
> It is enacted in the law of Venice,
> If it be proved against an alien
> That by direct or indirect attempts
> He seek the life of any citizen,
> The party 'gainst the which he doth contrive
> Shall seize the half his goods. The other half
> Comes to the privy coffer of the state.
> And the offender's life lies in the mercy
> Of the Duke only, 'gainst all other voice.
> In which predicament, I say, thou stand'st,
> For it appears, by manifest proceeding,
> That indirectly and directly too,
> Thou has contrived against the very life
> Of the defendant, and thou hast incurred

> The danger formerly by me rehearsed.
> Down, therefore, and beg mercy of the Duke [IV, i, 346–363].

Portia says, "down," like she's talking to a dog. Considering the anti–Semitism from beginning to end, the Duke's statement, "That thou shalt see the difference of our spirits," is ironic. In answer to Portia's question: "What mercy can you render him, Antonio?" one of his answers is that Shylock "presently become a Christian." But who would want to become a Christian as Christianity is practiced? Where's the mercy in that? It would be more of a punishment, and make him hate himself, like Christians hate Jews. So that, ironically, in the end, the Jew on the cross is Shylock, despised, rejected, and acquainted with grief.

Hamlet

There's no disputing the twenty-first-century currency of William Shakespeare and his disciple, Jonathan Swift, with regard to their intensely powerful, unmitigated condemnation of the African slave trade and the character of white people. Swift's condemnation is the subject of *Gulliver's Travels*, as revealed in *Gulliver as Slave Trader: Racism Reviled by Jonathan Swift*. Shakespeare's condemnation can be found in *Titus Andronicus*, *The Merchant of Venice*, *Othello*, *King Lear* and *The Tempest*. As to currency, one could have, for example, picked up the *New York Times* on March 20, 2007, and found an article titled: "Britain Confronts Legacy of Slave Trade," by Alan Riding. While making a comparison to the current film *Amazing Grace* about the feisty abolitionist, William Wilberforce, Riding calls our attention to "a series of exhibitions ... highlighting a far uglier back story: Britain's deep engagement in the slave trade in earlier centuries and the fundamental role this played in forging the nation's wealth and power." He goes on to say:

> With the support of the government and a $20 million grant from the Heritage Lottery Fund, national museums and community groups across Britain have begun re-examining what a new exhibition at the Victoria and Albert Museum in London calls these "Unfortunate Truths."

Riding adds:

> Although Prime Minister Tony Blair fell short of an apology, in November he went further than any other official by expressing "deep sorrow" for Britain's role in the slave trade. "It is hard to believe what would now be a crime against humanity was legal at the time," he noted.

It wasn't hard for Shakespeare and Swift to believe. What they would find incredible is the five centuries it has taken to make such an acknowledgment as Blair's, not to mention America's twenty-first century clinging to the slave trade's horrific legacy, as indicated by a March 20, 2006, *New York Times* article titled: "Plight Deepens for Black Men, Studies Warn." What Shakespeare and Swift exposed could unequivocally be considered prefigurative of this deepening plight. But even given their sixteenth-, seventeenth-, and eighteenth-century exposé of the fraud, cover-up, hypocrisy, and evil will of white people as characteristic, such abomination persisted in the nineteenth and twentieth centuries, and still persists in the twenty-first.

For example, one of the truths Riding mentions in his article Swift had already alluded to in *Gulliver's Travels*: that the African slave trade was "the foundation of Liverpool's enormous prosperity."[1] In addition, Riding tells of London and Bristol, also alluded to by Swift:

> Today the city takes this past seriously. In 1994, the Jerseyside Maritime Museum opened a Transatlantic Slavery Gallery to tell the story of Liverpool and slavery. This display will close in June [2007] to make way for Britain's first International Slavery Museum, which will open on August 23rd, named by the United Nations as Slavery Remembrance Day.
>
> London and Bristol, two other major slave-trading cities, are also probing their consciences this year. In October, the Museum of Docklands in London will open a permanent gallery called "London, Sugar, and Slavery," while the Bristol Industrial Museum has opened a Transatlantic Slavery gallery exploring how the city profited from the slave trade in the 17th and 18th centuries.

Riding describes twelve exhibitions in all. Both Shakespeare and Swift hold a mirror up to white people. Riding closes with mention of such a mirror:

> A photography exhibition at St. Paul's Cathedral through March 29th, "Slave Britain: The 21st Century Trade in Human Lives," holds just such a mirror to Britain today.

So, although in general there's nothing new about the universality and currency of Shakespeare, never before until now, except for historian Michael Woods' reference to *Othello*, has mention been made of the universality and currency of Shakespeare in the context of the African slave trade. It seems it took Britain until 2007 to confront what Shakespeare confronted Britain with in 1594, 1604, 1605, and 1611.

Another first, perhaps, is the "Trial of Hamlet," first created in 1994 by U.S. Supreme Court Justice Anthony M. Kennedy. According to the *New York Times* article of March 10, 2007, by Lynette Clemetson, "Was Dane's Madness Just Method? Jury to Decide." The central question of "The Trial of Hamlet" is whether Hamlet was sane at the time he killed Polonius. In other words, the issue is "the prince's criminal responsibility." The presiding judge in the trial, Anthony M. Kennedy, in a telephone interview says: "The trial provides a fascinating, oblique way in which to examine Hamlet, the legal process and the intellect of Shakespeare, who continues to speak to us in our own time." Clemetson informs us that "'The Trial of Hamlet' was originally to be presented in the Kennedy Center's 550-seat Terrace Theater, but tickets sold so quickly that it was moved to the 1,100-seat Eisenhower Theater; it again quickly sold out."

As to the prosecutor and the defense attorney, each believes he has "an incredibly strong case." Miles Ehrlich, the prosecutor, said: "Hamlet had a habit of talking to himself. It is almost an insult to suggest that someone of his insight was so impaired by mental disease that he could not comprehend or control his actions." According to the defense attorney, Abbe D. Lowell: "The cry for justice, as sincere as it is, should not have us try those with mental illness as serious criminals." Justice Kennedy adds: "It is clear to me that Shakespeare meant for this to be a puzzle. Each time I hear this trial, I see something new in the play and gain new insight into the way the law of criminal responsibility works."

Not everyone would agree with Justice Kennedy that "Shakespeare meant for this to be a puzzle." It seems fairly obvious that Hamlet's *feigned* madness is "just method," as he tells Horatio, Marcellus, and Bernardo, and later, Rosencrantz and Guildenstern. In the first instance he says: "I perchance hereafter shall think meet / To put an antic [mad] disposition on." In the later instance, Claudius says to Rosencrantz and Guildenstern: "Hamlet in madness hath Polonius slain" (IV, i, 34). But this, of course, is not true. Hamlet kills Polonius accidentally, mistaking him for Claudius. Hamlet does, however, admit to Polonius' bearing some responsibility in his own death. Upon lifting the arras and discovering the body of Polonius, Hamlet says:

> Thou wretched, rash, intruding fool, farewell!
> I took thee for thy better. Take thy fortune.
> Thou find'st to be too busy is some danger [III, iv, 32–34].

On one occasion, Guildenstern tells the king that Hamlet "with a crafty madness keeps aloof / When we would bring him on to some confusion / Of this true state" (III, i, 7–9). Rosencrantz and Guildenstern, betrayers of Hamlet, try to surreptitiously elicit information from Hamlet for the king, and the preceding is one of their reports. Hamlet is on to them, and one of his insightful responses proves him anything but mad:

> Why, look you now, how unworthy a thing you make of me! You would play upon me, you would seem to know my stops, you would pluck out the heart of my mystery, you would sound me from my lowest note to the top of my compass; and there is much music, excellent voice, in this little organ [recorder], yet cannot you make it speak. 'Sblood, do you think I am easier to be played on than a pipe? Call me what instrument you will, though you can fret me, you cannot play upon me [III, ii, 331–338].

Guildenstern is right; Hamlet's is a "crafty madness," of which Hamlet earlier makes us aware. So that, as far as "The Trial of Hamlet" is concerned, Hamlet is guilty of premeditated murder in the killing of Polonius, although he thought he was killing Claudius. "For out of the heart proceed evil thoughts, murders..." (Matt.15:19). Hamlet had premeditated murder in his heart to murder Claudius and, in his heart, he was murdering Claudius when he killed Polonius, and his reason consented to the murder.

But the killing of Polonius is of much greater significance than whether Hamlet was sane or not when he killed him. The killing of Polonius represents the fulfillment of Hamlet's desire and intent to kill the king ("As a man thinketh in his heart so is he"), as instigated by the ghost of Hamlet's father, and is thus the climax of the play.

This is to be understood in terms of Bernard's concept of the soul. "The soul has three faculties: the Memory, the Will, and the Reason. The three functions of the soul are thought, emotion and intention; residing respectively in the memory, the will and the reason":

> The "memory" is the thinking faculty. It is the most essential faculty, for without it the soul would not only fail to be a human soul, but would fail to be a soul at all.
>
> "Thoughts" arise from three sources: they originate in our own souls, or they are inspired in us by evil spirits, or they are inspired in us by God. We "speak," as it were, the thoughts which originate in us; that is, we are the cause of them. But we "hear" the thoughts which are inspired in us, for something external is the cause of them, and we are merely receptive.[2]

The death of Hamlet's soul is a dramatization of Bernard's explanation of how the soul dies:

> If a sin is suggested to the memory by thought, that is a blemish in the soul, although not a disease. But if the will is moved to the sin by an emotional desire for it, then the soul is diseased, although not fatally. But if the reason also is inclined to the sin by intention, so that the sin is consented to, then the soul dies.[3]

Applied to Hamlet: the sin of killing Claudius is suggested to Hamlet's memory by thoughts inspired in him by an evil spirit, his father's ghost. There's no doubt that Hamlet's will is moved to the sin by an emotional desire for it, he becomes obsessed with killing Claudius. To say Hamlet's "reason is inclined to the sin by intention, so that the sin is consented to" would be an understatement.

What brings us to the climax is Hamlet's tragic flaw, his listening to the wrong ghost, not the Holy Ghost. There are strict instructions on how to tell a ghost from heaven from a ghost from hell, instructions Shakespeare alludes to to expose Hamlet's ignoring or rejection of these instructions. When he has Hamlet cry out, upon first seeing his father's ghost,

> Angels and ministers of grace defend us!
> Be thou a spirit of health or goblin damned,
> Bring with thee airs from heaven or blasts from hell,
> Be thy intents wicked or charitable,
> Thou com'st in such a questionable shape
> That I will speak to thee [I, iv, 39–44],

Shakespeare is alluding to the following:

> Beloved, believe not every spirit, but try the spirits whether they are of God: because many false prophets are gone out into the world. Hereby know ye the Spirit of God: Every spirit that confesseth that Jesus Christ is come in the flesh is of God. And every spirit that confesseth not that Jesus Christ is come in the flesh is not of God: and this is that spirit of anti–Christ... [I John 4:1–3].

Shakespeare uses Hamlet's reaction to say the ghost of Hamlet's father is not of God but is "that spirit of anti–Christ," which Hamlet embraces, rejecting Christ. In addition, the "intents" of his father's ghost are obviously not "charitable," but "wicked." He commands Hamlet to "Revenge his foul and most unnatural murder," although "Vengeance is mine," saith to Lord, "I will repay." The Holy Ghost is the "Spirit of Truth," who, says Jesus "will guide you unto all truth" (John 16:13).

But our first clue that the ghost of Hamlet's father is an evil spirit is given to us by Marcellus in the beginning, when he says, after the ghost "faded on the crowing of the cock":

> Some say that ever 'gainst that season comes
> Wherein our Saviour's birth is celebrated,
> The bird of dawning singeth all night long.
> And then, they say, no spirit dare stir abroad,
> The nights are wholesome, then no planets strike
> So hallowed and so gracious is the time [I, i, 157–164].

Accordingly, the ghost would not have stirred abroad at all. And the nights are not wholesome, and the time is neither hallowed nor gracious; for, "Something is rotten in the state of Denmark" (I, v, 90) and "The times are out of joint" (I, v, 189). Plus the fact:

> 'Tis now the very witching time of night.
> When churchyards yawn and Hell itself breathes out
> Contagion to this world. Now could I drink hot blood,
> And do such bitter business as the day
> Would quake to look on [III, ii, 351–355].

But the death of Polonius is significant for a reason not yet mentioned: it is a symbol of Shakespeare's attack on patriarchy. The bigotry Shakespeare attacks in *Hamlet* is patriarchy and sexism. One could go so far as to say patriarchy, to an extent, destroys Hamlet. And patriarchy and sexism destroy Ophelia. Sexism destroys Hamlet's relationship with his mother and with Ophelia. What's even worse, sexism drives Hamlet close to matricidal thoughts. He is on his way to his mother's chamber when he harbors the thoughts quoted above: "Now I could drink hot blood, / And do such bitter business as the day / Would quake to look on."

Patriarchy is introduced almost from the very beginning, when Laertes, a young man, must seek permission from the King and from Polonius, his father, to return to France. When the king asks Laertes: "What wouldst thou have, Laertes?" he answers:

> Your leave and favor to return to France,
> from whence though willingly I came to Denmark
> To show my duty to your coronation,
> Yet, now, I must confess, that duty done,
> My thoughts and wishes bend again toward France
> And bow them to your gracious leave and pardon [I, ii, 50–56].

The King then asks: "Have you your father's leave? What says Polonius?" And although a simple "Yes, Your Grace" would do, Polonius answers:

> He hath, my Lord, wrung from me my slow leave
> By laborsome petition, and at last
> Upon his will I sealed my hard consent.
> I do beseech you give him leave to go [I, ii, 58–61].

Polonius' patriarchal advice to his son is famous for the irony in which it is framed, considering how enormously unlike his advice he himself is. He is as famous as a hypocrite as his advice is sound. His last bit of advice, especially, outrageously contradicts who he really is:

> This above all: To thine own self be true.
> And it must follow, as the night the day,
> Thou canst not then be false to any man [I, iii, 78–80].

He gives Ophelia the very opposite advice, which is not based on sound knowledge or evidence, but which is dangerous in her case because she is at the complete mercy of the patriarchy of the times, in which there is sexism involved as well. He asks her what Laertes said to her before he left. She tells him it was about Hamlet. Polonius then takes off on a tirade to destroy in Ophelia the possibility of believing anything amorous Hamlet says to her. He ends by forbidding her to even talk to Hamlet again. But later, he puts her up to being anything but true to herself or true to Hamlet, to playing a game of coquette that Hamlet sees right through, and never trusts her again as a result, and makes her a target of sexism by way of revenge. So that when her father is killed, she is lost, having been totally dependent upon him and never having been taught to think for herself. Moreover, her father had ruined her relationship with Hamlet, whom she loved. It's not surprising she goes mad, and has a questionable death, though beautifully described:

> There is a willow grows aslant a brook
> That shows his hoar leaves in the glassy stream.
> There with fantastic garlands did she come

> Of crowflowers, nettles, daisies, and long purples
> That liberal shepherds give a grosser name,
> But our cold maids do dead-men's fingers call them.
> There on the pendent boughs her coronet weeds
> Clambering to hang, an envious sliver broke,
> When down her weedy trophies and herself
> Fell in the weeping brook. Her clothes spread wide,
> And mermaidlike awhile they bore her up—
> Which time she chanted snatches of old tunes,
> As one incapable of her own distress,
> Or like a creature native and indued
> Unto that element. But long it could not be
> Till that her garments, heavy with their drink,
> Pulled the poor wretch from her melodious lay
> To muddy death [IV, vii, 167–184].

The sensitive beauty of this description of Ophelia's death rebukes the oppressive, stunting patriarchy, the root cause of the madness which led to her death and made her the target of Hamlet's sexism.

Patriarchy cast her in an unnatural role: above all, to her own self be "untrue," which made her the target of justifiable sexism. It was her fake change in attitude and behavior toward Hamlet, a change commanded by Polonius, that changed Hamlet and caused him to distrust her. She reports to Polonius, for example: "as you did command, I did repel his letters and denied / His access to me" (II, i, 107–109). Polonius, by command, even disrespects her privacy by reading her love letter from Hamlet, which can be taken for sincere, and then reads it to the king and queen, aloud. This leads to the plotting of another setup. Ophelia is planted where Hamlet is known to walk by. She is to pretend to be reading a book. Polonius, Claudius, and Gertrude are to hide within earshot. But Hamlet knows what's going on. So he plays a game of his own, speaking to her with sexism and incoherence, most notably in the "Get thee to a nunnery" portions. Ophelia falls for the act. But what else can Hamlet do, when he knows she's acting under false pretenses, and he knows why? He lets her conclude he is mad. The next time they are together he keeps up the act, only he adds lewdness to sexism in his addresses to her. So the relationship is over, thanks to her patriarchal father. What Hamlet is later to say over the dead body of Polonius is applicable to his dead relationship as well:

> Thou wretched, rash, intruding fool...
> Thou find'st to be too busy is some danger [III, iv, 31–33].

But Hamlet is also a victim of patriarchy. Shakespeare projects patriarchy as synonymous with "evil spirit," as in the case of the ghost of Hamlet's father and Polonius. Hamlet's soul is dead because he obeyed the command of the patriarch: "Revenge [my] foul and most unnatural murder," when he consented to do it, in other words, when he consented to murder. On top of that, Hamlet's soul is dead because he consented to the patriarch's command to "Remember me." As previously mentioned, the memory is the thinking faculty of the soul. "In the state of spiritual life the memory is devoted to thoughts of God."[4] But Hamlet vowed to wipe out every thought except thoughts of the ghost of the patriarch. That vow proves Hamlet is in the state of spiritual death. The ghost exits saying: "Adieu, adieu, adieu! Remember me." Hamlet responds:

> Remember thee!
> Aye, thou poor ghost, while memory holds a seat
> In this distracted globe. Remember thee!
> Yea, from the table of my memory
> I'll wipe away all trivial fond records,
> All saws of books, all forms, all pressures past,
> That youth and observation copied there,
> And thy commandment all alone shall live
> Within the book and volume of my brain,
> Unmixed with baser matter. Yes, by Heaven!
> * * *
> Now to my word.
> It is "Adieu, adieu! Remember me."
> I have sworn't [I, v, 95–112].

By comparison, one can see how much Bernard's complete definition is reflected in Hamlet's soliloquy:

> The "memory" is the thinking faculty. It is the most essential faculty, for without it the soul would not only fail to be a human soul, but would fail to be a soul at all. In the state of spiritual death the memory is devoted to thoughts which are not thoughts of truth; thoughts for the necessities of the body, which cannot be neglected but should be limited; thoughts concerned with our occupations; impure and evil thoughts of various sorts; and frivolous thoughts, which are not in themselves evil but which distract the soul. Sins exist in the memory even when past; and the memory of past sins is what constitutes the torment of hell, which is everlasting because the sins cannot be eradicated from the memory. Even the miraculous forgiveness of sins cannot delete them from the memory, for that would be to destroy the memory, but it brings it about that they no longer hurt the memory in which they exist. Hope of forgiveness, of grace, and of glory restores the dead memory, and in the state of spiritual life it is devoted to thoughts of God.[4]

But Hamlet says his thoughts will be devoted to thoughts of the ghost of his father. Note that Hamlet vows that the ghost's "commandment all alone shall live / Within the book and volume of my brain," not God's commandment, "Thou shalt not kill," and "'Vengeance is mine,' saith the lord, 'I will repay,'" which reveals again that Hamlet's memory is in the state of spiritual death. Moreover, it seems that Hamlet's father's spirit is "Doomed for a certain term to walk the night / And for the day confined to fast in fires / Till the foul crimes done in my days of nature / Are purged away," which means that the memory of his past sins is causing him to suffer the torments of hell. "Purged away" refers to his hope of forgiveness. But the main point is Hamlet's soul is dead because he consents to the commands of the spirit of his father, the patriarch, whose soul is dead.

When we first meet Hamlet we get the impression his soul is dead. His mother, the Queen, notes it well:

> Good Hamlet, cast thy knighted color off,
> And let thine eye look like a friend on Denmark.
> Do not forever with thy vailed lids
> Seek for thy noble father in the dust.
> Thou know'st 'tis common — all that lives must die,
> Passing through nature to eternity [I, ii, 68–73].

Hamlet's answer, focusing on "common," is morbidly sexist, in its being a veiled condemnation of his mother: "Aye, madam, it is common." Still thinking they are both talking about the death of Hamlet's father, Hamlet's mother responds: "If it be, / Why seems it so particular with thee?" Hamlet's answer proves the point, "You can't judge a book by its cover," and "Man judges by appearance, but God judges the heart." It's a fitting answer because outwardly Hamlet appears to be mourning the death of this father, but inwardly he is mourning his mother, and that's the crux of the matter. He says:

> Seems, madam! Nay, it is. I know not "seems."
> 'Tis not alone my inky cloak, good Mother,
> Nor customary suits of solemn black,
> Nor windy suspiration of forced breath —
> No, nor the fruitful river in the eye,
> Nor the dejected 'havior of the visage,
> Together with all forms, moods, shapes of grief —
> That can denote me truly. These indeed seem,
> For they are actions that a man might play.
> But I have that within which passeth show.
> These but the trappings and the suits of woe [I, ii, 76–86].

What he has within that passeth show is his sexist condemnation of his mother, which is grossly unnatural. To put it another way, of the three sources from which thoughts arise, "they originate in our own souls, or they are inspired in us by evil spirits, or they are inspired in us by God"[5]; Hamlet's unnatural thoughts about his mother originate in Hamlet's own soul and before his encounter with the ghost of his father, it's important to note. But because of the nature, unnaturalness, and evilness of his thoughts about his mother, Hamlet's memory is in the state of spiritual death. This becomes even more apparent when he is alone with his thoughts, for example the morbidity of his first famous soliloquy certainly reveals spiritual death. For, in the state of spiritual life, the memory, the thinking faculty, is devoted to thoughts of God, which is not the case here where suicide and sexism mix with unwitting, ironic allusions to God:

> Oh, that this too too solid flesh would melt,
> Thaw, and resolve itself into a dew!
> Or that the Everlasting had not fixed
> His canon 'gainst self-slaughter! Oh, God! God!
> How weary, stale, flat, and unprofitable
> Seem to me all the uses of this world!
> Fie on 't, ah, fie! 'Tis an unweeded garden.
> That grows to seed, things rank and gross in nature
> Possess it merely [entirely] [I, ii, 129–137].

This description of the world, by ironically echoing Scripture:

> Love not the world, neither the things that are in the world. If any man love the world, the love of the Father is not in him. For all that is in the world, the lust of the flesh, and the lust of the eyes, and the pride of life, is not of the Father, but is of the world [I John 2: 15–16],

seems to indicate Hamlet's thoughts are not devoted to God or he would have made known the similarity between his description and Scripture, so we would know his thoughts were inspired by God instead of being condemnatory thoughts of his mother originating in his own soul, such as those he speaks as he goes on:

> That it should come to this!
> But two months dead! Nay, not so much, not two.
> So excellent a King, that was, to this,
> Hyperion to a satyr. So loving to my mother
> That he might not beteem the winds of heaven
> Visit her face too roughly. Heaven and earth!
> Must I remember? Why, she would hang on him
> As if increase of appetite had grown
> By what it fed on. And yet within a month —
> Let me not think on 't.— Frailty, thy name is woman!—
> A little month, or ere those shoes were old
> With which she followed my poor father's body,
> Like Niobe all tears.— Why she, even she —
> Oh, God! A beast that wants discourse of reason
> Would have mourned longer — married with my uncle,
> My father's brother, but no more like my father
> Than I to Hercules. Within a month,
> Ere yet the salt of most unrighteous tears
> Had left the flushing in her galled eyes,

She married. Oh, most wicked speed, to post
With such dexterity to incestuous sheets!
It is not, nor it cannot, come to good.
But break, my heart, for I must hold my tongue! [I, ii, 129–159].

There is a Biblical precedence for a deceased man's brother marrying the deceased man's wife. That is, if the deceased man had no children. "The motive of this custom, widespread in primitive times, was to prevent the extinction of a family, for it was deemed a disaster if a man should be left without a descendant to perpetuate his name."[6] Claudius may be alluding to this when he refers to Hamlet as "my cousin Hamlet, and my son," and says to him:

... think of us
As a father. For let the world take note,
You are the most immediate to our throne,
And with no less nobility of love
Than that which dearest father bears his son
Do I impart toward you [I, ii, 103–112].

The Scripture reads:

Moses said, If a man die, having no children, his brother shall marry his wife, and raise up seed unto his brother [Matt. 22:24].

There is, of course, no precedence for the deceased man's being murdered.

But the seminal issue in Hamlet's soliloquy quoted above, is his condemnation of his mother. Such unnatural behavior is criticized in *King Lear* when Albany says to Goneril:

That nature which condemns its origin
Cannot be bordered certain in itself.
She that herself will sliver and disbranch
From her material sap [that sap which is part of herself],
Perforce must wither
And come to deadly use.[7]

This is Shakespeare's covert allusion to:

I am the vine, ye are the branches: He that abideth in me, and I in him, the same bringeth forth much fruit: for without me ye can do nothing. If a man abide not in me, he is cast forth as a branch, and is withered; and men gather them, and cast them into the fire, and they are burned [John 15:5–6].

In other words, Hamlet, in condemning his mother, is condemning his origin and disbranching from that sap which is part of himself. The same can be said for his origin in God ("God made man in his image and likeness"), starting with his memory being in the state of spiritual death, his Will and

Reason are soon to follow, as he goes next, to his encounter with the ghost of his father. He thus disbranches from God, his origin. Further proof is his associating his mother with "things rank and gross," suggestive of a whore, which is sexist, as is "Frailty, thy name is woman." And he speaks of her as lower than a beast, and accuses her of wickedness and incest. Such horrifying bigotry is a far cry from Scripture's "Honor thy father and thy mother" (Exo. 20:12), and "Judge not, that ye be not judged" (Matt. 7:1).

So Hamlet's thoughts reveal that the memory, the thinking faculty of his soul, is in the state of spiritual death even before Horatio, Marcellus, and Bernardo arrive to tell him they have seen the ghost of his father. Hamlet's reaction to what they describe suggests that the will, the emotional faculty of his soul, is in the state of spiritual death as well. Speaking of the ghost, he says:

> If it assume my noble father's person,
> I'll speak to it though Hell itself should gape
> And bid me hold my peace [I, ii, 244–246].

As previously pointed out, when he sees the ghost, Hamlet does not give it the litmus test for determining whether it "brings airs from Heaven or blasts from Hell." What is more, he does not seem to care where it's from. When it beckons, he says: "I'll follow thee." And this over vehement objections from Horatio and Marcellus. In spite of which, he says: "It waves me still. / Go on. I'll follow thee." And then:

> My fate cries out,
> And makes each petty artery in this body
> As hardy as the Nemean lion's nerve.
> Still am I called. Unhand me, gentlemen.
> By Heaven, I'll make a ghost of him that lets [hinders] me
> I say, away! Go on. I'll follow thee [I, iv, 82–87].

But it's not true that his "Fate cries out." Fate presupposes necessity, and Hamlet is not forced to follow the ghost. It's his will, the emotional faculty of the soul, that cries out. It's "I *will* follow thee." The will is free, it's voluntary. "Necessary" is contrary to "voluntary." "What is done by necessity does not derive from the will, and vice versa."[8] When Hamlet's patriarchal father commands him to "Revenge his foul and most unnatural murder," Hamlet does not have to be coaxed, he jumps to it; he is ready and *willing*. He says:

> Haste me to know 't, that I with wings as swift
> As meditation or the thoughts of love,
> May sweep to my revenge [I, v, 29–31].

He later tells Horatio: "It is an honest ghost, that let me tell you."

Hamlet's eagerness for revenge reveals a will in the state of spiritual death: the source of his thought of revenge is inspired in him by an evil spirit, the ghost of his father; his will is moved to revenge by an emotional desire for it. The soul is thus diseased, says Bernard, although not fatally. We are presented another portrait of Hamlet in the latter state. In this regard, Shakespeare satirizes the Renaissance for replacing God with man as the center of the universe. His soul's being in the state of spiritual death, Hamlet is far from seeing God as the center of the universe, without even realizing it. He says:

> I have of late — but wherefore I know not — lost all my mirth, forgone all custom of exercises, and indeed it goes so heavily with my disposition that this goodly frame the earth seems to me a sterile promontory. This most excellent canopy, the air, look you, this brave o'erhanging firmament, this majestical roof fretted with golden fire — why, it appears no other thing to me than a foul and pestilent congregation of vapors. What a piece of work is a man! How noble in reason. How infinite in faculty! In form and moving how express and admirable! In action how like an angel! In apprehension how like a god! The beauty of the world! The paragon of animals. And yet, to me, what is this quintessence of dust? Man delights not me — no, nor woman neither [II, ii, 306–321].

Hamlet glorifies man, but the psalmist glorifies God:

> O Lord, our Lord, how excellent is thy name in all the earth! who hast set thy glory above the heavens.... When I consider thy heavens, the work of thy fingers, the moon and the stars, which thou hast ordained; What is man, that thou art mindful of him? and the son of man, that thou visitest him? For thou hast made him a little lower than the angels, and hast crowned him with glory and honour. Thou madest him to have dominion over the works of thy hands; thou hast put all things under his feet: All sheep and oxen, yea, and the beasts of the field; The fowl of the air, and the fish of the sea, and whatsoever passeth through the paths of the seas. O Lord our Lord, how excellent is thy name in all the earth! [Ps. 8:1–9]

"Lest man should be absorbed in the contemplation of his own greatness, the concluding verse reminds him of his subordinate rank. Majesty and dominion are the prerogatives of God."[9]

Very soon after, Hamlet's mood changes, when he is told a company of players are on their way, coming to offer Hamlet service. But after asking the First Player: "Can you play 'The Murder of Gonzaga,'" and receiving an answer in the affirmative, he grows morose again. He begins to berate himself and succumb to self-doubt. But I think he is attempting "to find out the truth about himself." And to do this, Bernard says:

> There must be no dissimulation, no attempt at self-deception, but a facing up to one's real self without flinching and turning aside. When a man thus takes stock of himself in the clear light of truth, he will discover that he lives in a region where likeness to God has been forfeited, and

> groaning from the depths of a misery to which he can no longer remain blind, will he not cry out to the Lord as the Prophet did: "In your truth you have humbled me"? How can he escape being genuinely humbled on acquiring this true self-knowledge, on seeing the burden of sin that he carries, the oppressive weight of his mortal body, the complexitiesof earthly cares, the corrupting influence of sensual desires; on seeing his blindness, his worldliness, his weakness, his embroilment in repeated errors; on seeing himself exposed to a thousand dangers, trembling amid a thousand fears, confused by a thousand difficulties, defenseless before a thousand suspicions, worried by a thousand needs; one to whom vice is welcome, virtue repugnant? Can this man afford the haughty eyes, the proud lift of the head? With the thorns of his misery pricking him, will he not rather be changed for the better? Let him be changed and weep, changed to mourning and sighing, changed to acceptance of the Lord, to whom in his lowliness he will say: "Heal me because I have sinned against you." He will certainly find consolation in this turning to the Lord, because he is "the Father of mercies and the God of all comfort."[10]

For, although the above quote is more than a summary of what Hamlet actually does do, he does not cry out to the Lord as the Prophet did. And, although he would rather be changed for the better, it has nothing to do with acceptance of the Lord, to whom in his lowliness he will *not* say: "Heal me because I have sinned against you."[11] This use of Bernard just goes to show that in the Renaissance, God is not the center of the universe. Also, although Hamlet's finding out the truth about himself fits Bernard's format, the latter was used ironically for an evil purpose, certainly not for conversion to Christ, but for complete conversion to the Devil so that he can move without reservation to the murder of Claudius. Hamlet says, without dissimulation or attempts at self-deception, but a facing up to his real self without flinching and turning aside:

> Now I am alone.
> Oh, what a rogue and peasant slave am I!
> Is it not monstrous that this player here,
> But in a fiction, in a dream of passion,
> Could force his soul so to his own conceit
> That from her working all his visage wanned,
> Tears in his eyes, distraction in 's aspect,
> A broken voice, and his whole function suiting
> With forms to his conceit? And all for nothing!
> For Hecuba!
> What's Hecuba to him or he to Hecuba,
> That he should weep for her? What would he do
> Had he the motive and cue for passion
> That I have? He would drown the stage with tears
> And cleave the general ear with horrid speech,

Make mad the guilty and appal the free,
Confound the ignorant, and amaze indeed
The very faculties of eyes and ears [II, ii, 542–559].

Hamlet, as Bernard says, "on seeing his blindness, his worldliness, his weakness, his embroilment in repeated errors,"[12] goes on to say:

Yet I,
A dull and muddy-mettled rascal, peak
Like John-a-dreams, unpregnant of my cause,
And can say nothing—no, nor for a King
Upon whose property and most dear life
A damned defeat was made. Am I a coward?
Who calls me villain? Breaks my pate across?
Plucks off my beard and blows it in my face?
Tweaks me by the nose? Gives me the lie i' the throat
As deep as to the lungs? Who does me this?
Ha!
'Swounds, I should take it. For it cannot be
But I am pigeon-livered and lack gall
To make oppression bitter, or ere this
I should have fatted all the region kites
With the slave's offal. Bloody, bawdy villain!
Remorseless, treacherous, lecherous, kindless villain!
Oh, vengeance!
Why, what an ass am I! This is most brave,
That I, the son of a dear father murdered,
Prompted to my revenge by Heaven and Hell,
Must, like a whore, unpack my heart with words
And fall a-cursing like a very drab,
A scullion! [II, ii, 560–583].

So, Hamlet, as "one to whom vice is welcome, virtue repugnant ... with the thorns of his misery pricking him, would rather be changed for the better,"[13] and thoughts inspired in him by evil spirits, bring him to the change that is only for the betterment of his goal:

Fie upon 't! Foh! About, my brain! Hum, I have heard
That guilty creatures sitting at a play
Have by the very cunning of the scene
Been struck so to the soul that presently
They have proclaimed their malefactions;
For murder, though it have no tongue, will speak
With most miraculous organ. I'll have these players
Play something like the murder of my father
Before mine uncle. I'll observe his looks,
I'll tent him to the quick. If he but blench,
I know my course. The spirit that I have seen
May be the Devil, and the Devil hath power

> To assume a pleasing shape. Yea, and perhaps
> Out of my weakness and my melancholy,
> As he is very potent with such spirits,
> Abuses me to damn me. I'll have grounds
> More relative than this. The play's the thing
> Wherein I'll catch the conscience of the King [II, ii, 576–634].

Hamlet is wrong about the Devil being potent with weakness and melancholy spirits like Hamlet's, and abuses Hamlet to damn him. As Bernard tells us: "It is our own will that enslaves us to the devil, not his power."[14] Seeing that statement in context gives us deeper insight into Hamlet, especially to his will. Bernard speaks of the difference between a good and a bad free will:

> Created, then, to a certain extent, as our own in freedom of will, we become God's as it were by good will. Moreover, he makes the will good, who made it free; and makes it good to this end, that we may be a kind of first fruits of his creatures; because it would have been better for us never to have existed than that we should remain always our own. For those who wished to belong to themselves, became indeed like gods, knowing good and evil; but then they were not merely their own, but the devil's. Hence, free will makes us our own; bad will, the devil's; and good will, God's. This is the meaning of the words: "The Lord knows those who are his." For those who are not his he says "Amen I say to you, I do not know you." As long therefore, as by bad will we belong to the devil, we are, in a certain sense, no longer God's just as, when by good will we pass over to God, we cease to belong to the devil. "No one," in fact, "can serve two masters." Furthermore, whether we belong to God or to the devil, this does not prevent us from being also our own. For on either side freedom of choice continues to operate, and so the ground of merit remains, inasmuch as, when we are bad we are rightly punished, since we have become so of our own free choice, or when we are good we are glorified, since we could not have become so without a similar decision of our will. It is our will that enslaves us to the devil, not his power.[15]

Seeing Hamlet finding out the truth about himself, we would have to say he is his own — not merely his own but the devil's because he has the bad will to want to exact revenge upon Claudius, not to mention having berated himself for not having done so already.

But by the end of that soliloquy, he seemed fired up and ready to go, saying: "The play's the thing / Wherein I'll catch the conscience of the King." Since that resolve was made after his admitting to "weakness" and "melancholy," it seems puzzling to find him so soon after, in despair, and apparently considering suicide. He does not know God, so maybe this is Shakespeare's way of depicting Bernard's teaching: "Ignorance of God leads to despair."[16] This is emphasized again in this next soliloquy so soon after the last one. Hamlet alludes to the very answer to his questions and the very cure for his despair, which is Christ, but is ignorant of the fact he has alluded to Christ. It's as if in finding out the truth about himself, he questions if it's worth it to be:

> To be or not to be — that is the question.
> Whether 'tis nobler in the mind to suffer
> The slings and arrows of outrageous fortune,
> Or to take arms against a sea of troubles
> And by opposing end them. To die to sleep —
> No more, and by a sleep to say we end
> The heartache and the thousand natural shocks
> That flesh is heir to. 'Tis a consummation
> Devoutly to be wished. To die, to sleep,
> To sleep — perchance to dream. Aye, there's the rub,
> For in that sleep of death what dreams may come
> When we have shuffled off this mortal coil
> Must give us pause. There's the respect
> That makes calamity of so long life.
> For who would bear the whips and scorns of time,
> The oppressor's wrong, the proud man's contumely,
> The pangs of despised love, the law's delay,
> The insolence of office and the spurns
> That patient merit of the unworthy takes,
> When he himself might his quietus make
> With a bare bodkin? Who would fardels bear,
> To grunt and sweat under a weary life,
> But that the dread of something after death,
> The undiscovered country from whose bourn
> No traveler returns, puzzles the will,
> And makes us rather bear those ills we have,
> Than fly to others that we know not of?
> Thus conscience doth make cowards of us all,
> And thus the native hue of resolution
> Is sicklied o'er with the pale cast of thought,
> And enterprises of great pitch and moment
> With this regard their currents turn awry
> And lose the name of action [III, i, 56–88].

Shakespeare's answer to Hamlet's questions, and the cure for his despair, to which he unwittingly alludes in "Who would fardels [burdens] bear, / To grunt and sweat under a weary life," is offered by Christ:

> Come unto me, all ye that labour and are heavy laden, and I will give you rest. Take my yoke upon you, and learn of me; for I am meek and lowly in heart: and ye shall find rest unto your souls. For my yoke is easy, and my burden is light [Matt. 11:28–30].

The above soliloquy does seem to be a continuation of his finding out the truth about himself in the preceding soliloquy. In the preceding, he asked himself: "Am I a coward?" In the above, he seems to answer himself when he says that "conscience does make cowards of us all." The "resolution" he mentions above, in "And thus the native hue of resolution / Is sicklied o'er with the pale cast of thought," refers to the resolve he made in the preceding soliloquy: "The play's the thing / Wherein I'll catch the conscience of the King." But even if "resolution" and "enterprises of great pitch and moment" refer to Hamlet's resolve to kill the king, "the pale cast of thought" can turn their currents awry, and the resolution and enterprises lose the name of action. What Hamlet is implying and wants to do is turn his reason off, or at least put it to sleep. We are reminded of Macbeth when he said:

> From this moment
> The firstlings of my heart shall be
> The firstlings of my hand. And even now,
> To crown my thoughts with acts, be it thought and done
> [*Macbeth*, IV, i, 146–149].

But be the above soliloquy either melancholy or despair or reticence, the king is perceptive in his observation concerning Hamlet:

> There's something in his soul
> O'er which his melancholy sits on brood,
> And I do doubt the hatch and the disclose
> Will be some danger [III, i, 172–175].

The king's observation is soon to prove prophetic, for Hamlet goes on with his plan to catch the conscience of the king, and he does.

There is a secret hidden in Hamlet's advice to the players that is the key to Shakespeare's satire and irony. He uses the play *Hamlet* "to hold as 'twere the mirror up to nature — to show ... the very age and body of the time his form and pressure." And what he shows is that no one has "the accent of Christians nor the gait of Christians," and that one would think "some of Nature's journeymen had made men, and not made them well, they imitate humanity so abominably" (III, ii, 34–38).

Hamlet has the players reenact the murder of his father as related by the ghost. When the player pours the poison into the sleeper's ear, and Hamlet says to Ophelia, "You shall see anon how the murderer gets the love of Gonzaga's wife," the king rises, shouting, "Give some light. Away!" Hamlet has achieved his goal: the play has caught the conscience of the king. Polonius cries: "Lights, lights, lights!" Everyone exits except Hamlet and Horatio. Hamlet says to Horatio: "O good Horatio, I'll take the ghost's words for a thousand pound. Didst perceive?"

The Queen, "in most great affliction of spirit," sends for Hamlet. Given Hamlet's response, we discover what it is in Hamlet's soul "O'ver which his melancholy sits on brood." Not only is he in a regicide state of mind, he harbors matricide in his heart. Matricide, which is, of course, worse than regicide or the king's fratricide, and the most unnatural, seems to have the stronger pull. For we have never seen Hamlet so engulfed by such evil thoughts originating in his own soul:

> 'Tis now the very witching time of night,
> When churchyards yawn and Hell itself breathes out
> Contagion to this world. Now could I drink hot blood,
> And do such bitter business as the day
> Would quake to look on. Soft! Now to my mother.
> O heart, lose not thy nature, let not ever
> The soul of Nero enter this firm bosom.
> Let me be cruel, not unnatural.
> I will speak daggers to her, but use none.
> My tongue and soul in this be hypocrites,
> How in my words soever she be shent [rebuked],
> To give them seals [ratify words by actions] never, my soul consent!
> [III, ii, 406–417].

With such thoughts, Hamlet is on his way to his mother's closet. It's worth considering, matricide being the worst sin, that "David rightly mourned for his patricidal son, because he knew all exit from the pit of death was denied to him forever by the greatness of his sin."[18]

En route to his mother's chambers, Hamlet happens upon the king trying to pray. In the king's prayer is depicted the voice of God setting the soul before its own face, an image Bernard creates:

> ... for it is not only a Voice of power, but also a Ray of light, telling men of their sins, and enlightening the hidden things of darkness. Nor is there any difference betwixt the internal Voice and Light, the same Son of God being the Word of the Father, and the Splendor of his Glory; and the substance also of the Soul, in its kind spiritual, and uncompounded, without any distinction of senses is whole seeing, if we may call it a whole, and also in like manner whole hearing. For what is done by that either Ray of Light or Word, but that only the Soul is made to know it self? For the Book of Conscience is opened, the miserable order of the Life is unfolded, a sad Story is repeated, Reason is enlighten'd, and the unfolded Memory is exhibited to certain eyes, as it were of the Soul. But both is not so much any thing of the Soul, as the Soul it self: so that the same is both the beholder, and the beholded: the Soul set before her own face, and by sturdy apparitors, to wit, of thoughts sent into her, she is compelled, as a guilty Criminal, to appear before her own Tribunal. And who is able to undergo this Judgment without being troubled? and doest thou wonder that thou canst not be set before thy face without reprehension, without turbation, without confusion?[19]

The soul of the king is thus set before its own face in his attempt to pray as follows:

Oh, my offense is rank, it smells to Heaven.
It hath the primal eldest curse upon 't,
A brother's murder. Pray can I not,
Though inclination be as sharp as will.
My stronger guilt defeats my strong intent,
And like a man to double business bound,
I stand in pause where I shall first begin,
And both neglect. What if this cursed hand
Were thicker than itself with brother's blood,
Is there not rain enough in the sweet heavens
To wash it white as snow? Whereto serves mercy
But to confront the visage of offense?
And what's in prayer but this twofold force,
To be forestalled ere we come to fall
Or pardoned being down? Then I'll look up,
My fault is past. But oh, what form of prayer
Can serve my turn? "Forgive me my foul murder"?
That cannot be, since I am still possessed
Of those effects for which I did the murder—
My crown, mine own ambition, and my Queen.
May one be pardoned and retain the offense?
In the corrupted currents of this world
Offense's gilded hand may shove by justice,
And oft 'tis seen the wicked prize itself
Buys out the law. But 'tis not so above.
There is no shuffling, there the action lies
In his true nature, and we ourselves compelled
Even to the teeth and forehead of our faults
To give in evidence. What then? What rests?
Try what repentance can. What can it not?
Yet what can it when one cannot repent?
Oh, wretched state! Oh, bosom black as death!
Oh, limed soul, that struggling to be free
Art more engaged! Help, angels! Make assay!
Bow, stubborn knees, and heart with strings of steel,
Be soft as sinews of the newborn babe!
All may be well. [Retires and kneels.]
[Later rising.] My words fly up, my thoughts remain below.
Words without thoughts never to Heaven go [III, iii, 36–72, 97–98].

His offense, as he says, has the "primal eldest curse upon 't / A brother's murder," that of Abel by Cain. According to Bernard, when Cain murdered Abel, Cain had already murdered his faith. The same can be said about Claudius when he murdered his brother. In this regard, Shakespeare is perhaps implying Bernard's reaction to Cain: "Can you who murder your faith hope to please God?" "Without faith it is impossible to please God."[20] The two closing statements by Claudius above call to mind other statements by Bernard:

> There is certainly nothing righteous, but plainly impious, in giving Christ your tongue while surrendering your soul to the devil. Listen then to what he says: "That man honors me with his lips, but his heart is far from me." You cannot lift a head upwards that is weighed down by the devil's yoke.[21]

The foregoing is considered an unrighteous division. It's what is meant when Claudius says he's "like a man to double business bound." Perhaps Shakespeare is saying to Claudius through Bernard: "Divided as you are against yourself, it is no surprise that God pays you no heed."[22]

> Coming upon Claudius praying, Hamlet says:
> Now might I do it pat, now he is praying,
> And now I'll do 't. And so he goes to Heaven,
> And so am I revenged. That would be scanned:
> A villain kills my father, and for that
> I, his sole son, do this same villain send to Heaven [III, iii, 73–77].

This sounds like an excuse. Surely Hamlet knows what Claudius knows, that Claudius is not going to Heaven for committing a crime that smells to Heaven because "It hath the primal eldest curse upon 't / A brother's murder." In the end, Hamlet says:

> No.
> Up, sword, and know thou a more horrid hent [opportunity].
> When he is ... about some act
> That has no relish of salvation in 't... [III, iii, 73–96].

So Hamlet passes up this opportunity of killing Claudius, maybe because he has matricide on his mind. It's amazing the number of times he mentions "Heaven" in the above soliloquy, without introspection.

That's why it's ironic that, after the grave insult from the start—"You are the Queen, your husband's brother's wife, / And—would it were not so!—you are my mother" (III, iv, 15–16)—Hamlet has the audacity to say:

> Come, come, and sit you down. You shall not budge,
> You go not till I set you up a glass
> Where you may see the inmost part of you [III, iv, 18–20].

He needs to set up such a mirror himself. He would see worse than he implies she will see. With ironic clairvoyance the queen cries:

> What wilt thou do? Thou wilt not murder me?
> Help, help, ho! [III, iv, 21–22].

Hearing the queen cry for help, Polonius cries out from behind the arras where he's been hiding. Thinking it's the king, Hamlet makes a pass through the arras and kills Polonius. Without remorse, he speaks over the dead body of Polonius:

> Thou wretched, rash, intruding fool, farewell!
> I took thee for thy better. Take thy fortune.
> Thou find'st to be too busy is some danger [III, iv, 31–33].

Just those few remorseless words after killing someone, and then hardly missing a beat, Hamlet's right back on the attack with a scathing, judgmental, bigoted, sexist, abusive slander of his own mother. Shakespeare may have been inspired by what Bernard has to say about slanderers:

> They bear on their tongues the virus of death for their fellows, and gladly welcome the death that enters by their own ears. When with prattling mouths and itching ears we busy ourselves in administering the poisoned cup of slander to each other, we fulfill the Prophet's words: "Death has climbed in at our windows." I have no wish to be trapped in the plots of detractors, for the Apostle tells us they are hated by God: "Detractors, hateful to God." God himself through the Psalm confirms this judgment: "Him who slander his neighbour secretly I will destroy." No wonder if he should, since this vice is known to assail and victimize more bitterly than the others the love which is God, as you can see for yourself. For every slanderer first of all betrays that he himself is devoid of love. And secondly, his purpose in slandering can only be to inspire hatred and contempt in his audience for the victim of his slander. The venomous tongue strikes a blow at charity in the hearts of all within hearing, and if possible kills and quenches it utterly.... Hence the inspired Prophet said of such: "Their mouth is full of cursing and bitterness; their feet are swift to shed blood."[23]

It is ironic that Hamlet, who venomously slanders his own mother, should accuse Polonius, in so many words, of being a slanderer, which of course, he was the type.

As Hamlet is leaving his mother's closet he gives us a reason to believe we have reached the turning point in the play. Pointing to Polonius, he says:

> I do repent; but Heaven hath pleased it so,
> To punish me with this, and this with me,
> That I must be their scourge and minister.
> I will bestow him, and will answer well
> The death I gave him. So again good night.
> I must be cruel only to be kind.
> Thus bad begins, and worse remains behind [III, iv, 173–179].

The worse that remains behind is the deaths of Ophelia, Rosencrantz, Guildenstern, Laertes, Gertrude, Claudius, and Hamlet himself. But "Heaven" is not to blame for Hamlet's killing of Polonius. It's true he did not know Polonius was hiding behind the arras, and he did not mean to kill him, but Hamlet *did* mean to kill. The memory, will, and reason of his soul were united in murder, the murder of the king, or he wouldn't have, with such lightning spontaneity, made a pass through the arras, thinking it was the king.

So it seems we have a play with two villains: Hamlet and the king, each plotting the murder of the other, both with evil wills. Hamlet having just failed in his attempt to kill the king, it's the king's turn to kill Hamlet. Under the pretext of quickly removing Hamlet from suspicion regarding the death of Polonius, Hamlet is to be sent to England: "The bark is ready and the wind at help, / ...and every thing is bent / for England." Hamlet is to be accompanied by Rosencrantz and Guildenstern who will carry letters to the king of England from the king of Denmark, ordering the immediate death of Hamlet.

On his way to the ship that will carry him to England, Hamlet encounters the army of Fortinbras of Norway marching to Poland via Denmark. A captain tells Hamlet:

> We go to gain a little patch of ground
> That hath in it no profit, but the name.
> To pay five ducats, five, I would not farm it,
> Nor will it yield to Norway or the Pole
> A ranker rate should it be sold in fee [IV, iv, 18–22].

That is Shakespeare on the absurdity of war, but it inspires Hamlet to bloody thoughts:

> How all occasions do inform against me
> And spur my dull revenge! What is a man
> If his chief good and market of his time
> Be but to sleep and feed? A beast, no more.
> Sure, He that made us with such large discourse,
> Looking before and after, gave us not
> That capability and godlike reason
> To fust in us unused. Now whether it be
> Bestial oblivion, or some craven scruple
> Of thinking too precisely on the event—
> A thought which, quartered, hath but one part wisdom
> And ever three parts coward—I do not know
> Why yet I live to say "This thing's to do,"
> Sith I have cause, and will, and strength, and means
> To do 't. Examples gross as earth exhort me.
> Witness this army, of such mass and charge,
> Led by a delicate and tender Prince
> Whose spirit with divine ambition puffed
> Makes mouths at the invisible event,
> Exposing what is mortal and unsure
> To all that fortune, death, and danger dare,
> Even for an eggshell. Rightly to be great
> Is not to stir without great argument,
> But greatly to find quarrel in a straw
> When honor's at the stake. How stand I then,

That have a father killed, a mother stained,
Excitements of my reason and my blood
And let all sleep while to my shame I see
The imminent death of twenty thousand men
That for a fantasy and trick of fame
Go to their graves like beds, fight for a plot
Whereon the numbers cannot try the cause,
Which is not tomb enough and continent
To hide the slain? Oh, from this time forth,
My thoughts be bloody or be nothing worth! [IV, iv, 32–66].

Hamlet's thinking is all wrong, whether it's the absurdity of war, or the absurdity of finding quarrel in a straw when honor's at stake, or the value of human life, that he would be inspired by the prospect of two thousand men dying for a worthless patch of land too small to bury them in. As for Hamlet, the Scripture applies: "Wisdom will not enter an ill-willed soul" (Wis. 1:4). Bloody thoughts indicate an ill-willed soul, and a soul in the state of spiritual death. "In the state of spiritual life the Memory, the thinking faculty, is devoted to thoughts of God."[24] And as Hamlet's bloody thoughts originate in his own soul, his is an evil will. The two villains, Hamlet and Claudius, are both antagonists who stand directly opposed to Christ, the protagonist.

While Hamlet is away, the madness and death of Ophelia and the return of Laertes occur. While Claudius is counseling Laertes over the death of Polonius, Claudius receives word from Hamlet which signifies that his plot to have Hamlet murdered has gone awry. So he has to come up with another murder plot, and he does: a fencing match between Hamlet and Laertes, having heard of the superior skill of Laertes with the rapier. "You may choose / A sword unbated, and in a pass of practice / Requite him for your father" (IV, vii, 137–139), says Claudius to Laertes, who adds:

I will do 't.
And for that purpose I'll anoint my sword.
I bought an unction of a mountebank,
So mortal that but dip a knife in it,
Where it draws blood no cataplasm so rare,
Collected from all simples that have virtue
Under the moon, can save the thing from death
That is but scratched withal. I'll touch my point
With this contagion, that if I gall him slightly,
It may be death [IV, vii, 140–149].

Claudius doesn't want to take any chances: "If this should fail," he says:

Therefore this project
Should have a back or second, that might hold
If this did blast in proof. Soft! Let me see —

We'll make a solemn wager on your cunnings.
I ha 't.
When in your motion you are hot and dry —
As make your bouts more violent to that end —
And that he calls for drink, I'll have prepared him
A chalice for the nonce, whereon but sipping,
If he by chance escape your venomed stuck,
Our purpose may hold there [IV, vii, 153–163].

Hamlet later tells Horatio how the king's murder plot was foiled, that by stealth he obtained the packet with Claudius's royal command that Hamlet's "head should be struck off." Hamlet devises a new commission with instructions England "should the bearers put to sudden death. / No shriving time allowed." This was not carried out because Rosencrantz and Guildenstern insinuated themselves into a sea fight that cost them their lives. For that reason Hamlet says he does not have their deaths near his conscience, even though he had plotted their deaths. But Shakespeare may have in mind the teaching of Jesus: "As a man thinketh in his heart, so is he." But Hamlet does not know Jesus.

He proves this again when he misquotes the words of Jesus when he misapplies them to his misgivings about the duel with Laertes. When Horatio tells him, "If your mind dislike anything, obey it. I will forestall their repair hither and say you are not fit," Hamlet says:

> Not a whit, we defy augury. There's special providence in the fall of a sparrow. If it be now, 'tis not to come; if it be not to come, it will be now; if it be not now, yet it will come. The readiness is all. Since no man has aught of what he leaves, what is 't to leave betimes? Let be [V, ii, 230–235].

Hamlet is misquoting and misinterpreting Jesus's instructions to the apostles:

> Fear not them which kill the body, but are not able to kill the soul: but rather fear him which is able to destroy both soul and body in hell. Are not two sparrows sold for a farthing? and one of them shall not fall to the ground without your Father. But the very hairs of your head are all numbered. Fear ye not therefore, ye are of more value than many sparrows. Whosoever therefore shall confess me before men, him will I confess also before my Father which is in heaven [Matt. 10:28–32].

The point of the Scripture, as Shakespeare allusively and correctively applies it to Hamlet, is that Hamlet is right in not fearing being killed by Laertes, for Laertes can only kill the body, but is not able to kill the soul. Hamlet should fear God, for, as Biblical scholars concur: "the one who can destroy both soul and body in hell, is God."[25] It was believed, however, that "evil men and Satan could tempt one and so lead one to destruction,"[26] which is suggested by the ghost of Hamlet's father leading Hamlet to destruction, except that, according to Bernard: "It is our own will that enslaves us to the devil, not his power."[27] The problem for Hamlet is that he does not fear God, does not confess(KJV)/acknowledge (RVS) Christ before men, and did not "try the spirit" of his father "whether he is of God." ("Hereby know ye the spirit of God: Every spirit that confesseth that Jesus Christ is come in the flesh is of God. And every spirit that confesseth not that Jesus Christ is come in the flesh is not of God and this is that spirit of anti–Christ..." [John 4:13].) Scripture brings us full circle. For, neither Hamlet, nor the spirit of his father, confesses Jesus Christ before men. They, as well as Claudius, are "that spirit of anti–Christ."

Shakespeare's ultimate concern, *real* Christianity, is brought to bear in his satire of the Renaissance, and in Hamlet's downfall, in a manner best revealed through seeing Hamlet as a Renaissance Everyman in contrast to the medieval Everyman in *Everyman*. Given Shakespeare's attack on Renaissance man for usurping the place of God as the center of the universe, all three themes can seem to crystallize in the Prologue to *Everyman*:

> I perceive, here in my majeste
> How that all creatures be to me unkinde....
> Drowned in sinne, they know me not for their God.
> They fere not my rightwysnes, the sharpe rod.
> My love that I shewed whan I did for them died
> They forgete clene, and shedinge of my blode rede.
> I hanged bitwene two theves, it cannot be denied;
> To get them life I sueffred to be deed;
> I heled their fete, with thornes hurt was my heed.
> I could do no more than I dide, truely;
> And nowe I se the people do clene forsake me....
> * * *
> They thanke me not for the pleasure that I to them ment,
> Nor yet for their beings that I them have lent.
> I profered the people grete multitude of mercy,
> And few there be that asketh it hertly.[28]

And the end is in this beginning, as a comparison of Hamlet's death with the death of Everyman will show. Hamlet dies like his father: "No reckning made, but sent to my account / With all my imperfections on my head." It's not enough for Horatio to make Hamlet's reckoning for him, as Hamlet asks him to. Every man has to make his own reckoning. If we compare Hamlet's death to Everyman's death, we have to assume that Hamlet goes to Hell and not to Heaven like Everyman. When Everyman dies, flights of angels sing him to his rest:

> THE AUNGELLS (above or within). Come, excellente electe
> Spouse to Jesu!
> Here—above thou shalt go,

> Bicause of thy singuler vertue.
> Now thy soule is taken thy body fro,
> Thy rekeninge is crystall clere.
> Now shalte thou into the hevenly sphere,
> Unto the whiche all ye shall come
> That liveth well before the daye of dome.[29]

("Methinketh that I here aungelles singe, / And make grete joy and melody / Where Everymannes soule received shall be" [Bevington, pg 963, 11. 891–893].)

Horatio's reverent eulogy, "Good night, sweet Prince, / And flights of angels sing thee to thy rest," is wishful thinking. Flights of angels will not be singing Hamlet to his rest. On top of everything else, he has no "singuler vertue" nor "liveth well" and makes no "rekeninge," and every man has to:

> For, after dethe, amendes may no man make,
> For than mercy and pite doth him forsake.
> If his rekeninge be not clere whan he doth come,
> God will saye: "Ite, maledicti, in ignem aeternum!"[30]

Translated, the latter means: "Depart, ye cursed, into everlasting fire."

Othello

This play is not about jealousy. It's about racism, Shakespeare's protest of racism. Expounding on his "strategic opacity" theory, Stephen Greenblatt says: "Though *Othello* is constructed around the remorseless desire of the ensign Iago to destroy his general, the Moor, Shakespeare refused to provide the villain with a clear and convincing explanation for his behavior."[1] Nothing could be farther from the truth. The clear and convincing explanation for Iago's behavior provided by Shakespeare is *racism*, which is made obvious by the language and behavior Shakespeare gives Iago. The play is about how the white man destroys the black man through racist menticide. The cunning malicious Iago is a mirror held up to white people, reflecting the arch-racist; the arch-white supremacist; the arch–African slave trader; the arch-anti–Christ — all genocidal and menticidal racists. Othello's tragedy is not due to any tragic flaw in Othello. Quite the contrary. He is depicted as a great warrior, a great general, in fact, to demonstrate that racism is more devastating than war, and against which even a great warrior is defenseless. Like Iago, racism is "more fell than anguish, hunger, or the sea," (as in Katrina), as Shakespeare presents it. Racism destroys soul and body. Othello asks in the end: "Will you, I pray, demand that demi-devil / Why he hath thus ensnared my soul and body?" Othello's tragedy, his madness, the killing of his beloved and himself was caused by lethal racism, Iago's work. Iago is projected as the soul and character of western civilization.

It's not difficult to see racism as menticide, and Iago as the personification combining both. He's a racist mind-killer. "Menti" means mind; "cide" means killer. The definition of "menticide" is easily applicable to Iago's racist destruction of Othello:

> "Menticide" is a systematic and intentional undermining of a person's conscious mind for the purpose of instilling doubt and replacing that doubt with attitudes and ideas directly inimical to his normal ideas and attitudes by subjecting him to mental and physical torture, extensive interrogation, suggestion, training and narcotics.[2]

It's not difficult to see Iago as systematically and intentionally undermining Othello's conscious mind for the purpose of instilling doubt and replacing that doubt with attitudes and ideas directly inimical to Othello's normal ideas and attitudes by subjecting him to mental torture: suggestion, implication, intimidation, insinuation, fraud, projection, set-up, manipulation, insidiousness, deception, treachery, hatred, jealousy, and false pretense. One critic in particular speaks of what amounts to menticide when he says: "Iago works for the substitution of Othello's view of himself by a narrative drawn from racist discourse." In *Shakespeare Against Apartheid*, Martin Orkin goes on to say:

> Othello, as his sense of betrayal intensifies, intermittently appears to recognize the racism which, present in his world, must lurk at the edges of his consciousness or identity. Iago, aware of this, attempts to penetrate the integrity of Othello's sense of self and encourages the general's acceptance of a construction of himself and his interaction with other's drawn from the discourse of racism.[3]

In other words, in his depiction of Othello, Shakespeare reveals one of the fatal effects of menticide, which is that black people, in their understanding of themselves, internalize the attitudes of white racists. That is, they see themselves as white people see them, buying into the racist myths, or are forced to act as if they do for the sake of survival. It is by Iago's slow, sneaky, steady undermining of Othello's born-again or reinvented post–African slave-self to return him to the slave-self created by white people, to get him to internalize that self, that Iago destroys Othello, driving him into extreme schizophrenia and paranoia, and ultimately to the killing of his beloved. Racist critics consider that act proof of what they call the black man's "innate barbarism." But the barbarism is Iago's. Shakespeare makes that only too clear. It's like Tony Morrison puts it:

> It wasn't the jungle blacks brought with them to this place from the other (livable) place. It was the jungle whitefolks planted in them. And it grew. It spread.[4]

One of the ironies Shakespeare exposes is that not only are black people driven to schizophrenia by menticide, white people are schizophrenic in their desires. They cling to the stereotypes *they* created to prove that blacks lack the capacity for equality with whites. But when black people like Othello demonstrate the qualities white people esteem, white people still don't accept them, and see only the stereotypes they prefer. There's an old sick joke that black people tell amongst themselves. The question is asked: "What do you call a black PhD?" The answer is: "Nigger." This is certainly symbolized by inferior Iago's treatment of that superior human being, Othello, as Shakespeare intended he be seen. Othello is Shakespeare's most tragic figure. He is the poster person for black innocence crucified, symbolic of black victims of the most inhuman atrocities in the history of mankind.

It is the innocence of Othello that is at the heart of his tragedy, the fact that he has no tragic flaw. There is no flaw or defect in his character that causes his downfall. "Honesty hath no fence against superior cunning,"[5] says Swift. I don't think Shakespeare intended Iago's success at menticide to be viewed as due to a tragic flaw in Othello, but, rather, to the superior diabolical cunning of Iago. Nor is Iago to be praised for "improvisation." Othello's internalizing the attitudes of white racists does not constitute a tragic flaw because it was achieved through menticide. In addition, there was a layer under the undermined layer, when Othello was a slave, a condition not attributable to a slave's tragic flaw.

It seems to me immoral and insensitive to describe Iago's inhuman, evil machinations as "improvisation," as does Greenblatt, according to Orkin:

> Stephen Greenblatt has described the skill which Iago displays, not merely in hiding his motives but in using language in order to manipulate and redirect the behavior of others, of his skill in taking advantage of the opportune and unprepared-for moment, as characteristic of a Renaissance tendency, which he calls improvisation.... Greenblatt suggests that among Iago's skills are to be found "a sharp eye for the surfaces of social existence ... a reductive grasp of human possibilities." He is "sensitive to habitual and self-limiting forms of discourse" and "demonically sensitive to the way individuals interpret discourse, to the signals they ignore and those to which they respond." ... Greenblatt argues that this skill of improvisation displays the ability both to capitalize on the unforeseen and to transform given material into one's own scenario ... what is essential is the Europeans' ability again and again to insinuate themselves into the pre-existing political, religious, even psychic structures of the natives and to turn those structures to their advantage ... such improvisation depends upon the ability and willingness to play a role, to transform oneself, if only for a brief period and with mental reservations, into another. This necessitates the acceptance of disguise, the ability to effect a divorce, in Ascham's phrase, between the tongue and the heart. Such role-playing in turn depends upon the transformation of another's reality into a manipulable fiction.[6]

The example Greenblatt gives of the use of these improvisational skills by Europeans is the egregious conning of the entire population of islands, now the Bahamas, into boarding ships and being taken as slaves to the gold mines of Hispaniola. The use of "improvisation" to color such "skills" (Iago's skills) is to countenance the African slave trade and racism, which is the contrary opposite of Shakespeare's intent and demonstration in *Othello*.

Racist critics disagree. As I see it, only a racist interpretation of *Othello*, and there have been many, could deny its being about the racist destruction of the black man by the white man. Michael Neill says that "Shakespeare would surely have been puzzled to understand the claim that his play 'opposes racism,' cast as it is in a language peculiar to the politics of our own century."[7]

> The play doesn't "oppose racism," but (much more disturbingly) illuminates the process by which such visceral superstitions were implanted in the very body of the culture that informed us.[8]

Of course the play opposes racism. If it didn't, Iago would be the hero instead of the arch villain, and Shakespeare would be promoting evil as good. Obviously, he illuminates the process by which racism destroys, for the very purpose of opposing racism. It goes without saying that I agree with Orkin, who says:

> In its fine scrutiny of the mechanisms underlying Iago's use of colour prejudice, and in its rejection of human pigmentation as a means of identifying worth, the play, as it always has done, continues to oppose racism.[9]

Neill focuses on what he calls "the shocking iconic power of the bed in the play," and says the ending of the tragedy is unendurable because it "lays naked the scene of forbidden desire in the unity between a black man and a white woman and the bed on which it was made."[10] But I say the ending is unendurable because it exposes the unendurable, the naked, unnatural, monstrous, menticidal face of racism. And it's Iago's work. With an apparent obsessive aversion to miscegenation, most of Neill's commentary focuses on "the bed" and projects as unnatural, illegitimate and adulterous the marriage of Othello and Desdemona. The title of Neill's essay is some indication: "Unproper Beds: Race, Adultery, and the Hideous in *Othello*."

Although history and tradition substantiate Neill's concerns, Shakespeare condemns such history and traditions as evil, poisonous, and destructive of the good, especially when buttressed by racism and religion. Going back to the Middle Ages, on into the Renaissance, Desdemona's marriage to a Jew, a Mahometan, or a pagan would have been as adulterous as her marriage to Othello is deemed to be, but not by Shakespeare. He has Bassanio say in *Merchant of Venice*:

> In law, what plea so tainted and corrupt
> But being seasoned with a gracious voice,
> Obscures the show of evil? In religion,
> What damned error but some sober brow
> Will bless it and approve it with a text
> Hiding the grossness with fair ornament?[11]

The latter is especially pertinent to the evil, tainted, and corrupt justification, and the damned, gross, religious error justification, for the inhuman treatment of and regard for black people. For example, "blackness was originally visited upon the offspring of Noah's son Cham as a punishment" for having sex with his wife in the Ark, which was forbidden. So that,

> all his posteritie after his should be so black and lothsome, that it might remain a spectacle of disobedience to all the worlde. And of this blacke and cursed Chus came all these blacke Moors which are in Africa.[12]

Obviously Shakespeare doesn't view Othello in light of such ignorance, and protests all forms of bigotry, whether religiousized, legalized, or institutionalized. And he protests racism and the African slave trade in at least five of his plays: *Titus Andronicus*, *Merchant of Venice*, *Othello*, *King Lear* and *The Tempest*. Anyone who can't see that just doesn't want to see it. In his satire of the Renaissance, Shakespeare is greatly to be praised for his rejection of Aristotle who "was looked upon as the guide to almost everything,"[13] and whose philosophy of slavery was the basis and justification for the African slave trade; his despicable, outrageous arrogance the nauseating foundation for "white supremacy." In his protest of the African slave trade, Shakespeare is perhaps the first abolitionist; and in his protest of racism and the dehumanization and animalization of black people, Shakespeare more than earns the title of Harold Bloom's *New York Times* bestseller: *Shakespeare: The Invention of the Human*. By contrast, Aristotle's philosophy of slavery can accurately be called "the invention of the inhuman or nonhuman":

> a slave is a sort of living piece of property ... those whose condition is such that their function is the use of their bodies and nothing better can be expected of them, those, I say, are slaves by nature. It is better for them to be ruled thus.... The use made of slaves hardly differs at all from that of tame animals; they both help with their bodies to supply our essential needs.... It is clear then that by nature some are free, others slaves, and for these it is both just and expedient that they should serve as slaves.[14]

We can point to Iago's identifying Othello with animals. Aristotle's philosophy was challenged, but the challenge, rational as it was, failed to move him: "Some had argued that 'the rule of a master over slaves is contrary to nature, and that the distinction between master and slave exists only by law ... and, being an interference with nature, is thus unjust.'"[15] This is the basis of the argument Shakespeare is making with his portrayal of Othello. What Iago and Brabantio call "unnatural" and "unjust" only reveals, ironically, how humanly unnatural and morally unjust they are. Racism is so reviled by Shakespeare that, in Iago, he presents one of the most vividly ugly and alarming life-sized portraits of unequivocal racist hatred of black people in literature, unmistakably to end racism. It is shocking that most critics, except for racist critics, have not discussed or even mentioned the racism in *Othello*, and Shakespeare's opposition to racism.

There's no denying that racism was the motivation, the means, and the ends in Iago's systematic destruction of Othello. Without Iago's racism we wouldn't have the same play. We wouldn't have a black leading man of Othello's stature. Or, we would have the usual stereotypical situation of a jealous, barbaric black man obsessed with a lily-white, angelic white woman, presumably every black man's desire, and the audience would be happy that Shakespeare is as racist as they are. Iago would not have tried to destroy his white general for passing him over for Cassio. He would just have done what he ultimately did do: find some way to set up Cassio and take Cassio's place as his white general's "Lieutenant." Racist critics of *Othello* justify and validate Shakespeare's attack on racism by demonstrating in the criticism the blindness, ignorance, and degeneracy racism fosters, and thereby they encourage menticide and genocide. One of the very first critics of *Othello*, Thomas Rymer in 1693 stressed the "improbability" of the match between Othello and Desdemona, using Horace as his authority: "But not the soft and savage to combine, / Serpents to doves, tigers to lambskins join."[16] To imply that Othello is "savage" is racist. To see him as he is presented by Shakespeare is *not* to see him as "savage" and therefore not an "improbable" mate for a soft white senator's daughter who is not a racist. Shakespeare sees racists as savage. Shakespeare is well aware that racism is probable; it's the very issue he's addressing. He gives the black man attributes a racist would consider improbable to demonstrate that racism destroys black people, destroys those attributes designed to give birth to the probable. Ironic proof of Rymer's complete ignorance of the meaning of *Othello* and of Shakespeare is abundant in his question: "The ending is nothing but blood and butchery. What can remain with the audience to carry home with them from this sort of poetry for their use and edification?"[17] The answer is obvious: a determination to end racism by any means necessary! This is Shakespeare's whole point in writing *Othello*. Iago is a mirror of what is; Othello is a mirror of what could and should be.

In commenting on Rymer's criticism, Charles Gildon (1665–1724) comes to the same conclusion. In response to Rymer's statement regarding the improbability that Venice would "set a Negro to be their general. With us a blackamoor might rise to be a trumpeter."[18] Gildon states:

> 'Tis granted a Negro here does seldom rise above a trumpeter, nor often perhaps at Venice. But then that proceeds from the vice of mankind, which is the poet's duty as he informs us to correct, and to represent things as they should be, not as they are. Now 'tis certain there is no reason in the nature of things why a Negro of equal birth and merit should not be on an equal bottom with a German, Hollander, Frenchman, etc. The poet, therefore, ought to do justice to nations as well as persons and set to rights, which the common course of things confound.... The poet has therefore well chosen a polite people to call off this customary barbarity of confining nations, without regard to their virtue and merits, to slavery and contempt for the mere accident of their complexion.[19]

With keen insight into Shakespeare, Gildon goes on to chastise Rymer for arguing the improbability of Desdemona's loving Othello. Gildon's chastisement is an excellent reading of the inspiration and motivation behind Shakespeare's characterizations. He says there are black Africans in Africa who are "much better Christians than we of Europe generally are." He goes on to say:

> After all this, Othello being of "royal blood" and a Christian, where is the disparity of the match? If either side is advanced, 'tis Desdemona. And why must this Prince, though a Christian and of known and experienced virtue, courage, and conduct, be made such a monster that the Venetian lady can't love him without perverting nature?[20]

It is amazing, not to mention troubling if not distressing, that with this kind of magnanimity and verity, Shakespeare's and Gildon's, that racism prevails even into the twentieth century, let alone the twenty-first.

And to think that Coleridge was a racist is most disappointing. But I do agree with him in one point, which has to do with my main point:

> let me repeat that Othello does not kill Desdemona in jealousy but in a conviction forced upon him by the almost superhuman art of Iago—such a conviction as any man would and must have entertained who had believed Iago's honesty as Othello did.[21]

But Coleridge also says the following, which is racist:

> Can we imagine Shakespeare so utterly ignorant as to make a barbarous negro plead royal birth—at a time, too, when negroes were not known except as slaves? ... It would be something monstrous to conceive this beautiful Venetian girl falling in love with a veritable negro. It would argue a disproportionateness, a want of balance, in Desdemona, which Shakespeare does not appear to have in the least contemplated.[22]

One thing this does prove is that Coleridge did not understand *Othello*, and did not know Shakespeare. "He regarded Desdemona's love, in effect, as Brabantio regarded it, and not as Shakespeare conceived it."[23]

Charles Lamb's (1775–1834) conclusion, drawn from emphasizing the enormous difference between reading *Othello* and seeing it performed, is most disturbing, especially considering its presentation as the only logical, natural, and commonsense conclusion to draw. He speaks of "dramatic personages in Shakespeare" who are "improper to be shown to our bodily eye."[24] Pivotal to his point are the distinctions he makes between the imagination and the senses. Building to his main point and describing the experience of reading *Othello*, Lamb mentions Desdemona's marriage to a "coal black man," and then qualifies the oncoming blow by saying parenthetically:

> (for such he is represented ... though the Moors are now well enough known to be by many shades less unworthy of a white woman's fancy.)[25]

But his main point is that the good or noble feeling we may derive from reading about "a young Venetian lady of highest extraction" falling in love and marrying a "coal black Moor," is "the perfect triumph of virtue over accidents, of the imagination over the senses."[26] But that when we *see* the play on the stage we are bound to "find something extremely revolting in the courtship and wedded caresses of Othello and Desdemona."[27] His reasoning is that the impact upon the senses would be too powerful to be overcome by the imagination. The implication is, however, that white people are constituted or hard-wired to be so overcome, that is, constituted to be racists.

Conversely, A. C. Bradley's (1851–1935) retort is an awesome tribute to Shakespeare's "glorious conception": Desdemona, whom racist critics sell short when they are repulsed by her marriage to "a coal black man." Bradley's commentary is exquisite and bears repeating and remembering; except for the last phrase:

> Desdemona, the "eternal womanly" in its most lively and adorable form, simple and innocent as a child, ardent with the courage and idealism of a saint, radiant with that heavenly purity of heart which men worship the more because nature so rarely permits it to themselves, had no theories about universal brotherhood, and no phrases about "one blood in all the nations of the earth" or "barbarian, Scythian, bond and free"; but when her soul came in sight of the noblest soul on earth, she made nothing of the shrinking of her senses, but followed her soul until her senses took part with it, and "loved with the love which was her doom."... She met in life with the reward of those who rise too far above our common level; and we continue to allot her the same reward when we consent to forgive her for loving a brown man, but find it monstrous that she would love a black one.[28]

But Shakespeare does not want us to find it monstrous that Desdemona loves a black man, and doesn't think we should find it so. It would defeat his purpose in writing the play if we found it monstrous that Desdemona loved coal-black Othello. Bradley says her love "was not prudent," that, "It even turned out tragically."[29] But, her love *was* prudent, as Shakespeare intended. She and Othello were a perfect couple, as Shakespeare presented them. Their love never ended. Their tragedy was the work of Iago and the fertile racism he could count on.

It's true that Iago is "absolute evil," as Bradley states. And he asks the questions, speaking of Iago: "Why is the representation tolerable, and why do we not accuse its author either of untruth or of a desperate pessimism?"[30] Racism is absolute evil, and Iago is symbolic of the arch-racist and is therefore "absolute evil." But Shakespeare does not present Iago as tolerable, except to other racists. It is shocking that Bradley asks such questions considering his life span. There was slavery when he was born, and Jim Crow when he died. So we can hardly accuse Shakespeare of untruth. And this doesn't even take into account the enormity of the African slave trade, the "gigantic international operation"[31] that transpired before, during, and after Shakespeare wrote *Othello*, which Bradley would have known of. We also cannot accuse Shakespeare of "desperate pessimism" because he is presenting the stark-naked truth in his depiction of Iago as the symbol of the arch-racist and the white man's hatred and destruction of black people. Through his characterization of Othello and Desdemona, and his depiction of their love, Shakespeare presents what should be, which is outrageously optimistic, but hopeful and possible, and corrective. But we are ever mindful of the fact that, if Othello had been created white, we would not have this play. To show how lethal racism is, Shakespeare created two stalwart, spiritually stellar human beings, Othello and Desdemona, in an unlikely but pure love relationship made unlikely, not by any defect in them, but by racism from the outside, which destroyed it.

One of the most telling ironies in the play's attack on racism is the projection of Iago as the devil, a switch from the racist tradition of reserving that title for the black man. By making Iago's evil actions archetypically befitting the devil, Shakespeare calls attention to the racist absurdity of stereotyping the devil by black skin rather than by evil actions. In this regard three clues in the very beginning are significant: (1) Iago's hatred of Othello; (2) Iago's ominous indication of his intent: "Were I Othello I would not be Iago"; and (3) "I am not what I am." G. B. Harrison's gloss on the latter is: "I am in secret a devil."[32] These are clues that tell us whether Iago or black Othello is the devil. In, "Were I Othello I would not be Iago," Shakespeare reveals the plot for the play's controlling theme of racist menticide. The plot is triggered ironically by "What a full fortune does the thick-lips own / If he can carry 't thus!" (I, i, 66). Roderigo is referring to Othello's marriage to Desdemona, whether Othello can carry it off. But it's bad fortune of which Othello becomes full, to which "thick-lips" is a clue. Apparently inspired by Roderigo's words, Iago initiates the action by proposing it, then immediately acting upon his proposal:

> Call up her father,
> Rouse him. Make after [Othello], poison his delight
> Proclaim him in the streets. Incense her kinsmen,
> And though he in a fertile climate dwell,
> Plague him with flies. Though that his joy be joy,
> Yet throw such changes of vexation on 't
> As it may lose some color [I, i, 67–73].

Iago is accurately confident Brabantio wouldn't want his daughter to marry a black man. By his tone it's safe to say Iago and Roderigo rush to Brabantio's house. And the plot takes off! And there's no slowing it down.

By pouring on thick, traditional racist epithets, and animalizing Othello, appealing to Brabantio's racism, Iago inflames Brabantio's racism even more than if Iago had just said: "Your daughter is married to a black man," instead of:

> Even now, now, very now, an old black ram
> Is tupping your white ewe. Arise, arise,
> Awake the snoring citizens with the bell,
> Or else the Devil will make a grandsire of you.
> Arise, I say [I, i, 88–92].

This plumbs the depths of Brabantio's racism, its never having occurred to him that anything so repulsively unnatural could be possible, notwithstanding his original fondness for Othello. There's irony in Iago's referring to Othello as "the Devil," which is not the pot calling the kettle black, for that would put Othello on the same level as Iago, which is far from being the case. Only a racist would see Othello, because he is black, as "the Devil," and overlook, because he is white, the evil perpetrated by Iago, who possesses all of the known characteristics of "the Devil." This is one of Shakespeare's proofs, racist Iago, the self-proclaimed Devil, referring to Othello as "the Devil," that the racist sees things not as they are but as he is. There is nothing about black skin that can be equated with evil, which is what Shakespeare is saying in depicting black Othello as possessing impeccable character; that his tragedy is Iago's work, the work of racism, which is menticide.

Roderigo tells Brabantio his daughter is in "the gross clasp of a lascivious Moor"; yet, Roderigo doesn't even know Othello except as "thick-lips." Iago is able to use Roderigo and extort money from him because Roderigo is a racist in love with Desdemona. Brabantio is roiled by the news Iago and Roderigo bring. He hastens to search the house for Desdemona. In the meantime, Iago, to add to his other diabolical character traits, shiftily departs, saying to Roderigo:

> Farewell, for I must leave you.
> It seems not meet, nor wholesome to my place,
> To be produced — as if I stay I shall —
> Against the Moor
> * * *
> Though I do hate him as I do Hell pains,
> Yet for necessity of present life
> I must show out a flag and sign of love,
> Which is indeed but sign [I, i, 145–148, 155–158].

The Renaissance was much taken with appearance and reality, and in the latter regarding "sign" we are reminded of Hamlet's words to his mother regarding "seems" ("But I have that within which passeth show, / These but the trappings and the suits of woe."[33] Iago proceeds to tell Roderigo to lead Brabantio and the "raised search" to the Sagittary where he will be with Othello. Iago knows that Brabantio will raise special officers with weapons and set out to arrest Othello. And that's exactly what happens once Brabantio discovers Desdemona is gone. He at once turns to Roderigo, the same Roderigo he moments before vehemently barred from his house, yelling, in no uncertain terms: "My daughter is not for thee," which, "In honest plainness" he has told Roderigo on prior occasions. But now, Roderigo is "good Roderigo," and "Oh, would you had had her!" In other words, *any* white man would be better than a black man.

And so, in response to Brabantio's question, "Do you know / Where we may apprehend her and the Moor?" and in compliance with Iago's plot, Roderigo takes Brabantio and his "good guard" to the Sagittary to arrest Othello. Meanwhile, Iago is working his sadistic, malicious mojo on Othello. As in "Artificer of Fraud," as self-proclaimed by Milton's Satan, Iago slyly seeks to ingratiate himself with Othello by feigning feelings he isn't even capable of; professing a conscience he doesn't even have, that prevents him from doing what he is deliberately in the process of doing. Simultaneously, he is setting up Cassio and bearing false witness against him. It is not dramatic irony, nor is it the irony of self-betrayal, for he knows exactly what he is plotting, and he knows full well he is deliberately lying when he says he hasn't the conscience to contrive a murder, when he is in the very process of contriving the destruction of Othello. He says, for example, going into his act:

> Though in the trade of war I have slain men,
> Yet do I hold it very stuff o' the conscience
> To do no contrived murder [I, ii, 1–3].

As he goes on, disingenuously lying, he plants the seed for setting up Cassio, and he feigns affection for Othello:

> I lack iniquity
> Sometimes to do me service. Nine or ten times
> I had thought to have yerked him here under
> ribs [I, ii, 3–6].

When Othello says: "'Tis better as it is," Iago lies on Cassio:

> Nay, but he prated
> And spoke such scurvy and provoking terms
> Against your honor
> That, with the little godliness I have,
> I did full hard forbear him [I, ii, 1–10].

He may have a "little godliness (pagan)" but *no* Godliness (Christian). Iago then abruptly changes the subject. Hoping to unsettle Othello, he asks him if he is securely married. And then, feigning concern for Othello, he patronizingly attempts to reduce Othello to a former slave status, slyly insinuating his having a slave-mentality-fear of white authority. He tells Othello that the "Magnifico" has twice the power of the Duke and will divorce him or use the law (against miscegenation) to restrain him, another example of racism, the Law, which Swift defines as "that insatiable gulf of injustice and oppression."[34] Shakespeare provides Othello a slap in the face of racism, in the latter's declaration that not only will his service to the state outweigh the Magnifico's complaints, but that he "fetches his life and being from men of royal siege"; that, "his merits are such that he need show deference to no man,"[35] and that he has had as proud a fortune as the one he has presently reached. In other words, he in no way fits the racist stereotype of black inferiority. The presumption of "white superiority," Shakespeare is saying, is an absurdly false presumption and the only way white people are superior is in superior cunning, as he demonstrates with Iago. And in this regard, Shakespeare also demonstrates what Swift gleaned from him in *Gulliver's Travels*, that, "honesty hath no fence against superior cunning."[36] So that, when Iago tells Othello that Brabantio and friends are approaching, and tries again to insinuate a slave-mentality-fear, warning Othello, "You were best go in," Othello is fatally vulnerable in a general sense, although he prevails in this particular instance:

> Not I, I must be found.
> My parts, my title, and my perfect soul
> Shall manifest me rightly [I, ii, 30–32].

But Othello is, for the time being spared the confrontation, for it is Cassio who approaches, bringing a message from the Duke, requiring Othello's presence posthaste. Moments later, Brabantio, Roderigo, and officers are approaching. Not to miss any opportunity to instill his poison drop by drop, Iago, seeking again to undermine Othello's self-confidence by instilling fear, deceptively alerts Othello: "It is Brabantio. General, be advised, / He comes to bad intent." Ironically, of course, it is Iago who comes, not so much to bad intent as to worst intent. Othello treats the drawn swords of Brabantio et. al. with contempt.

In response, Brabantio hurls a barrage of traditional racist epithets and stereotypes at Othello. There is irony in Brabantio's attack in that what he accuses Othello of doing reminds us of what Iago is doing to Othello, and the motivation in both instances is racism. Shakespeare does not let us forget that this play is about racism, and how the white man destroys the black man through racism. And the racism in Brabantio's barrage is so blatant it can't be missed, and could hardly be said to a white man:

> O thou foul thief, where hast thou stowed my daughter?
> Damned as thou art, thou hast enchanted her.
> For I'll refer me to all things of sense
> If she in chains of magic were not bound,
> Whether a maid so tender, fair, and happy,
> So opposite to marriage that she shunned
> The wealthy curled darlings of our nation,
> Would ever have, to incur a general mock,
> Run from her guardage to the sooty bosom
> Of such a thing as thou, to fear, not to delight.
> Judge me the world if 'tis not gross in sense
> That thou hast practiced on her with foul charms,
> Abused her delicate youth with drugs or minerals
> That weaken motion... [I, ii, 62–75].

In this attack on Othello, Brabantio makes implied allusions to the stereotype of the black man being the Devil, which calls attention to the real Devil, Iago, who is white.

To emphasize the profound depth of culturally ingrained racism, Shakespeare has Brabantio rank racism as more urgently important than war. Learning by messenger of the Duke's urgent need of Othello, Brabantio exclaims:

> How! The Duke in Council!
> In this time of the night! Bring him away.
> Mine's not an idle cause. The Duke himself,
> Or any of my brothers of the state,
> Cannot but feel this wrong as 'twere their own.
> For if such actions may have passage free,
> Bondslaves and pagans shall our statesmen be [I, ii, 93–99].

Like racism, Brabantio persists. When he, Othello, Iago, Roderigo, and officers enter the Duke's council chamber, the urgency the Duke immediately addresses is "Valiant Othello, we must straight employ you / Against the general enemy Ottoman." Nevertheless, Brabantio proceeds to stress the first-things-first urgency of racism:

> my particular grief
> Is of so floodgate and o'erbearing nature
> That it engluts and swallows other sorrows,
> And it is still itself [I, iii, 55–58].

To the Duke, Brabantio emphasizes the racist aspect more than any other concern. He accuses Othello of witchcraft in the theft of his daughter, witchcraft being traditionally associated with the Devil and with Africa. But the deepest racist cut is the claim his daughter would have to have been "deficient, blind, or lame of sense," "For nature so preposterously to err," that she would even consider marrying Othello, which is to say, Othello isn't even human. Of course, Iago was the first to make that claim, with "Barbary horse," etc.

Critics agree that the language Shakespeare gives Othello throughout the play "is so resoundingly beautiful," it has been called "the Othello music."[37] So that when Othello is called upon to answer the charges made by Brabantio, it does seem ironic, therefore, at least at first glance, that he disparages somewhat that very language. He says, for example:

> Rude am I in my speech,
> And little blest with the soft phrase of peace....
> And little of this great world can I speak,
> More than pertains to feats of broil and battle,
> And therefore little shall I grace my cause
> In speaking for myself [I, iii, 81–89].

Some critics have seen self-doubt in these lines. But I disagree. I think Shakespeare is satirizing polished, florid, and duplicitous language, and suiting the language to the character, further defining Othello through his language. In this regard, Robert Graves later said:

> To write English well, it is generally agreed, is to evolve a style peculiarly suited to one's own temperament, environment and purpose. It's a moral matter.[38]

Othello's language is modest, honest, straightforward, unpretentious, unadorned, clear, functional, practical, simple, neat, and sincere, as befits his character. He admits to not knowing the ways of the world, but I don't think Shakespeare intended this to be interpreted as self-doubt, naiveté perhaps. In answering the charges against him, he tells the Duke: "I will a round unvarnished tale deliver...." Harrison's gloss on "round, unvarnished tale" is: "direct, unadorned account."[39] Othello's purpose is to convey a message without his language including anything that will distract the reader or audience from the message.

He is rudely interrupted by Brabantio, whose language is proof again that language is a moral matter. Brabantio's language is well suited to his hateful, ignorant, bigoted, intolerant, white-supremacist, ugly, racist temperament. His blatantly insensitive language is full of distortions, prejudice, distractions, and vicious, destructive, dehumanizing and false accusations. Shakespeare emphasizes the irony, that the more dehumanizing Brabantio's language is, the more inhuman he reveals himself to be. It goes without saying his language is anti–Christian, not to mention the fact that Othello is a Christian. Of course, to be a racist is to be an anti–Christ. Christ quite clearly states: "As you do unto the least of my brethren, you do unto me." Moreover, what Brabantio also reveals, as he rudely interrupts Othello, is that he doesn't even know his own daughter, which is no doubt attributable to the evil defect in his character and judgment, as indicated by his racism. He describes Desdemona as "A maiden never bold, / Of spirit so still and quiet that her motion / Blushed at herself." But this is not Desdemona. Desdemona is a liberated woman. She is Mary in the Mary and Martha story of the New Testament. By her very nature, it is not at all unlikely that she should fall in love with a man like Othello. She even wants to go off to war with him. This is *not* "A maiden never bold," as her father describes her. So, inasmuch as he does not even know Desdemona's nature, he really can't legitimately say what would be contrary to it. However, in demonstration of the ignorance and heinousness of racism, he does say:

> and she — in spite of nature,
> Of years, of country, credit, everything —
> To fall in love with what she feared to look on!
> It is a judgment maimed and most imperfect
> That will confess perfection so could err
> Against all rules of nature, and must be driven
> To find out practices of cunning Hell
> Why this should be. I therefore vouch again
> That with some mixtures powerful o'er the blood,
> Or with some dram conjured to this effect,
> He wrought upon her [I, iii, 96–106].

Since we know this did not happen, Shakespeare here attacks racism, sexism, and patriarchy in one fell swoop, especially racism. For, as the Duke states, in part defining racism:

> To vouch this is no proof
> Without more certain and more overt test
> Than these thin habits and poor likelihoods
> Of modern seeming do prefer against him [I, iii, 107–110].

The First Senator asks questions of Othello that echo the Duke's statement in being non-racist and open to the same possibilities as would exist between two white people "soul to soul":

> But, Othello, speak.
> Did you by indirect and forced courses
> Subdue and poison that young maid's affections?
> Or came it by request, and such fair question
> As soul to soul affordeth? [I, iii, 110–114].

Othello's answer is to let Desdemona speak for herself, and if he is found "foul in her report," he is willing to give up his office and his life. While the Duke's order to "Fetch Desdemona hither" is carried out by Iago, Othello presents his side of the story. He begins with Shakespeare's calling attention to Brabantio's racism, the old "You wouldn't want your daughter to marry one" shtick:

> Her father loved me, oft invited me,
> Always questioned me the story of my life
> From year to year, the battles, sieges, fortunes,
> That I have passed [I, iii, 128–131].

He goes on to tell how Desdemona would "seriously incline" to hear his story, leaving her house affairs "she'd come again, and with a greedy ear / Devour up [his] discourse." This sounds a bit like the Mary/Martha story. Mary sits at the feet of Jesus, listening to his teachings, while Martha tends to the house affairs and complains to Jesus that Mary is not helping with the preparations for dinner.

We get further insight into how it all began between Othello and Desdemona, and who was the aggressor, when Othello relates that, after he finished his story, she said "She wished / That heaven had made her such a man." She bade me, says Othello, "if I had a friend that loved her,"

> I should but teach him how to tell my story
> And that would woo her. Upon this hint I spake.
> She loved me for the dangers I had passed,
> And I loved her that she did pity them.
> This only is the witchcraft I have used.
> Here comes the lady, let her witness it [I, iii, 162–170].

So it was Desdemona who came, saw, and conquered. This is not the Desdemona her father described as being "never bold" and "so shy that she blushed at the slightest cause." But that is a racist stereotype of white women as pure, innocent, and irresistible to make the black man seem like a monster prone to desiring this lily-white, still, quiet (never bold), blushing, blond, blue-eyed creature. Later, as a victim of menticide, Othello sees Desdemona according to the stereotype, just before he kills her, having internalized the racist stereotypes of black men.

In the question he gives Brabantio when the bold Desdemona enters—"Do you perceive in all this noble company / Where most you owe obedience?"—Shakespeare attacks patriarchy, as he does in *Merchant of Venice*, *Hamlet*, and *King Lear*. Desdemona answers her father's question with forthright honesty, boldly and without blushing, like Othello would answer. She speaks of a divided duty. And as she ends one sentence with a period and begins the next with a "But," the "But" tells us where she most owes her "obedience": "I am hitherto your daughter. But here's my husband." This is also an attack on sexism. For, at the time, it would have been quite unexpected and unusual for a daughter to have responded in this manner, which is one of the reasons, the primary reason being racism, it ultimately kills Brabantio. He expected a daughter more like Ophelia. With a broken heart, he says to Desdemona: "God be with you! I have done." And to the Duke whose affairs his racism has interrupted, he says: "Please it your Grace, on to the state affairs." And to Othello he says with implied racism, as there was no other reason to reject the marriage:

> Come hither, Moor.
> I here do give thee that with all my heart
> Which, but thou hast already, with all my heart
> I would keep from thee [I, iii, 192–195].

This is a purely racist resignation. If Othello had been a white man, one of "The wealthy curled darlings" of Venice, possessed of Othello's impeccable character and sterling qualities, Brabantio would have considered his daughter lucky, and he would have loved the white Othello, as even he loved the black Othello before the latter married his daughter, the remotest possibility of such a union never having entered the father's racist mind. So it is important to note in this regard, that the white Duke does not possess racism's "troubled vision"[40] and would not find such a union troubling, even if it were his white daughter. For, after hearing Othello's story of how the union came about, the Duke states: "I think this tale would win my daughter too," and he is not in the least horrified at the thought.

Shakespeare amplifies the Duke's point with the voice of Desdemona, the poster woman for the twenty-first century, here speaking about the poster man for the twenty-first century. They are so much alike, they're not only a poster couple, they're poster human beings. Shakespeare is showing us what real human beings can be if we transcend categories and labels, which, after all, are artificial and politically or religiously imposed from the outside, usually for purposes of power or greed or both. With the same strength, integrity, directness, simplicity, and power, as in Othello's language, Desdemona, upon hearing that her husband is being sent to war with the Turks, addresses the Duke:

> That I did love the Moor to live with him,
> My downright violence and storm of fortunes
> May trumpet to the world. My heart's subdued
> Even to the very quality of my lord.
> I saw Othello's visage in his mind,
> And to his honors and his valiant parts
> Did I my soul and fortunes consecrate.
> So that, dear lords, if I be left behind,
> A moth of peace, and he go to the war,
> The rites for which I love him are bereft me,
> And I a heavy interim shall support
> By his dear absence. Let me go with him [I, iii, 249–260].

As a woman she is unique in taking this position. It reflects Shakespeare's attack on sexism. Desdemona has a mind of her own, she is inner-directed, she is true to herself and she is not limited by the prescribed boundaries and limitations of her sex or paternity. One could say she echoes Christ when he said to his parents, who made him aware they had been looking for him: "What have I to do with thee? I must be about my Father's business." And even though the stand Desdemona takes is impractical and unrealistic, Othello respects her for having a mind of her own, and he says to the Duke, "Let her have your voice," not for any selfish reasons of his own, "But to be free and bounteous to her mind." So that, feasible or not, the irony is, if Othello's warrior bride had gone with him, this play might not have been a tragedy. Desdemona would not have been left in the hands of a monster, of whom Othello speaks as:

> A man he is of honesty and trust.
> To his conveyance I assign my wife... [I, iii, 284–285].

The cause of this misjudgment, residing in the Duke's praise of Othello, suggests a clue to the root cause of Othello's downfall. The Duke says to Brabantio:

> If virtue no delighted beauty lack
> Your son-in-law is far more fair than black [I, iii, 289–290].

And this is how Shakespeare presents Othello, as far more white, as white is usually stereotyped, than black, as black is usually stereotyped. But, taken with his misjudgment of Iago, it's Othello's virtue that is the root cause of his downfall. His virtue leaves him wide open for monsters to rush in, stereotyping his blackness. "Honesty hath no fence against superior cunning,"[41] which is a truth Swift, influenced by Shakespeare it seems, made known in *Gulliver's Travels.* In other words, Othello's virtue, ironically, is the opening that enables the monster Iago to rush in and build the foundation for his plot. Iago says, for example:

> The Moor is of a free and open nature
> That thinks men honest that but seem to be so,
> And will as tenderly be led by the nose
> As asses are [I, iii, 405–408].

But before the foundation is laid, there is a precursory instigation, which, like the poison of the serpent, makes "the ear death's first gateway."[42] It's when the racist Brabantio pours poison into Othello's ear:

> Look to her, Moor, if thou hast eyes to see.
> She has deceived her father, and may thee [I, iii, 293–294].

This, of course, is a lie. Othello believes in her. With the utmost confidence, his response is: "My life upon her faith!" Iago overhears this exchange, and later reminds Othello of Brabantio's malicious warning, with "deadly effect."[43]

In the meantime, Iago also takes the role of the serpent, ultimately proving the ear was death's first gateway. In trying to conceive a plot to get Cassio's place, and "to plume up my will / In double knavery," he thinks out loud:

> — How, how?— Let's see.—
> After some time, to abuse Othello's ear
> That [Cassio] is too familiar with his wife.
> He hath a person and a smooth dispose
> To be suspected, framed to make women false.
> The Moor is of a free and open nature
> That thinks men honest that but seem to be so.
> And will be as tenderly led by the nose
> As asses are.
> I have 't. It is engendered. Hell and night
> Must bring this monstrous birth to the world's light [I, iii, 400–410].

Thus ends Act I.

Awaiting Othello's return from the war with Turkey are Desdemona, Emilia, Iago, and Roderigo. When Cassio arrives, having been parted from Othello by a storm, he gallantly greets Desdemona and takes her by the hand. Intending to make something of this, Iago says in an aside: "He takes her by the palm.... With as little a web as this will I ensnare as great a fly as Cassio." He goes on to say things that reveal his jealousy of Cassio. So we know the first strategic step in the plot he has "engendered." His second step is the set-up of the lovelorn Roderigo. He tells Roderigo Desdemona is in love with Cassio, and he taps into Roderigo's racism to support his strategy. Speaking of Desdemona, Iago says:

> Her eye must be fed, and what delight shall she have to look on the Devil? When the blood is made dull with the act of sport, there should, again to inflame it and to give satiety a fresh appetite, loveliness in favor, sympathy in years, manners, and beauties, all which the Moor is defective in. Now, for want of these required conveniences, her delicate tenderness will find itself abused, begin to heave the gorge, disrelish and abhor the Moor. Very nature will instruct her in it and compel her to some second choice. Now, sir, this granted — as it is a most pregnant and unforced position — who stands so eminently in the degree of this fortune as Cassio does? [II, i, 227–240].

Roderigo agrees to do his part of the scheme to set up Cassio to dishonor himself by fighting, thus lose his position so to be replaced by Iago. Made to believe this will give him a chance with Desdemona, Roderigo has no idea he is being set up to be killed. When he leaves to put this part of the plot into action, Iago is left alone and we are made privy to more of his evil plotting. Again we are confronted with the irony that Othello's virtues do not serve him well in the face of superior cunning. And these are virtues, as we have seen, that even Iago gives countenance to, which makes him even more monstrous. He says, for example:

> The Moor, howbeit that I endure him not,
> Is of a constant, loving, noble nature,
> And I dare think he'll prove to Desdemona
> A most dear husband [II, i, 296–300].

Iago's asides and soliloquies are to assure us his thoughts "originate in his own soul," so to confirm for us his consummate evilness, that *he* is *the* evil spirit. His thoughts are not "inspired in him by evil spirits" or "by God," the other two of the "three sources from which thoughts arise," according to Bernard.[44] He devises another reason for destroying Othello that is not credible and has nothing to do with the vengeance against Othello for passing him over for Cassio. He plans to "put the Moor into a jealousy so strong / That judgment cannot cure." He will:

> Make the Moor thank me, love me, and reward me
> For making him egregiously an ass
> And practicing upon his peace and quiet
> Even to madness [II, i, 317–320].

The method will be menticide. It's important to note again that the kind of menticide used to destroy Othello could not have been used to destroy a white man, because of the racism factor. That is why it is difficult not to conclude that, in its protest of racism, this play exposes how the white man is virtually praised for his superior intelligence, especially by Harold Bloom, who never even mentions the word racism. But superior cunning is not the same as superior intelligence. For example, that is what the Scripture means when it speaks of those (like Iago), who "have none understanding," who "are wise to do evil, but to do good they have no knowledge" (Jer. 4:22).

Accordingly, Iago is not of superior intelligence, as critics say, for to do good he has no knowledge. He is only wise to do evil, which means he has superior cunning, which is why his plots succeed as conceived and instigated. His setup of Cassio, Roderigo, and Montano proves very effective. He gets Cassio's job which he's envied by getting Cassio out of favor with Othello, which enables Iago to use Cassio pivotally in the plot to destroy Othello. His success thus far is heightened ironically by Othello's virtuous misjudgment of him. After Iago perversely pretends to cover for Cassio when reporting to Othello the details of the contrived brawl, Othello, with misguided magnanimity, says:

> I know, Iago,
> Thy honesty and love doth mince this matter,
> Making it light to Cassio. Cassio, I love thee,
> But never more be officer of mine [II, iii, 247–250].

Now Iago has gotten what he's wanted, replacing Cassio as Othello's lieutenant; and the professed cause of his hatred of Othello is now removed; and he has succeeded in winning Othello's love and esteem. So what provokes him to go on with his destruction of Othello? Is it Othello's blackness, which is provocation enough for a racist? Or is it just that an evil person doesn't need a reason to be evil? But there is a certain inevitability about Iago's destruction of Othello. This inevitability is caused by color, by Othello's blackness. Blackness is fate. "Blackness carries with it enough cultural prejudgments to make the vengeance of a god seem meager."[45] Inevitability makes it possible to identify Othello, because he is black, with Christ:

> On the plane of reality, the life and death of Christ have all the basic traditional elements of tragedy — especially inevitability. His death was foreseen and forecast, and was a "forgone conclusion." And even Christ was very nearly without hope. His cry of agony and despair from the Cross was the final proof, so to speak, of the authenticity of his human condition.[46]

Shakespeare's portrayal in the seventeenth century of the inevitable in Othello's tragedy proves to have been prophetic, given the color prejudice in each succeeding century to the present, and the neverending destruction of black people because of it.

Othello's belief in the honesty of Iago raises again the issue of tragic flaw. Othello's belief in the honesty of the most dishonest character is tragic irony, not a tragic flaw. Othello's error or mistaken judgment is not a flaw in his character; it is hamartia, which is often mistaken for tragic flaw. Also, Othello is not the only one who misjudges Iago. So too does Brabantio, Roderigo, Cassio, Montano, and Desdemona.

The plot thickens. Iago's success in the first setup of Cassio makes possible the second setup of Cassio, which brings Iago closer to his goal of destroying Othello. And, typical of the devil, he has no qualms, no scruples, and no compunctions about it, nor about pouring poison into the ear, "death's first gateway," for, he says:

> How am I ... a villain
> To counsel Cassio to this parallel course
> Directly to his good? Divinity of Hell!
> When devils will the blackest sins put on,
> They do suggest at first with heavenly shows,
> As I do now. For whiles this honest fool
> Plies Desdemona to repair his fortunes,
> And she for him pleads strongly to the Moor,
> I'll pour this pestilence into his ear,
> That she repeals him for her body's lust.
> And by how much she strives to do him good,

She shall undo her credit with the Moor.
So will I turn her virtue into pitch,
And out of her own goodness make the net
That will enmesh them all [II, iii, 354–368].

We've known Iago to speak of the goodness of Othello, and in the above he speaks of the goodness of Cassio and Desdemona. It is tragically ironic that their goodness, like the goodness of Jesus, cannot save them from destruction because they erroneously believe in the goodness of Iago, the Devil, in whom there is no goodness. This is one of the ways Shakespeare emphasizes Othello's innocence in the tragedy of Othello. But, as an indication of how grossly misunderstood *Othello* is, the movie *Othello* was shown during the entire trial of O. J. Simpson, to project O.J. in the presumed but erroneous stereotypical role of Othello. Ironically, however, it was the racist rush to judgment that acquitted O. J. Simpson.

It is also ironic, as previously mentioned regarding the goodness of Desdemona, that her innocence and sterling character lead to her downfall, beginning with the following expression of friendship to Cassio who has asked her to intervene on his behalf to Othello in hopes of being reinstated. She guarantees him he will be restored to his position:

Assure thee,
If I do vow a friendship, I'll perform it
To the last article. My lord shall never rest.
I'll watch him tame and talk him out of patience,
His bed shall seem a school, his board a shrift.
I'll intermingle every thing he does
With Cassio's suit. Therefore be merry, Cassio,
For thy solicitor shall rather die
Than give thy cause away [III, iii, 20–28].

In the face of patriarchy, which is contrary to "real Christianity," Desdemona followed the teaching of Jesus: "A man shall leave father and mother and cleave to his wife" (Matt. 19:5). In the above, she follows the teaching of Jesus concerning friendship: "Greater love hath no man than this, that a man lay down his life for his friends" (John 15:13). In alluding to these Scriptures through Desdemona, Shakespeare is projecting equality between man and woman, since the Scriptures mention "man" only, instead of "person."

As Desdemona completes her declaration, Othello and Iago are seen approaching at a distance, at which cue Cassio is seen leaving. Othello asks Iago: "Was not that Cassio parted from my wife?" Iago, through the power of suggestion, insinuates doubt in the trusting mind of Othello:

Cassio, my lord! No, sure, I cannot think it,
That he would steal away so guilty-like,
Seeing you coming [III, iii, 37–39].

Howbeit innocently, Desdemona couldn't have made a worse choice of words than "suitor," considering the suggestive implications in a diabolical situation. She says to her husband: "I have been talking with a suitor here, / A man that languishes in your displeasure." Ironically, she is laying the groundwork for the arousal of Othello's suspicions later. Also in this regard, she pushes her cause too hard, too altruistically, and too annoyingly. This must be considered a tragic flaw in Desdemona, a defect in her character that leads to her downfall. Her nagging forces Othello to dismiss her, and to make a declaration after she exits, which, on its face, reads like dramatic irony prefigurative of his downfall. But it's not, because he never stops loving her, and Chaos never comes again, "that utter confusion that existed before order was established in the universe."[47] This is not to be confused with the chaos of madness, in which condition he also never stops loving Desdemona. He says:

> Excellent wretch! Perdition catch my soul
> But I do love thee! And when I love thee not,
> Chaos is come again [III, iii, 90–92].

Iago hears this declaration and goes right into demolition mode, planting seeds of jealousy, and for the first time he begins to make inroads into Othello's interior and mind. Or, as seen in Bernardian terms, his soul, which is composed of memory, will, and reason. Shakespeare ingeniously uses the irony of self-betrayal to depict Othello by what he says, unwittingly exposing his own ignorance, especially when what he says is true, significant and insightful, but he does not know it. For example, when Iago starts making incomplete suggestive statements, and repeating Othello's whys and wherefores without answering, Othello says: "By Heaven, he echoes me / As if there were some monster in his thought / Too hideous to be shown." There is! And the more unsettled he becomes and correct in his assessments, the more exploitable he becomes. He says to Iago, after accurately projecting "some monster" in Iago's thought, "too hideous to be shown":

> Thou dost mean something.
> I heard thee say even now thou likedst not that
> When Cassio left my wife. What didst not like?
> And when I told thee he was of my counsel
> In my whole course of wooing, thou criedst "Indeed!"
> And didst contract and purse thy brow together
> As if thou then hadst shut up in thy brain
> Some horrible conceit....
> And for I know thou'rt full of love and honesty
> And weigh'st thy words before thou givest them breath,
> Therefore these stops of thine fright me the more.
> For such things in a false disloyal knave

Are tricks of custom, but in a man that's just
They're close delations [concealed accusations] working from the heart,
That passion cannot rule [III, iii, 108–124].

He's of course talking to that "false disloyal knave," unawares, sad to say. Iago, setting up Othello, says he thinks Cassio is honest. After Othello agrees, he says, full of insinuation: "Men should be what they seem, / Or those that be not, would they might seem none [not seem to be honest men]." This is to imply Cassio is not, after just saying he is, for the purpose of jerking Othello around, to lose him from his moorings. Iago is slowly but slyly building up to the subject of jealousy, using innuendos, beating around the bush, veiled allusions, inferences, equivocations, until Othello, losing control, in frustration demands: "By Heaven, I'll know thy thoughts." Given this outburst, Iago knows he's succeeding, and thrusts in the subject of jealousy while Othello is a little off balance:

Oh, beware, my lord, of jealousy.
It is the green-eyed monster which doth mock
The meat it feeds on. That cuckold lives in bliss
Who, certain of his fate, loves not his wronger.
But, oh, what damned minutes tells he o'er
Who dotes, yet doubts, suspects, yet strongly loves! [III, iii, 165–170].

Such a vision evokes the desired reaction in Othello: "Oh, misery!" This response is not yet personalized, but it leaves him open to Iago's poison, for we know that Iago is plotting to "put the Moor ... into a jealousy so strong / That judgment cannot cure," so he needs to know how vulnerable Othello is when it comes to jealousy. Their conversation on the subject gives us a clue to the truth of Othello's statement in the end, which Shakespeare intended us to see as truth: Othello's speaking of himself as "one not easily jealous, but being wrought, / Perplexed in the extreme...." The conversation on jealousy being described at present marks the beginning of Othello's "being wrought." The late medieval definition of "wrought," which was in use is Shakespeare's day, is "worked into shape or condition. Created, shaped, moulded,"[48] which means that Shakespeare deliberately chose the word "wrought" so as to indicate that jealousy did not come naturally to Othello, but that Iago created the jealousy, and worked Othello into a jealous condition, "an example of thoughts inspired in him by evil spirits" (Iago).[49] So that, before Othello is "wrought," Shakespeare would have us believe Othello when, answering Iago, he says (ignorant of Iago's machinations):

Why, why is this?
Think'st thou I'd make a lie of jealousy,
To follow still the changes of the moon
With fresh suspicions? No, to be once in doubt

Is once to be resolved. Exchange me for a goat
When I shall turn the business of my soul
To such exsufflicate and blown surmises,
Matching thy inference....
Nor from mine own weak merits will I draw
The smallest fear or doubt of her revolt,
For she had eyes, and chose me. No, Iago,
I'll see before I doubt, when I doubt, prove,
And on the proof, there is no more but this—
Away at once with love or jealousy! [III, iii, 180–188, 191–196].

This is not to say Othello does not know himself but that he does not know Iago, who immediately begins to work Othello into a jealous condition, and, ironically, as laid out by Othello's unsuspecting honesty and openness, "mine own weak merits," "see, doubt, prove." Iago moves right in with the undermining of Othello's confidence by instilling doubt, using Othello's self-assurance regarding jealousy as an opening. But it is worth noticing that Othello introduces the realism of racism, internalizing racist stereotyping, when he speaks of "mine own weak merits" in connection with "For she had eyes, and chose me." Exploiting Othello's vehement repudiation of jealousy, wily Iago dissembles:

I am glad of it, for now I shall have reason
To show the love and duty that I bear you
With franker spirit. Therefore, as I am bout,
Receive it from me. I speak not yet of proof.
Look to your wife. Observe her well with Cassio.
Wear your eye thus, not jealous nor secure [overconfident].
I would not have your free and noble nature
Out of self-bounty be abused, look to 't.
I know our country disposition well.
In Venice they do let Heaven see the pranks
They dare not show their husbands. Their best conscience
Is not to leave 't undone, but keep 't unknown [III, iii, 193–204].

Bewildered, Othello asks: "Dost thou say so?" To strategically shore up his front, Iago quickly adds: "She did deceive her father, marrying you. / And when she seemed to shake and fear your looks, / She loved them most." But we have no account of the latter. It's an established racist presumption by which, given "mine own weak merits," Othello has already been brainwashed, which is why he agrees with Iago, saying: "And so she did." To buttress the racist claim of Brabantio, Iago amplifies it to undermine Othello's faith in Desdemona. The amplification is as absurd as the claim. Brabantio's eyes were already "seeled" by racism. Iago next smokescreens what he's implied, with affectation:

She that so young could give out such a seeming
To seel her father's eyes up close as oak—

> He thought 'twas witchcraft — but I am much to blame.
> I humbly do beseech you of your pardon
> For too much loving you [III, iii, 209–213].

The success of Iago's treachery can be measured by the irony of Othello's response: "I am bound to thee forever" (like a slave). This is the beginning of the end. We know it, not only by the foregoing statement of Othello's, but by the breakdown signs of menticide buffeted by racism, which begin immediately. Iago projects the destruction he is perpetrating by cruelly calling Othello's attention to it as a way of measuring his (Iago's) progress. For example, Iago says to Othello: "I see this has a little dashed your spirits." Othello answers, unconvincingly: "Not a jot, not a jot." As this exchange continues, and by the time it ends, we notice a bit of a crack in Othello's armor, verified by the use of the word "much":

> IAGO: I' faith, I fear it has.
> ... but I do see you're moved ...
> My lord, I see you're moved
> OTHELLO: No, not much moved. I do not think but Desdemona's
> honest... And yet, how nature erring from itself
> [III, iii, 219–231].

He thus ends his part of the conversation revealing the lethal effects of racism, internalizing the taught racist abomination that claims black people, and therefore miscegenation, to be unnatural.

The racist Iago couldn't be happier. Othello's statement provides him an arsenal of ammunition with which to destroy Othello. In fact, I don't think Iago could have destroyed Othello without the debilitating racism factor. It is pivotal and central. Just listen to Iago responding to "nature erring from itself":

> Aye, there's the point. As— to be bold with you —
> Not to affect many proposed matches
> Of her own clime, complexion, and degree,
> Whereto we see in all things nature tends—
> Foh! One may smell in such a will most rank,
> Foul disproportion, thoughts unnatural.
> But pardon me. I do not in position
> Distinctly speak of her, though I may fear
> Her will, recoiling to her better judgment,
> May fall to match you with her country forms,
> And happily repent [III, iii, 228–238].

The foregoing, added to "nature erring from itself" and "mine own weak merits" and what is to follow in this vein, constitute a classic example of "a systematic and intentional undermining of a person's conscious mind for the purpose of instilling doubt and replacing that doubt with attitudes and ideas directly inimical to his normal ideas and attitudes by subjecting him to mental torture, suggestion, etc."[50] and a classical example of menticide by racism. Racism has systematically and intentionally undermined Othello's conscious mind for the purpose of instilling and replacing that doubt with attitudes and ideas directly inimical to his normal ideas and attitudes, such as:

> Haply [by chance], for I am black
> And have not those soft parts of conversation
> That chamberers have, or for I am declined
> Into the vale of years—yet that's not much—
> She's gone, I am abused, and my relief
> Must be to loathe her [III, iii, 267–272].

Racism has him thinking of himself in racist terms as inferior and unnatural; his identity is reduced to "thick-lips." This is not the same Othello who was once proud of his accomplishments and his blackness. The self-doubt and self-disparagement he has come to has replaced his undermined normal self-confidence and self-possession. Instead of "mine own weak merits," his normal attitude is revealed in the following statement:

> I fetch my life and being
> From men of royal siege, and my demerits [deserts]
> May speak unbonneted to as proud a fortune
> As this that I have reached.
> * * *
> My parts, my title, and my perfect soul
> Shall manifest me rightly [I, ii, 21–24, 31–32].

His attitude toward Desdemona and marriage has also been by racism cunningly undermined and replaced with doubt and attitudes inimical to his normal ideas and attitudes. Whereas once he declared:

> For, know, Iago
> But that I love the gentle Desdemona,
> I would not my unhoused free condition
> Put into circumscription and confine
> For the sea's worth [I, ii, 24–28].

He comes to say not only that he loathes her, but also: "Oh, curse of marriage," and "Why did I marry?"

With Othello's consideration ("the intention of the mind when it is searching for the true"[51]): "This fellow's of exceeding honesty, (Iago) / And knows all qualities with a learned spirit, / Of human dealings," we are reminded again of the hamartia: "the mistaken judgment through which the fortunes of the hero of a tragedy are reversed."[52] Iago is far from being of "exceeding honesty," but, ironically, he does know "all qualities with a learned spirit, of human dealings," which knowledge augments his superior cunning.

For, he is "wise to do evil, but to do good he has no knowledge."[53] The reversal caused by Othello's mistaken judgment of Iago occurs when Othello is reduced to the racist stereotype of the black man, with which his subconscious mind identifies him from an old racist tape played over and over while he was an African slave. In undermining Othello's conscious mind, the reinvented Othello, Iago tapped into Othello's subconscious mind, the repository of days of slavery, where doubt and destructive attitudes instilled by former slave masters are stored, which Iago reawakens in Othello. This reawakening causes Othello to become irrational, wrought into jealousy, and sunk into madness. When he was strong, confident, and rational, he would bet his life on Desdemona's faithfulness: "My life upon her faith." But after the reversal and Iago's poison begins to work, and he is no longer the Othello we knew, it is: "She's gone, I am abused, and my relief / Must be to loathe her." But then, as she approaches, it's "If she be false, oh, the Heaven mocks itself! / I'll not believe it."

We know there is a change in Othello because Desdemona tells us. Almost immediately after the foregoing soliloquy, she enters cheerfully, reminding him of a dinner guest, and he says, without context or pertinence: "I am to blame." She says: "Why do you speak so faintly? / Are you not well?" No, he is not well. And in his distracted state, he, ironically, causes her to drop the very handkerchief, the fatal handkerchief, he later abuses her for losing. Before Iago even sees Othello again, he says: "The Moor already changes with my poison." And when he does see Othello, he says: "Look where he comes!"

> Not poppy, nor mandragora,
> Nor all the drowsy syrups of the world,
> Shall ever medicine thee to that sweet sleep
> Which thou owedst yesterday [III, iii, 329–333].

Iago's poison has caused Othello to see himself as racist whites, like Iago, see him, which makes him blame himself for Desdemona's supposed infidelity, and makes him see marrying her as "nature erring from itself," and makes him see that when she came to her senses and compared his black self to white men, like Cassio, she would naturally repent marrying black Othello. These are ideas directly inimical to Othello's normal ideas, and they were created to inculcate doubt, the sense of inferiority instilled by Iago while he systematically undermined Othello's conscious mind. So that, Othello's "I am to blame," although a sign of mental illness, is simply not true. The root cause of his vulnerability to Iago's poison is his having been in the past an African slave. And although he reinvented himself, and the ideas and attitudes of his reinvented conscious mind constitute what is normal to him, Iago's replacing them with inimical ideas and attitudes is causing Othello to suffer a schizophrenic split. He goes back and forth from the normal to the inimical. He is not well, and we can track his decline. The next sign is his "Ha! Ha! False to me?,"—after just saying above: "If she be false, oh, then Heaven mocks itself! / I'll not believe it." Not knowing what a righteous thing he's doing, he even turns on Iago to whom he said he was "bound to forever." He says to Iago: "Avaunt! Be gone! Thou hast set me on the rack. / I swear 'tis better to be much abused / Than but to know 't a little" (III, iii, 334–337). Iago certainly doesn't want to hear that.

A sure sign the reinvented Othello, the valiant Othello, the Othello the Duke praised, the Othello Desdemona fell in love with is gone (the willful, aware, upper level of mental life, the conscious mind, having been systematically undermined by Iago) is famously affirmed by Othello himself:

> I had been happy if the general camp,
> Pioneers and all, had tasted her sweet body,
> So I had nothing known. Oh, now forever
> Farewell the tranquil mind! Farewell content!
> Farewell that plumed troop and the big wars
> That make ambition virtue! Oh, farewell,
> Farewell the neighing steed and the shrill trump,
> The spirit-stirring drum, the ear-piercing fife,
> The royal banner and all quality,
> Pride, pomp, and circumstance of glorious war!
> And, O you mortal engines, whose rude throats
> The immortal Jove's dread clamors counterfeit,
> Farewell! Othello's occupation's gone! [III, iii, 345–357].

Crazed by anguish and torture, Othello is now, like King Lear on the heath, "unaccommodated man, the thing itself," naked, without the sophisticated, adulterated, artificial "pride, pomp, and circumstance of glorious war" and imperialism. (Shakespeare is satirizing both war and imperialism as well as "accommodated man.") Also like Lear, unaccommodated and on the brink of madness, Othello, in this state, "sees better," and has, ironically, moments of striking lucidity. For the first time, for example, he sees Iago for the villain he is:

> Villain, be sure thou prove my love a whore,
> Be sure of it, give me the ocular proof.
> Or by the worth of man's eternal soul,
> Thou hadst been better have been born a dog
> Than answer my waked wrath!...
> Make me to see 't, or at least so prove it
> That the probation bear no hinge nor loop
> To hang a doubt on, or woe upon thy life![54]

And in this lucid state, Othello reveals Shakespeare's message: the white man's destruction of the black man, which Iago's destruction of Othello symbolizes, is the worst sin:

> If thou does slander her and torture me,
> Never pray more, abandon all remorse.
> On horror's head horrors accumulate,
> Do deeds to make Heaven weep, all earth amazed,
> For nothing canst thou to damnation add
> Greater than that [III, iii, 368–372].

It is ironic that even in his lucidity, Othello exposes unawares his own ignorance to Iago. In condemning "slander," Shakespeare is alluding to the condemnation of slander in Scripture: "Him who slanders his neighbour secretly I will destroy" (Vulgate, Ps. 100:5). Or, "Whoso privily slandereth his neighbour, him I will cut off" (KJV, Ps. 101:5). In obviously including Othello as a victim of racist slander, Shakespeare is alluding to Bernard's teaching on slander and its application to the "black but beautiful bride" of Christ, thus Shakespeare's application to Othello. Considering Bernard's description of slander, combined with Scripture's "privily" and "secretly," it's not at all far-fetched to think of this kind of slander as a kind of torture, especially since Iago so very much resembles Bernard's characterization of the slanderer. Bernard refers to slander as "this most deadly vice," and uses Herod and Pilate as examples of slanderers:

> for the Gospel says of them that they became friends with each other that very day, that is, on the day of the Lord's passion. When they meet thus together it is not to eat the Lord's supper, but rather to offer to others "the cup of demons" and to drink of it themselves. They bear on their tongues the virus of death for their fellows, and gladly welcome the death that enters by their own ears.... No wonder if God should destroy "Him who slanders his neighbour secretly," since this vice is known to assail and victimize more bitterly than the others the love which is God. For every slanderer first of all betrays that he himself is devoid of love. And secondly, his purpose in slandering can only be to inspire hatred and contempt in his audience for the victim of his slander. The venomous tongue strikes a blow at charity in the hearts of all within hearing, and if possible kills and quenches it utterly; even the absent are contaminated by the flying word that passes from those present to all within reach. See how easily and in how short a time this swift-moving word can infect a great multitude of men with its sickly malice. Hence the inspired Prophet said of such: "Their mouth is full of cursing and bitterness; their feet are swift to shed blood."[55]

Iago also fits another of Bernard's descriptions of the slanderer:

> Some will spew out, with barefaced disrespect, any wicked slander that enters their heads; others try to hide an irrepressible evil purpose under the guise of simulated modesty. See the prelude of deep sighs, the mingled gravity and reluctance blazoned on his unhappy face, the downcast eyes and sombre tones, as the slanderer tells his tale, all the more per-

> suasive, the more the audience believes that he speaks with regret and with sympathy rather than malice.[56]

In using Bernard, Shakespeare is saying that nothing "assails and victimizes more bitterly ... the love which is God" than the racist destruction of black people by white people, which he demonstrates with Iago's destruction of Othello. And Shakespeare has characterized Iago according to Bernard as being "devoid of love," and as having as his purpose "to inspire hatred and contempt" and destruction, in that he "bears on his tongue the virus of death" for Othello. One of the most outrageously sickening examples of Iago's fitting Bernard's description of "trying to hide an irrepressible evil purpose under the guise of simulated modesty" is Iago's response to Othello's threatening echo of God's damnation of secret slanderers and torturerers like Iago, quoted above:

> Oh, grace! Oh, Heaven defend me!
> ... O wretched fool,
> That livest to make thine honesty a vice!
> O monstrous world! Take note, take note, O world,
> To be direct and honest is not safe.
> I thank you for this profit [profitable lesson], and from hence
> I'll love no friend, sith love breeds such offense [III, iii, 377–384].

In this mocking apostasy, Shakespeare seems to have alluded to a fitting response to Iago in the same sermon by Bernard quoted above:

> Though not yet your brother's murderer, you have murdered your own faith. How can you be right when, while raising up your hand to God, your heart is drawn to earth by envy and fraternal hate? How can you be right when your faith is dead, your purpose to kill, your heart empty of devotion and laden with bitterness?[57]

But, ironically, there is some truth in Iago's outburst although the source is false. The lesson he speaks of is one for Othello, howbeit too late for the learning: "To be direct and honest is not safe." Proof he hasn't learned it is his response to Iago: "Nay, stay. Thou shouldst be honest." The operative word being "shouldst."

Iago is not yet Othello's murderer, but through menticide he's on his way to being it. He certainly has Othello confused and Othello proves in practice that "To be direct and honest is not safe." For he directly and honestly reveals his confusion to Iago, leaving himself wide open for Iago to slip the knife in farther:

> I think my wife be honest, and think she is not.
> I think that thou art just, and think thou art not.
> I'll have some proof. Her name, that was as fresh
> As Dian's visage, is now begrimed and black
> As mine own face [III, iii, 384–388].

Shakespeare's point is in Swift's words, "Honesty hath no fence against superior cunning."[58]

Sticking the knife in farther, Iago, to aggravate, cunningly calls attention to the deliberately provoked confused state evident in Othello: "I see, sir, you are eaten up with passion." In this state, Othello asks for "a living reason [Desdemona's] disloyal." From this moment on, wrought by Iago, who tells Othello of Cassio's talking in his sleep about making love to Desdemona, we witness Othello's rather rapid and horrific descent back to the Chaos of the African slave trade, than which nothing better resembles the original Chaos. Othello's step-by-step descent is traceable. After the monster's fraudulent dream narration, Othello cries, "Oh, monstrous! Monstrous!"—unaware how befitting the narrator. Iago adds that the dream "may help to thicken other proofs / That do demonstrate thinly," which elicits from Othello: "I'll tear her to pieces." Iago next cunningly mentions the handkerchief, and its speaking against her with the other proofs. Othello's agony in response completes his descent to the Chaos of the African slave trade, making the menticide complete:

> Oh, that the slave had forty thousand lives!
> One is too poor, too weak, for my revenge.
> Now do I see 'tis true. Look here, Iago,
> All my fond love thus do I blow to Heaven—
> 'Tis gone.
> Arise, black Vengeance, from thy hollow cell!
> Yield up, O Love, thy crown and hearted throne
> To tyrranous hate! Swell, bosom, with thy fraught [load],
> For 'tis of aspics tongue! [III, iii, 442–449].

He calls out "Oh, blood, blood, blood!" Presented the viciously ironic supposition, "Your mind perhaps may change," Othello, kneeling, makes a solemn vow of revenge, after violently objecting to the supposition:

> Never, Iago...
> ... my bloody thoughts, with violent pace,
> Shall ne'er look back, ne'er ebb to humble love,
> Till that capable and wide revenge
> Swallow them up. Now, by yond marble Heaven,
> In the due reverence of a sacred vow
> I here engage [pledge] my words [III, iii, 457–466].

With these words, Othello reveals another indication of menticide, to swear by Heaven what is forbidden by Heaven: "Vengeance is mine," saith the Lord, "I will repay." The reinvented Othello had become Christian, but through menticide his Christianity was undermined and replaced by ideas and attitudes inimical to Christianity, as demonstrated by the foregoing "engaged words." There's no denying this as Othello makes a pact with the devil, Iago, the two of them kneeling together, victim and perpetrator of menticide.

In Othello's menticidally changed state, Shakespeare provides insight into the justifiable rage of an African slave, especially one of royal lineage. The African slave is certainly justified in the urge to kill. ("A Time to Kill" [Eccl. 3:3].) After all, the African slave thrived on menticide, which didn't stop with the African slave trade. As a consequence of his changed state, Othello wants to kill Desdemona, and have Cassio killed. He is obviously out of his mind.

As the scene ends with the parting of Othello and Iago, Othello orders Iago "to furnish [him] with some swift means of death" for Desdemona. As the next scene opens, we are made privy to a conversation between Desdemona and Emilia, in which we learn of Desdemona's distress over losing the handkerchief Othello gave her. In this conversation, Emilia is revealed to be an accomplice in the death of Desdemona. When Desdemona asks: "Where should I lose that handkerchief, Emilia?" the answer from Emilia is: "I know not, madam," which is a lie. She knows she gave that handkerchief to Iago. What Desdemona goes on to say characterizes Othello before "being wrought":

> Believe me, I had rather have lost my purse
> Full of crusades. And, but my noble Moor
> Is true of mind and made of no such baseness
> As jealous creatures are, it were enough
> To put him to ill thinking [III, iv, 25–28].

When asked: "Is he not jealous?" Desdemona answers: "Who he? I think the sun where he was born / Drew all such humors from him." This is true of his original state, and is corroborated by him in the end when he speaks of himself as "one not easily jealous, but being wrought, / Perplexed in the extreme." And he exhibits the latter state as he enters the scene we are now discussing, in that his discourse is rather incoherent. Desdemona breaks off from it to remind Othello of his promise. He says: "What promise, chuck." In his right mind, Othello would never have debased Desdemona to the level of "chuck." And more and more the focus is on his not being in his right mind.

When she cannot produce the handkerchief he gave her, he tells her a frightening voodoo-type story about the handkerchief that ends ironically with prefigurative omens:

> To lose 't or give 't away were such perdition
> As nothing else could match [III, iv, 67–68],

and a mummy's curse. She notices the change in his tone: "Why do you speak so startling and rash?" But she persists in aggravating him, and then she lies to him. He asks her if the handkerchief is lost, and she lies, saying for the second time: "I say it is not lost." When he tells her to "Fetch 't, let me see it," she says:

> Why, so I can, sir, but I will not now.
> This is a trick to put me from my suit.
> Pray you let Cassio be received again [III, iv, 87–89].

She is digging her own grave. He insists: "Fetch me the handkerchief. My mind misgives." But she persists, making matters worse:

> DESDEMONA: Come, come, / You'll never meet a more sufficient man.
> OTHELLO: The handkerchief!
> DESDEMONA: I pray talk me of Cassio.
> OTHELLO: The handkerchief!
> DESDEMONA: man that all his time
> Hath founder his good fortunes on your love,
> Shared dangers with you —
> OTHELLO: The handkerchief!
> DESDEMONA: In sooth, you are to blame.
> OTHELLO: Away!
> (Othello exits.) [III, iv, 92–101].

Even under normal circumstances this is overkill on the part of Desdemona, in addition to lying. Again we are confronted with a tragic flaw in Desdemona. It's a long shot, but perhaps Shakespeare confirmed the tragic flaw in her dying answer to Emilia, who asks: "Oh, who hath done this deed." Desdemona answers: "Nobody, I myself. Farewell." It seems pretty obvious that Shakespeare did not intend that Othello be held responsible for Desdemona's death.

Othello's first self-awareness of his own mental illness occurs in the heated exchange just described, when he says: "My mind misgives," which, in addition to other signs, should have alerted Desdemona to back off, and to be more concerned about her husband than about her friend, especially since she'd already noticed a difference or change in his tone which prompted her to ask him: "Why do you speak so startingly and rash?" She and Emilia are a big help to Iago. For the most part unwittingly, yes, but lying is a conscious act, and their lies made it possible for Iago to succeed. If, for example, upon finding the handkerchief she knew was highly valued by Desdemona, Emilia had given the handkerchief to its rightful owner, instead of to Iago, Iago would not have had the crucial proof he needed. Or, if Emilia, aware as she was of Desdemona's distress over the loss of the handkerchief, had not lied to Desdemona concerning the whereabouts of it, and told her the truth, Iago would have been stymied. Also, if Desdemona had been honest with Othello about losing the handkerchief, instead of lying to him (especially since he knew Cassio had the handkerchief), while at the same time persistently pushing Cassio's case, things could have turned out differently, she might well have saved her own life. And given the situation just described, any sane man would have been jealous. Needless to say, it's becoming more and more obvious that Othello is no longer the sane man he was when we first met him. Not only does he notice the change within himself—"My mind misgives"—Desdemona notices it as well.

After Othello sends Desdemona away, and Emilia says to her, "Is not this man jealous?" Desdemona answers: "I ne'er saw this before." When Cassio arrives, having been sent for by Desdemona to plead his case with Othello, she tells Cassio:

> Alas, thrice-gentle Cassio!
> My advocation is not now in tune.
> My lord is not my lord, nor should I know him
> Were he in favor as in humor altered...
> I have spoken for you all my best
> And stood within the blank of his displeasure
> For my free speech!...
> What I can do I will, and more I will
> Than for myself I dare [III, iv, 122–131].

In other words, Othello is not Othello, even to finding displeasure in Desdemona, something he'd originally given every indication he'd be incapable of. The urgency of her tone prompts Iago to feign surprise: "Is my lord angry?" He then craftily pays Othello a left-handed compliment by praising his courage, then undercutting the praise with a racist comparison of Othello with the Devil:

> Can he be angry? I have seen the cannon
> When it hath blown his ranks into the air,
> And, like the Devil, from his very arm
> Puffed his own brother, and can he be angry?
> Something of moment then. I will go meet him.
> There's matter in 't indeed if he be angry [III, iv, 135–140].

There is indeed "matter," that only he and Othello are privy to. But Desdemona, ignorant, of course, of their plot, gives "matter" a political meaning, which, ironically, enables her to blame herself for Othello's anger. She says:

> Beshrew me much, Emilia,
> I was, unhandsome a warrior as I am,
> Arraigning his unkindness with my soul,
> But now I find I had suborned the witness,
> And he's indicted falsely [III, iv, 150–154].

The irony here, is that Desdemona *is* to blame for Othello's anger, only not in the way she thinks.

The climactic moment in Othello's mental decline occurs when he is wrought to such an extreme that he passes out. Iago's crafting of an image of Cassio lying in bed with Desdemona takes Othello over the brink. Breaking into "incoherent muttering" before passing out, he says:

> Lie with her! Lie on her!—We say lie on her when they belie her.—Lie with her! 'Zounds, that's fulsome! Handkerchief—confessions—handkerchief! To confess and be hanged for his labor. First to be hanged, and then to confess. I tremble at it. Nature would not invest herself in such shadowing passion without some instruction. It is not words that shake me thus. Pish! Noses, ears, and lips. Is 't possible?—Confess?—Handkerchief?—Oh, devil! [Falls in a trance.][59]

Iago's inhuman ruthlessness is beyond description. He is the consummate monster. Seeing Othello lying in a trance, he gloats:

> Work on,
> My medicine, work! Thus credulous fools are caught.
> And many worthy and chaste dames even thus,
> All guiltless, meet reproach [IV, i, 45–48].

Soon after, Iago plants Othello where he can overhear Cassio talking about Bianca, not Desdemona, as Iago has Othello believing. Bianca enters talking about the fatal handkerchief she found in Cassio's chambers. Listening to all of this, Othello becomes schizophrenic, exhibiting a separation between his intellect and his emotion so that his feeling and his expression of them seem inappropriate to the situation at hand. For example, to make Othello feel worse about what he has overheard regarding the handkerchief, Iago exaggerates the lie by saying: "And see how he prizes the foolish woman your wife! She gave it to him, and he hath given it to his whore," Othello's intellect says, "I would have him nine years a-killing." But his emotions, by contrast, say: "A fine woman! A fair woman! A sweet woman!"—about his wife. And again, when Iago says, "Nay you must forget that," Othello says:

> OTHELLO: Aye, let her rot, and perish, and be damned tonight, for she shall not live. No, my heart is turned to stone, I strike it and it hurts my hand. Oh, the world hath not a sweeter creature. She might lie by an emperor's side, and command him tasks.
> IAGO: Nay, that's not your way.
> OTHELLO: Hang her! I do but say what she is, so delicate with her needle, and admirable musician—oh, she will sing the savageness out of a bear—of so high and plenteous wit and invention—
> IAGO: She's the worse for all this.
> OTHELLO: Oh, a thousand thousand times. And then, of so gentle a condition!
> IAGO: Aye, too gentle.

OTHELLO: Nay, that's certain. But yet the pity of it, Iago! O Iago, the pity of it, Iago!
IAGO: If you are so fond over her iniquity, give her patent to offend, for if it touch not you, it comes near nobody.
OTHELLO: I will chop her into messes! Cuckold me!
IAGO: Oh, 'tis foul in her.
OTHELLO: With mine officer!
IAGO: That's fouler.
OTHELLO: Get me some poison, Iago, this night. I'll not expostulate with her, lest her body and beauty unprovide me again. This night, Iago.
IAGO: Do it not with poison, strangle her in her bed, even the bed she hath contaminated.
OTHELLO: Good, good. The justice of it pleases. Very good [IV, i, 177–205].

This exchange is interrupted by a trumpet announcing the arrival of Lodovico on state business. Desdemona gets to him first, and apprises him of the rift between Othello and Cassio, about which Lodovico confronts Othello. Before Othello can answer, Desdemona intrudes, regarding the division, with: "A most unhappy one. I would do much / To atone them for the love I bear to Cassio." The unfortunate latter remark provokes Othello's anger to the extent he ultimately slaps her, in front of Lodovico, and we are reminded again of the enormous change in Othello. Lodovico says:

My lord, this would not be believed in Venice
Though I should swear I saw 't [IV, i, 240–241].

After Othello orders Desdemona away, and makes a few arrangements for the state, he utters remarks that call his wits into question. He says to Lodovico: "You are welcome, sire to Cyprus. Goats and monkeys!" Othello exits, and Lodovico says to Iago:

Is this the noble Moor whom our full Senate
Call all-in-all sufficient? This the nature
Whom passion could not shake? Whose solid virtue
The shot of accident nor dart of chance
Could neither graze nor pierce? [IV, i, 275–279].

He has it on the best authority, as Iago confirms: "He is much changed." But Lodovico persists: "Are his wits safe? Is he not light of brain?"

Nowhere is this more evident than when Othello stands over the sleeping Desdemona preparatory to killing her. That is when the separation between intellect and emotion, as the dictionary defines schizophrenia, seems essentially complete. In Bernardian terms, however, to which Shakespeare alludes, the relationship between the will and the reason is at issue; the will being the emotional faculty, the reason, the choosing faculty. It is clearly obvious, as Othello stands over Desdemona, that he loves her and does not want to kill her, but that this is contrary to the counsel and judgment of his reason, which amounts to rationalizing a cause to justify killing her: "It is the cause, it is the cause, my soul, / ...she must die, else she'll betray more men."

According to Bernard,

> The reason distinguishes good and bad, true and false, expedient and inexpedient. It does so infallibly so long as it is illumined by the light which created it. But when it has lost that light it makes errors. Being thus fallible, it cannot restore itself by its own power, but must be aided by faith, which infallibly makes those distinctions which corrupt reason is no longer able to make.[60]

As Othello continues, Bernard's words can be heard to echo throughout, beginning with his adoration of Desdemona, like a pilgrim at a shrine:

> Yet I'll not shed her blood,
> Nor scar that whiter skin of hers than snow
> And smooth as monumental alabaster [V, ii, 3–5],

which immediately changes to:

> Yet she must die, else she'll betray more men.
> Put out the light, and then put out the light.
> If I quench thee, thou flaming minister,
> I can again thy former light restore,
> Should I repent me. But once put out thy light,
> Thou cunning'st pattern of expelling nature,
> I know not where is that Promethean heat
> That can thy light relume. When I have plucked
> the rose,
> I cannot give it vital growth again,
> It needs must wither. I'll smell it on the tree.
> [Kissing her] [V, ii, 6–15].

Given the fact Othello had become Christian, to demonstrate that due to menticide, Othello's reason has lost the light which created it, Shakespeare has Othello ironically confuse Prometheus with Christ while unwittingly alluding to Christ "the light of the world." In his use of "quench" in the above, the allusion is to Jesus as prophesied by Isaiah: "smoking flax [candle] shall he not quench, till he send judgment unto victory" (Matt. 12:20). "Quench" is also used by the Apostle Paul in "Quench not the Spirit" (I Thess. 5:19), which associates the Holy Spirit with fire. Othello's use of "repent" is a timely allusion to Christ's message: "Except ye repent ye shall all perish." The Resurrection associates Jesus with "restoring" and "reluming" life, as Othello uses those terms, and with eternal life: as Truth, Jesus bears witness saying: "This is life eternal, that they might know thee the true God, and Jesus Christ whom thou hast sent." When Othello uses the word "wither" with regard to plucking the rose, "vital growth," and "tree," he is alluding to the words of Christ's affirmation:

> If a man abide not in me, he is cast forth as a branch, and is withered; and men gather them, and cast them into the fire, and they are burned ... for without me ye can do nothing [John 15:6].

In other words, as Bernard states: Reason "cannot restore itself by its own power, but must be aided by faith."[61]

As Othello kisses Desdemona again, with unspeakable poignancy, he proves all the more the absence of the will to kill her:

> Ah, balmy breath, that dost almost persuade
> Justice to break her sword! One more, one more.
> Be thus when thou art dead, and I will kill thee,
> And love thee after. One more, and this the last.
> So sweet was ne'er so fatal. I must weep,
> But they are cruel tears. This sorrow's heavenly,
> It strikes where it doth love. She wakes [V, ii, 16–22].

A further explanation by Bernard of the relationship between the will and the reason explains the satiric point Shakespeare makes with the above lines, especially if we consider Iago as reason and racist, and the effect of African slavery and racism as to Othello's no longer being master of his own reason nor retaining the use of his own will. Bernard explains, for example, that:

> Reason is given to the will for instruction, not destruction. It would be to the destruction of the will, however, were it to impose any necessity on it which would prevent it from moving freely in accordance with its judgment. Such necessity might push it (consenting to appetite or evil spirit) toward wrong, making an animal of it, not knowing, or even actively resisting the things which are of the spirit of God; or (following grace) toward right, making it spiritual, able to judge all things, but itself judged by no one. If, I say, the will were incapable of reaching out to any of these because of some prohibition of the reason, it would no longer be will. For, the presence of necessity means the absence of will.[62]

Racism is a structure of reason that makes man inhuman, not human. Following Aristotle, Thomas Aquinas said that "what is essential for man is his intellect, which means his ability to live in meanings and structures of reason; not the will but the intellect makes him human."[63] Not according to Bernard:

> Do you not think that man endowed with reason but failing to live reasonably is more of a beast than the beasts themselves? For if the beast does not control himself by reason he has an excuse based on his very nature, for that gift was totally denied to him; but man has no excuse, because reason is a special prerogative of his nature. A man in this con-

> dition is rightly judged to go forth from the company of other living creatures and drop to a lower level, since he is the only creature who violates the laws of his nature by a degenerate way of life.... It is demonstrably clear therefore, that man is inferior to the herds ... by the depravity of his nature (Iago, for example).[64]

Racism is a degenerate way of life. The Renaissance followed the Aristotelian-Thomist view, which is another reason why Shakespeare satirizes the Renaissance. Bernard had said it is the will that makes man human, that God is will, and the will of God is love.

Othello's mental state seems to worsen once he kills his wife. The ironic conflict between what he has done and what he did not will to do is overwhelming. His immeasurable love for her as perfection is such that he unwittingly identifies her death with the death of Christ:

> My wife! My wife! What wife? I have no wife.
> Oh, insupportable! Oh, heavy hour!
> Methinks it should be now a huge eclipse
> Of sun and moon, and that the affrighted globe
> Should yawn at alteration [V, ii, 97–101].

Scripture describes what Othello is unwittingly alluding to:

> Jesus, when he had cried again with a loud voice, yielded up the ghost. And, behold, the veil of the temple was rent in twain from the top to the bottom; and the earth did quake, and the rocks rent [Matt. 27:50–51].

Desdemona's dying words echo the dying words of Christ on the cross: "Father, into thy hands I commend my spirit." Desdemona says: "Commend me to my kind lord. Oh farewell!" This, coming after her answer to Emilia's wanting to know who killed her: "Nobody, I myself," is an implied reminder of Christ's words regarding his killers: "Father forgive them for they know not what they do." In other words, Shakespeare has Desdemona forgive Othello, for, Shakespeare is saying Othello, in his mental state and the kind of mental state it is, and what caused it, knew not what he was doing.

The focus on Othello's madness as a black victim of racist menticide who, as such, kills his beloved wife, is for the purpose of exonerating the black victim, Othello. In this projection, Shakespeare has Bernard as his authority, who says:

> On what basis, in fact, can one impute anything to a man, whether good or bad, if he is not known to have the free disposal of himself? Necessity excuses from both. For necessity's presence means freedom's absence; and where there is no freedom, neither is there merit, nor consequently judgment.... That is why we impute nothing they do, whether good or ill, to the mentally deficient ... because, even as they are no longer masters of their reason, so neither do they retain the use of their own will, nor consequently the judgment of freedom.[65]

These words support, needless to say, Shakespeare's unequivocal protest of the African slave trade and racism; that is, the white man's destruction of the black man, a protest he especially underscores with Othello's demand to know why Iago "hath thus ensnared my soul and body," which is how the white man destroys the black man. Shakespeare also has Othello allude to the African slave trade with "journey," "sea mark," "sail," and "oh, cursed slave!"

> Here is my journey's end, here is my butt
> And very sea mark of utmost sail.
> * * *
> Oh, cursed, cursed slave! [to himself] [V, ii, 270–271, 279].

We are again reminded of his devastating change when Lodovico asks: "Where is this rash and most unfortunate man?" and Othello answers: "That's he that was Othello. Here I am."

Clearly, Shakespeare does not intend that Othello be held responsible for the death of Desdemona. This he has made known in several ways, even at the very end, when he has Lodovico say, as he views the dead bodies of Othello and Desdemona, speaking to Iago: "This is thy work."

> O Spartan dog,
> More fell [cruel] than anguish, hunger, or the sea!
> Look on the tragic loading of this bed,
> This is thy work [V, ii, 362–365].

But Shakespeare does intend to expose the residual devastation resulting from racist menticide: black people's hatred of themselves. We have only to turn to the twentieth century (during the sixties) and the twenty-first century (2007), for proof of the validity of Shakespeare's protest: the experiment using five-year-old black children, who, when asked to choose between a black doll and a white doll, chose the black doll as the bad doll and the white doll as the good doll. And when asked to choose the doll most like themselves, they all chose the black doll.

Through Othello's holding himself responsible for Desdemona's death; his self-hatred; his self-condemnation; and his suicidal despair, the unforgivable sin; Shakespeare exposes the residual devastation resulting from racist menticide. As previously stated, Shakespeare, using Bernard, demonstrates that Othello's "reason cannot restore itself by its own power, but must be aided by faith,"[66] which, due to menticide, Othello no longer possesses. His loss of faith is indicated ironically by his allusions to Christian doctrine unaware of what he is saying. He condemns himself wrongly and despairingly, for example, when he says to the dead body of Desdemona:

> Now, how dost thou look now? O ill-starred wench!
> Pale as thy smock! When we shall meet at compt [Judgment Day],

> This look of thine will hurl my soul from Heaven
> And fiends will snatch at it. Cold, cold, my girl!
> Even like thy chastity. Oh, cursed slave!
> Whip me, ye devils
> From the possession of this heavenly sight!
> Blow me about in winds! Roast me in sulphur!
> Wash me in steep-down gulfs of liquid fire!
> O Desdemona! Desdemona! Dead!
> Oh! Oh! Oh! [V, ii, 272–282].

This is— it goes without saying — a broken and contrite heart. And although,

> The Lord is nigh unto them that are of a broken heart; and saveth such as be of a contrite spirit [Ps. 34:18],

> The sacrifices of God are a broken spirit, a broken and a contrite heart, O God, thou wilt not despise [Ps. 51:17],

Othello does not turn to God, his faith having been through menticide undermined and replaced by ideas and attitudes inimical to faith, which means "the turning of the heart to God," the condition of salvation."[67] In addition, he condemns himself, although Scripture tells us:

> If our heart condemn us, God is greater than our heart, and knoweth all things. Beloved, if our heart condemn us not, then have we confidence toward God [John 3:20–21].

Also, his despair, obvious in "in my case, 'tis happiness to die," is blasphemously indicative of the lack of faith, and of dementia, which is emphasized when he identifies himself with Judas Iscariot, the betrayer of Christ who committed suicide in despair. Actually, it's an erroneous comparison made possible only because of Othello's madness. On that level, they both do "throw a pearl away / Richer than all his tribe." The allusion is to one of the parables of Jesus:

> the kingdom of heaven is like unto a merchant man, seeking goodly pearls: Who, when he had found one pearl of great price, went and sold all that he had, and bought it [Matt. 13:45–46].

Through their lack of faith, their despair, and their suicide, Othello and Judas throw away the pearl of great price: Heaven. "Ignorance of God," says Bernard, "leads to despair, the greatest evil of all."[68] And applicable to mad Othello is Bernard's "opinion that all those who lack knowledge of God are those who refuse to turn to him."[69] But Othello's refusal is not willful refusal, it's dementia. Even in describing his tears he is ironically unaware he is alluding to Christ. Othello says to speak of him as—

> one whose subdued eyes,
> Albeit unused to the melting mood,

> Drop tears as fast as the Arabian trees
> Their medicinal gum [V, ii, 348–351].

Myrrh, a valuable gift brought to the baby Jesus by wise men in celebration of his birth, is a medicinal gum which drops from Arabian trees.

Othello's next lines are a prelude to suicide, but not committed by the real Othello, just as the real Othello did not kill Desdemona. Both acts were committed by the mad Othello that racism created. He proves that racism is "more cruel than anguish, hunger, or the sea," which is why *Othello* is one of the most tragic of all of Shakespeare's tragedies. The hero did nothing to precipitate or cause his own downfall except to be black.

King Lear

King Lear has long been considered Shakespeare's greatest play. It's been called "a sublime account of the human condition"[1]; also, "one of the profoundest of all artistic explorations of the human condition"[2]; and, it is said of the play: "there is something terrifying in the grandeur of the tragedy and its immense pessimism."[3] It cannot be said, however, that Lear is a more tragic figure than Othello. For, unlike Lear, Othello has no tragic flaw. Also, Shakespeare did not intend that "immense pessimism" be found in the play. On the contrary, he depicts the human condition as it is without Christ, and there is no pessimism in Christ. Shakespeare speaks as a satirist and ironist exhortatively, not as a storyteller; the story had already been told. It was a well known old story Shakespeare could have found in Holinshed's *Chronicles*, and in Spenser's *Fairie Queene*, and in contributions from Sidney's *Arcadia*. But to make his point, Shakespeare invented Lear's madness, Kent's loyalty, the storm, the fool, the Gloucester plot, and the tragic ending to serve his purpose in satire and irony. Chiefly he targets the Renaissance for its embrace of Aristotle's system of knowledge, which Shakespeare depicts as the root cause of bigotry; madness; the failure to know oneself, one's neighbor, and God; unnatural and degenerate human behavior; and humans becoming monsters. According to Aristotle, "The soul has to receive impressions from the external world."[4] Shakespeare attacks this system with Bernard's "The First Step of Pride, Curiosity," which is described as "a new disease in the soul, which has tired of introspection and which neglect of self makes curious toward others."

> For, as it knows not itself, it is sent forth to feed its kids. I shall rightly have called the eyes and ears kids, which signify sin; for just as death enters into the world by sin, so by these windows it enters into the mind. The curious man, therefore, occupies himself with feeding these, no longer curious to know how he has left himself within.... Hearken to Solomon, thou curious fellow; hearken to the wise man, thou fool. "Keep thy heart," he says, "with all diligence;" let all thy sense be alert for keeping that out of which "are the issues of life."[5]

Bernard's "Curiosity" explains the importance of "seeing" and "eyes" in the play. When Kent says: "See better, Lear," Shakespeare means for Lear to see better than his Aristotlean way of seeing. For, as Shakespeare implies:

> The eye is not dependable either for truth or wisdom, for Isaiah says: "Woe to you who are wise in your own eyes." Can wisdom which is accursed be good? It is of the world, and for that reason is folly in God's sight.... Do not look for wisdom with your eyes of flesh, because flesh and blood will not reveal it to you, but the Spirit.... Faith discerns truths unknown to the senses, beyond the range of experience.... With the power to understand invisible truths, faith does not know the poverty of the senses; it transcends even the limits of human reason, the capacity of nature, the bounds of experience. Why do you ask the eye to do what it is not equipped to do?[6]

The truth is revealed through irony when Lear says:

> Doth any here known me? This is not Lear.
> ... Where are his eyes? ... Who is it that can
> tell me who I am? [I, iv, 246–250].

In this, Shakespeare emphasizes the cause and effect relationship between eyes/seeing and Knowing Oneself, the First Step of Truth, to show that Aristotle's philosophy, feeding the eyes and ears, not only prevents Knowing Yourself, but also Knowing your Neighbor and Knowing God. For example, not only does Lear not know himself, he does not know his own daughters; but Cordelia, not ignorant of the Second Step of Truth, Knowing Your Neighbor, knows her sisters well. She says:

> The jewels of our father, with washed eyes
> Cordelia leaves. I know you what you are,
> And, like a sister, am most loath to call
> Your faults as they are named. Use well our father.
> To your professed bosoms I commit him.
> But yet, alas, stood I with his grace,
> I would prefer him to a better place [I, i, 271–277].

Eyes and ways of seeing, and the three steps of truth, are key motifs throughout the play.

Beginning with Lear's bigoted commercialization of marriage, Shakespeare, in giving us clues to his meaning, takes us from Bernard's "Curiosity," alluded to at the very beginning, to Goneril and Regan's feigned profession of love, which panders to the First Commandment expectations of their father, which Lear, presuming the divine right of kings, expects of Cordelia: "Thou shalt love the Lord thy God with all thy heart, and with all thy soul, and with all thy mind" (Matt. 22:37). Jonathan Swift accurately articulates Shakespeare's satire of the concept of the divine right of kings as personified by Lear:

> Among other theological arguments made use of in those times in praise of monarchy, and justification of absolute obedience to a prince, there seemed to be one of a singular nature; it was urged, that Heaven was gov-

erned by a monarch, who had none to control his power, but was absolutely obeyed: then it followed, that earthly governments were the more perfect, the nearer they imitated the government in Heaven. All which I look upon as the strongest argument against despotick power, that ever was offered; since no reason can possibly be assigned, why it is best for the world, that God Almighty has such power, which does not directly prove that no mortal man should ever have the like.[7]

The irony, of course, which emphasizes Shakespeare's satire, is that Lear does not know God. This is revealed in his angry reaction to Cordelia's failure to demonstrate the First Commandment, when he heretically puts diabolical creatures and planets in place of God:

by the sacred radiance of the sun,
The mysteries of Hecate, and the night,
By all the operation of the orbs
From whom we do exist and cease to be,
Here I disclaim all my paternal care,
Propinquity, and property of blood,
And as a stranger to my heart and me
Hold thee from this forever. The barbarous Scythian,
Or he that makes his generation messes
To gorge his appetite shall to my bosom
Be as well neighbored, pitied, and relieved
As thou, my sometime daughter [I, i, 108–119].

Lear thus disbranches his daughter because she does not love him with all her heart, and with all her soul, and with all her mind, as he requires.

Kent's caring, sensitive reprimand of Lear puts the issues in enlightening perspective when he speaks of Lear as "power bowing to flattery"; as "majesty falling to folly"; as needing to "check" his "hideous rashness"; and tells him to "See better, Lear." Kent implores Lear to "let me still remain, / The true blank of thine eye," which would have made all the difference, for Kent sees better than Lear. Rightfully, he says to Cordelia that she "justly thinkst, and hast most rightly said," in her answer regarding her love for her father. Kent sees better implicitly in his farewell insinuations to Goneril and Regan: "And your large speeches may your deeds approve. / That good effects may spring from words of love."

France "sees better" than Burgundy, who states that choosing Cordelia without her dowry, her third of the kingdom, would be impossible. France, on the other hand, finds it impossible to believe that Cordelia could do anything so monstrous as to cause such a contrary reversal of affection by her father, which to believe of her "Must be a faith that reason without miracle / Could never plant in me," says France. Cordelia's defense, which follows, proves his and her ability to "see better." She states:

I yet beseech your Majesty—
If for I want that glib and oily art,
To speak and purpose not, since what I well intend
I'll do 't before I speak—that you make known
It is no vicious plot, murder, or foulness,
No unchaste action or dishonored step,
That hath deprived me of your grace and favor,
But even for want of that for which I am richer,
A still-soliciting eye, and such a tongue
As I am glad I have not, though not to have it
Hath lost me in your liking [I, i, 227–236].

In response, Lear, in his divine-right-of-kings posture, blasphemously claiming the attributes of deity, makes a monstrous (as in unnatural) statement for a father, even for a patriarchal father: "Better thou / Hadst not been born than not to have pleased me better." It's an ironic reminder of Christ's warning: "Woe unto that man by whom the Son of man is betrayed! It had been good for that man if he had not been born" (Matt. 26:24). Lear's bigotry is a betrayal of Christ.

That France "sees better" is again revealed in his statement to Burgundy:

My Lord of Burgundy,
What say you to the lady? Love's not love
When it is mingled with regards that stand
Aloof from the entire point. Will you have her?
She is herself a dowry [I, i, 240–244].

Burgundy does not "see better," he sees as a mercenary, sexist bigot, saying to Lear:

Royal Lear,
Give but that portion which yourself proposed,
And here I take Cordelia by the hand,
Duchess of Burgundy [I, i, 245–247].

Lear, of course, with the obstinate intolerance of a bigot, does not "see better": "Nothing. I have sworn, I am firm."

The irony in Burgundy's response: "I am sorry then you have so lost a father / That you must lose a husband," not only confirms he does not "see better," but that he is blind to the fact that Cordelia hasn't lost but only gained. She hasn't lost a father, only a patriarchal, sexist, unloving bigot. She hasn't lost a husband, only a sexist, mercenary, unloving bigot who wouldn't be a husband even if he had her "portion" because he obviously doesn't love her. And even according to his own criteria she hasn't lost, for, it's certainly a gain to be Queen of France compared to being Duchess of Burgundy. But her greatest gain is love. Thus she's gained a "real" husband. And, as always, Cordelia "sees better." For, she says to Burgundy:

> Peace be with Burgundy!
> Since that respects of fortune are his love,
> I shall not be his wife [I, i, 250–252].

Shakespeare's irony emphasizes the gain in the response by France, which is further proof France "sees better":

> Fairest Cordelia, that art most rich being poor,
> Most choice forsaken, and most love despised,
> Thee and thy virtues here I seize upon,
> Be it lawful I take up what's cast away.
> Gods, gods! 'Tis strange that from their cold'st neglect
> My love should kindle to inflamed respect.
> Thy dowerless daughter, King, thrown to my chance,
> Is Queen of us, of ours, and our fair France.
> Not all the dukes of waterish Burgundy
> Can buy this unprized precious maid of me.
> Bid them farewell, Cordelia, though unkind.
> Thou losest here, a better where to find [I, i, 249–260].

Lear stays in character, the character that is his tragic flaw. Such traits as "hideous rashness," intolerance, obstinancy, and bigotry are indicative. He does not "see better," as he proves in the following:

> Thou hast her, France. Let her be thine, for we
> Have no such daughter, nor shall ever see
> That face of hers again. Therefore be gone
> Without our grace, our love, our benison [I, i, 261–264].

His two daughters Goneril and Regan, evil though they are, testify to the above-mentioned character traits of their father: "He always loved our sister most, and with what poor judgment he hath now cast her off appears too grossly." "'Tis the infirmity of his age. Yet he hath ever but slenderly known himself." The latter is crucial, revealing his ignorance of the First Step of Truth, Knowing Yourself, which Shakespeare makes crucial for the reason Bernard explains:

> I wish therefore that before everything else a man should know himself, because not only usefulness, but right order demand this. Right order, since what we are is our first concern; and usefulness, because this knowledge gives humility rather than self-importance, it provides a basis on which to build. For unless there is a durable foundation of humility, the spiritual edifice has no hope of standing. And there is nothing more effective, more adapted to the acquiring of humility, than to find out the truth about oneself. There must be no dissimulation, no attempt at self-decep-

> tion, but a facing up to one's real self without flinching and turning aside. When a man thus takes stock of himself in the clear light of truth, he will discover that he lives in a region where likeness to God has been forfeited, and groaning from the depths of a misery to which he can no longer remain blind, will he not cry out to the Lord as the Prophet did: "In your truth you have humbled me"?[8]

We are reminded of this passage when Lear is on the heath, except that he does not cry out to the Lord, nor is he humbled. What is added to the statement above: "Yet he hath ever but slenderly known himself"—"The best and soundest of his time hath been but rash," comprise the essence of Lear's tragic flaw.

One of the salient Renaissance mottos was "know thyself," not derived from Bernard's First Step of Truth, but from Aristotle's system of knowledge. Shakespeare satirizes the latter derivation ironically in his depiction of the hypocrite Polonius, especially in Polonius's advice to Laertes, his son. Like Polonius, Lear doesn't know himself for the fool he is, which is why Shakespeare created a Fool to teach him. As it turns out, Lear is proven to be a bigger fool than the Fool himself. Part and parcel of what the Fool teaches him combine to reveal Lear as a fool because he does not know himself; because he does not "see better"; and because he embodies the wisdom of Aristotle, the wisdom of the world, which is foolishness with God. He thus, like Aristotle, focuses on the external instead of the internal, which is why, needless to say, he doesn't know himself. His focus on the external preoccupies him with appearance instead of reality, the difference between the two being another major Renaissance theme. Hamlet's distinctions are symbolic. Being the only one still mourning his father's death, his mother asks: "Why it seems so particular with thee?" Hamlet replies:

> Seems, madam! Nay, it is. I know not "seems."
> 'Tis not alone my inky cloak, good Mother,
> Nor customary suits of solemn black,
> Nor windy suspiration of forced breath—
> No, nor the fruitful river in the eye,
> Nor the dejected 'havior of the visage,
> Together with all forms, moods, shapes of grief—
> That can denote me truly. These indeed seem,
> For they are actions that a man might play.
> But I have that within which passeth show.
> These but the trappings and the suits of woe.[9]

Lear, however, is concerned with "seems"; with appearance rather than reality; with the trappings and show rather than the real thing; with "The name and all the additions [titles of honor] to a king," but not "all the large effects /

That troop with majesty" (I, i, 133). Cordelia has "that within which passeth show," but Lear chooses the appearance of love, what "seems" love, the flattery of Goneril and Regan, over the real thing. We discover more about Lear by means of his foil, Gloucester, who, by significant contrast, sets off Lear to even greater disadvantage.

I mentioned earlier that Cordelia "sees better." She also possesses Bernard's three steps of truth, which is why she "sees better." She could never be heard to say, like Lear: "Who is it can tell me who I am?" She first demonstrates the First Step of Truth upon hearing her sisters' false protestations of love. She says: "Then poor Cordelia, / And yet not so, since I am sure my love's / More ponderous [profound] than my tongue" (I, i, 74–76). When Lear asks: "What can you say to draw / A third more opulent than your sisters?" she answers: "Nothing, my lord," because she knows herself well enough to know she can't be as opulently phoney as her sisters, let alone more so. She goes on to say with self-knowledge (in addition to what she has already stated about herself):

> Unhappy that I am, I cannot heave
> My heart into my mouth. I love your Majesty
> According to my bond, nor more nor less....
> You have begot me, bred me, loved me. I
> Return those duties back as are right fit,
> Obey you, love you, and most honor you.
> Why have my sisters husbands if they say
> They love you all? Haply, when I shall wed,
> That lord whose hand must take my plight shall carry
> Half my love with him, half my care and duty.
> Sure, I shall never marry like my sisters,
> To love my father all [I, i, 90–92, 95–103].

In creating Cordelia incapable of giving her father First Commandment love, Shakespeare is attacking the bigotry of patriarchy and "the divine right of Kings." The latter was established by Constantine the Great together with Pope Sylvester I in 330.[10] When Cordelia speaks of herself as "So young, my lord, and true," Lear answers: "Let it be so. Thy truth then be thy dower." And so it is, ironically, to her good fortune.

Cordelia demonstrates the Second Step of Truth, Knowing Your Neighbor, when she bids farewell to her sisters, which was quoted earlier. Her knowledge of the Third Step of Truth, Knowing God, is demonstrated by Shakespeare's making her the Christ figure in the play, in her forgiveness, in her crucifixion, and in her image suggestive of the Pieta.

Act 1, Scene 2 opens with an ironic attack upon another kind of bigotry, that of the perverse unnaturalness of labeling a human being "illegitimate," not to mention the prejudice legitimized thereby. It is the so-called "bastard" son of Gloucester who protests, and whose protest is to thrust into the face of the wisdom of the world, the "bastard" it created:

> Thou, Nature, art my goddess, to thy law
> My services are bound. Wherefore should I
> Stand in the plague of custom, and permit
> The curiosity of nations to deprive me,
> For that I am some twelve or fourteen moonshines
> Lag of a brother? Why bastard? Wherefore base?
> When my dimensions are as well compact,
> My mind as generous and my shape as true,
> As honest madam's issue? Why brand they us
> With base? With baseness? Bastardy? Base, base?
> Who in the lusty stealth of nature take
> More composition and fierce quality
> Than doth, within a dull, stale, tired bed,
> Go to the creating a whole tribe of fobs
> Got 'tween asleep and wake? Well then,
> Legitimate Edgar, I must have your land.
> Our father's love is to the bastard Edmund
> As to the legitimate—fine word, "legitimate!"
> Well, my legitimate, if this letter speed
> And my invention thrive, Edmund the base
> Shall top the legitimate. I grow, I prosper.
> Now, gods, stand up for bastards! [I, ii, 1–22].

Shakespeare's use above of the word "curiosity" is an allusion to Bernard's Curiosity, the first step of pride, perfect in an attack on Aristotle's philosophy from which bigotry is derived. But it also attacks the primary importance Plato perceives "curiosity" to be.

Edmund's protest introduces us to a story of filial ingratitude to which Lear's story pales by comparison, which it is the purpose of the Gloucester/Edmund/Edgar episode to expose. It is interesting to note that the play virtually opens with it, Gloucester is almost the very first character to speak. Ironically, given the title of the play, the real tragedy is Gloucester's, not Lear's, to set off the nature of Lear's responsibility for his own tragedy. The words Cordelia utters in the end apply to herself and to Gloucester, not to Lear, as they seem to: "We are not the first / Who with best meaning have incurred the worst" (V, iii, 4–5). Lear did not have "best meaning," Gloucester did.

Concerning Edmund, we don't know, of course, how long Gloucester has "so often blushed to acknowledge him"; although, as the play opens, he says, "now I am brazed to it," that is to say, brazen about acknowledging Edmund as his son. "Brazed" would seem to imply an activist attitude in opposition to or in protest of bigotry as it relates to the perverse stigma of human "illegitimacy." In the same vein, Gloucester makes it clear to Edmund and to us regarding both his sons: "the one by order of law," Edgar, and "the whoreson," Edmund, that one is no dearer to him than the other. Moreover, by all indications, Edgar loves Edmund like a "legitimate" brother. So it does seem that Edmund's justifiable quarrel is solely with the law, "that insatiable gulf of injustice and oppression, the law,"[11] not with Gloucester, not with Edgar, but he makes them suffer for the law's injustice. Also, he has no justifiable claim to the land, not because he is "illegitimate" but because he was not the first born, which has to do with another unjust law as well, sexist bigotry. It seems ironic that Shakespeare would attack bigotry by depicting a victim of bigotry who personifies the very stereotypes bigots associate with illegitimacy even though illegitimacy is not the cause of the victim's villainy, villainy makes him a bastard idiomatically. In other words, being "illegitimate" does not prevent Edmund's being loved by his family, nor does it prevent his owning the land, thus is not casual in his heinousness, unless he is just mad at the world for its opprobrious stigma. As for causality, two thoughts come to mind: Land is more important to him than love; in fact, love is not important to him at all; and he knows himself. As he explains himself he reminds us of Iago. His explanation attacks the wisdom of the world, correcting it with an allusion to Bernard on the difference between necessity and free will: Edmund says:

> This is the excellent foppery of the world, that when we are sick in fortune — often the surfeit of our own behavior — we make guilty of our disasters the sun, the moon, and the stars, as if we were villains by necessity ... and all that we are evil in, by a divine thrusting on — an admirable evasion of whoremaster man, to lay his goatish disposition to the charge of a star. My father compounded with my mother under the dragon's tail, and my nativity was under Ursa Major, so that it follows I am rough and lecherous. But, I should have been that I am had the maidenliest star in the firmament twinkled on my bastardizing [I, i, 128–144].

Edmund's saying "I am what I am means I am what I will." That is, he is a villain by will not by necessity. "The consent of the will, being voluntary, not necessary, makes us just or unjust," says Bernard:

> For, the presence of necessity means the absence of will. What is done by necessity does not derive from the will and vice versa. He is not forced to be evil by some other cause, but simply chooses to be so at the behest of his own will. It is our own will that enslaves us to the devil, not his power.[12]

After maliciously turning Gloucester against Edgar, and setting up Edgar, his speech in a soliloquy reminds us of Iago:

> A credulous father, and a brother noble,
> Whose nature is so far from doing harms

That he suspects none, on whose foolish honesty
My practices ride easy. I see the business.
Let me, if not by birth, have lands by wit.
All with me's meet that I can fashion fit [I, ii, 95–100].

The scene thus ends with Edmund plotting against his father and brother, as the next scene opens with Goneril plotting against her father.

Perhaps the most significant difference between Edmund's ingratitude and the ingratitude of Goneril and Regan is in the value of what Edmund was given: love, compared to the value of land, which Goneril and Regan were given. Lear places no value on love, just the appearance of it. There is a conspicuous absence of love in Goneril and Regan and the rest of the characters except for Edgar, Gloucester, Kent, Cordelia, and France. The play could be said to symbolize ingratitude to benefactors and, like Ixion, fathering monsters via Aristotle's system of knowledge. Reflected implicitly is ingratitude to the ultimate benefactor: Christ. Pivotally relevant to the satire as well in this regard is the implied Scripture: "He that loveth not knoweth not God; for God is love." We are also given the reason for the gratitude expected:

> In this was manifested the love of God toward us, because that God sent his only begotten Son into the world, that we might live through him. Herein is love, not that we loved God, but that he loved us, and sent his Son to be the propitiation for our sins [John 4:8–10].

Seen in this light, it seems the only real ingratitude in the play is that of Edmund toward Gloucester, not of Goneril and Regan toward Lear, who, in his presumptions of divine right, missed the point: it's "not that we loved God but that he loved us." In other words, Lear placed his emphasis, in determining his giving, on how much his daughters loved him, rather than on how much he loved them. And in his expectations of them, and his judgment of Cordelia especially, he demonstrated his own ingratitude to his benefactor: Christ. We are reminded of the influence on Shakespeare of medieval drama with its purpose of teaching Scripture through plays. These plays dealt with all the major events in Christianity, from creation and the fall of man to the resurrection. "Mystery cycles" survived in parts of England into the late sixteenth century. Stephen Greenblatt observes: "In 1579, when Shakespeare was fifteen, he and his family could still have seen them performed at Coventry. Something of their power — their way of constructing a shared community of spectators, their confidence that all things in the heavens and the earth can be represented onstage, their delicious blending of homeliness and exaltation — left its mark upon him."[13] Just as it is important to note the historical and traditional background of Shakespeare's Scriptural allusions, it is fitting to view Lear in the context of his presumptions while criticizing those presumptions in the context of the Scriptures he purports to embody.

Following Edmund's Iago-like soliloquy, there is a very brief scene, seemingly for the purpose of exposing Goneril's machinations against Lear, and her uttering the basis for an image of Lear the development of which establishes the need for a Fool. Goneril says:

> Idle old man,
> That still would manage those authorities
> That he hath given away! [I, iii, 16–18].

She writes to her sister to support her in her scheme. The attitudinal genesis of the scheme that breaks Lear lies embedded in her words that follow:

> Now, by my life,
> Old fools are babes again, and must be used
> With checks as flatteries when they are seen abused [I, iii, 18–20].

Goneril's telling observation and scheme provide insight into the character of Lear, particularly into his pride and self-ignorance. She is correct in saying he "still would manage those authorities / That he hath given away." Authority is pretty much what makes a king a king. Lear only knows himself as a king; he does not know himself as no longer a king, which means he does not know himself. To be treated like an "old fool" or a "babe," or to be humored as a person of no consequence, is more than his pride can endure.

In the next scene we see this brewing, but we also see Lear still thinking he's king, bigoted, tyrannical, with "hideous rashness" ordering people around contemptuously as if they are of no consequence, referring to Goneril's man Oswald as "blockhead," "mongrel," and "slave." When he asks, speaking of Oswald, "Why came not the slave back to me when I called him?" Lear gets a reality check from one of his knights:

> My lord, I know not what the matter is, but, to my judgment, your Highness is not entertained with that ceremonious affection as you were wont. There's a great abatement of kindness appears as well in the general dependents as in the Duke himself also and your daughter [I, iv, 61–67].

Lear gives a profoundly revealing response, especially considering Shakespeare's third use of "curiosity" in this first act. Lear's "own conception," which he justly blames on his Aristotelian "jealous curiosity," is indicative of his inability to "see better":

> Thou but rememberest me of mine own conception. I have perceived a most faint neglect of late, which I have rather blamed as mine own jealous curiosity than as a very pretense and purpose of unkindness. I will look further into 't but where's my fool? I have not seen him this two days [I, iv, 66–71].

Proof that his Fool "sees better" than Lear is brought to light by the knight in answer to Lear's question concerning his Fool's whereabouts: "Since my young lady's going into France, sir, the fool hath much pined away." Lear doesn't want to hear it: "No more of that, I have noted it well." But the most telling blow to his pride is delivered by Oswald. Lear asks him: "Who am I, sir?" Oswald answers: "My lady's father." Lear is livid: "My lady's father! My lord's knave! You whoreson dog! You slave! You cur!" Lear strikes him.

Once Oswald is pushed out, Lear's Fool enters to demonstrate what a fool Lear is. After much bandying about with less than subtle hints, Lear comes right out and says to his Fool: "Dost thou call me fool, boy?" His Fool answers: "All thy other titles thou hast given away, / That thou wast born with." The Fool sings three insinuating songs, and when Lear asks since when was he so full of songs, the Fool answers: "ever since thou madest thy daughters thy mother." Another thrust home is the Fool's affirmation: "I had rather be any kind of thing than a fool. And yet I would not be thee, Nuncle. Thou hast pared thy wit o' both sides and left nothing i' the middle. Here comes one o' the parings." Goneril enters.

The Fool keeps up a steady, exposing commentary during the exchange between Lear and Goneril. When Lear says to Goneril "How now, Daughter! What makes that frontlet on? Methinks you are too much of late i' the frown." The Fool comments wisely:

> Thou wast a pretty fellow when thou hadst no need to care for her frowning. Now thou art an O without a figure. I am better than thou art now. I am a fool, thou art nothing [I, iv, 210–215].

Goneril obviously has no respect for Lear as her father, let alone as King. In keeping with her strategy, as previously noted, she reprimands him as if he were a child or a ward, and threatens to take measures that would be considered shameful towards a father but that she deems justifiable as a necessity. She speaks of his "all-licensed fool" and his "insolent retinue" who "hourly carp and quarrel, breaking forth in rank and not to be endured riots." This treatment, of course, isn't nearly as gross as the way Lear treated his daughter, Cordelia, without provocation, whom even Goneril had said was "cast off too grossly." The question also arises whether, given Lear's obstinately wrongheaded treatment of Kent and Cordelia, Goneril and Regan were not justified in originally planning precautionary steps which now seem to be taking effect. Goneril had said: "The best and soundest of his time hath been but rash." And then, referring to the "temper which has long been part of his nature,"[14] she added:

> Then must we look to receive from his age not alone the imperfections of long-ingrafted condition, but therewithal the unruly waywardness that infirm and choleric years bring with them.... Such unconstant starts are we like to have from him as this of Kent's banishment [I, ii, 298–304].

But Lear, having "ever but slenderly known himself" (I, ii, 297), is in stunned disbelief at Goneril's attack. The perceived overbearing insolence to a father and the contemptuous effrontery to a king combine to throw Lear into a state of discombobulation or outraged indignation. He asks Goneril: "Are you our daughter?" She answers patronizingly:

> Come, sir,
> I would you would make use of that good wisdom
> Whereof I know you are fraught, and put away
> These dispositions that of late transform you
> From what you rightly are [I, iv, 239–243].

The Fool puts her remarks in proper perspective: "May not an ass know when the cart draws the horse?" As for Goneril, she "holds forth in the style of the master she has learned from,"[15] her father.

Lear says:

> Doth any here know me? This is not Lear.
> Doth Lear walk thus? Speak thus? Where are his eyes?
> Either his notion weakens, his discernings
> Are lethargied — Ha! Waking? 'Tis not so.
> Who is it that can tell me who I am? [I, iv, 246–250].

There is irony here. His pride can't believe that he, as "divine right" king and patriarchal father, is being attacked as he is by Goneril, so the questions are indignantly rhetorical. But also, he has never known who he is. He doesn't know himself as the arrogant, "divine," tyrannical bigot he is, which also means he does not know God. Shakespeare again exposes this by Lear's questions about his eyes and understanding, which are allusions to those who believe not in Jesus and why.

> Therefore they could not believe, because that Isaiah said again, He hath blinded their eyes, and hardened their heart; that they should not see with their eyes, not understand with their heart, and be converted, and I should heal them [John 12:39–40].

In other words, "God's just but hidden judgment neither washes away the evil deeds of the wicked nor is placated by their good deeds," (as with Edmund as he "pants for life": "Some good I mean to do, / Despite mine own nature" [V, iii, 243]). "He even hardens their hearts lest they should repent, take stock of themselves, and be converted and he would heal them." Bernard recalls God's words to the angels when they ask: "Shall we show favor to the wicked.... Will he not, then, learn to do justice?" God answers: "No," and gives the reason: "He does evil in the land of the upright, and he will not see the glory of the Lord."[15] With the same contemptuous arrogance as her father, Goneril calls Lear's reaction "pretended with astonishment," and continues to rail at him and threaten more, in no uncertain, insensitive terms. Then, Lear blows his top:

> Darkness and devils!
> Saddle my horses, call my train together.
> Degenerate bastard! I'll not trouble thee.
> Yet have I left a daughter [I, iv, 273–276].

"Degenerate 'bastard,'" ironically, significantly applies to Edmund. Not only is "bastard" a generalized term of abuse, it doesn't apply to Goneril because she is "legitimate," but she *is* "degenerate." Still, Lear's disbranching her, in a sense deprives her of legitimacy, which, for all intents and purposes, makes her a bastard in both uses of the word. Actually, she, Regan, and Edmund are all monsters, ungrateful to their benefactors. All are lacking in natural human feeling. Lear says:

> Ingratitude, thou marble-hearted fiend,
> More hideous when thou show'st thee in a child
> Than a sea monster! [I, iv, 281–283].

This is true, but, ironically, not in the way he thinks. Ingratitude may be more hideous in a child, but not in his child; rather, in Gloucester's child, Edmund. Lear only has devastated pride to complain of; Gloucester has the putting out of his eyes to complain of.

But at the point at which we have now arrived, the focus is on Lear's rage and pride, the latter seeming to bring on the first signs of madness in him. He defends his hundred knights and squires in a fierce attack on Goneril, which, for the first time affords a bit of introspection on his part:

> Detested kite! Thou liest.
> My train are men of choice and rarest parts,
> That all particulars of duty know,
> And in the most exact regard support
> The worships of their name. O most small fault,
> How ugly didst thou in Cordelia show!
> That, like an engine, wrenched my frame of nature
> From the fixed place, drew from my heart all love

And added to the gall. O Lear, Lear, Lear!
Beat at this gate, that let thy folly in
[Striking his head]
And thy dear judgment out! [I, iv, 284–294].

For the first time Lear sees no small fault in himself. Rage, extreme indignation and extreme regret compete for control of him. What he is now calling "a most small fault" inspired a "hideous rashness" in his behavior toward Cordelia, and only proves how all out of proportion to the circumstances his behavior really was. He is pathetic. There is perhaps nothing worse than being forced to hate yourself, especially when you compare the gem you have thrown away with the cheap imitation you have chosen to replace it. But, inasmuch as Cordelia was never wrong in the first place, we can only suppose his fury at her had its origins in pride and selfishness. Like he said: "I loved her most, and thought to set my rest / On her kind nursery."

Lear's striking his own head, symptomatic of the first signs of madness, suggests Bernard's description of a man who hates himself:

> Notwithstanding, this hatred as well of the Body as of the Soul, is rather in effect than affection. So the phrenetick man hates his own flesh, when he endeavours to mischief himself; the deliberation of Reason being asleep in him. But can there be a worse phrensie than impenitency of the heart, and an obstinate resolution to go on in sin? For such an one lays violent hands upon himself; nor does he tear and gnaw his flesh, but his mind.... So we tear and wound our unhappy Souls with our own hands; but with this difference, that we wound them so much the more grievously, by how much a spiritual Creature is more excellent, and more hardly cured. We do this out of a stupid internal insensibility. For the Soul being poured out abroad, it has no sense of its internal damages; because it is not within itself.... And what wonder, if the Soul feel not its own wounds, when forgetful of it self, and wholly absent from it self, it was gone into a far Country? But the time will come, when returning home to it self, it shall understand how cruelly it tore out its own very bowels [heart].[16]

The time *has* come, and Lear's soul is returning home to itself, and is beginning to understand how cruelly it tore out its own very heart: "like an engine, wrenched my frame of nature / From the fixed place, drew from my heart all love." The root cause as described demonstrates Shakespeare's use of Bernard to satirize the Renaissance worship of Aristotle who said the soul must receive impressions from the external world; which Bernard and Shakespeare are saying cause "a stupid internal insensibility." The soul's receiving impressions from the external world is "the soul being poured out abroad, gone into a far country, having no sense of its internal damages because it is not within itself, is forget of itself, and wholly absent from itself, so that it feels not its own wounds." Through Lear's first signs of madness, Shakespeare shows us what happens when Lear returns home to himself and begins to understand how cruelly he tore out his own very heart. He also has Lear answer Bernard's question: "But can there be a worse phrensie than impenitency of heart, and an obstinate resolution to go on in sin?" Lear answers with a horrible curse on his daughter, Goneril:

> Hear, Nature, hear, dear goddess, hear!
> Suspend thy purpose if thou didst intend
> To make this creature fruitful.
> Into her womb convey sterility.
> Dry up in her the organs of increase,
> And from her derogate body never spring
> A babe to honor her! If she must teem,
> Create her child of spleen, that it may live
> And be a thwart disnatured torment to her.
> Let it stamp wrinkles in her brow of youth,
> With cadent tears fret channels in her cheeks,
> Turn all her mother's pains and benefits
> To laughter and contempt, that she may feel
> How sharper than a serpent's tooth it is
> To have a thankless child! Away, away! [I, iv, 297–311].

Lear's tirade doesn't end with the preceding. When he discovers that Goneril has given orders for fifty of his train to depart within a fortnight, he starts in again. If he didn't regard his dignity so highly, he perhaps would not feel so destroyed. It is all about pride, or at least essentially about pride, as it began. "Thankless child" must be weighed in the balance:

> Life and death! I am ashamed
> That thou hast power to shake my manhood thus,
> That these hot tears, which break from me perforce,
> Should make thee worth them. Blasts and fogs upon thee!
> The untented woundings of a father's curse
> Pierce every sense about thee! Old fond eyes,
> Beweep this cause again, I'll pluck ye out
> And cast you with the waters that you lose
> To temper clay. Yea, is it come to this?
> Let it be so. Yet have I left a daughter
> Who I am sure is kind and comfortable.
> When she shall hear this of thee, with her nails
> She'll flay thy wolfish visage [I, iv, 318–330].

He *is* mad if he thinks Regan will be any better than Goneril, but his pride won't allow him to think any differently. He makes other empty threats before leaving, such as taking back his kingdom by force. The last things he says as the scene closes are ominous: "Oh, let me not be mad, not mad, sweet Heaven! /

Keep me in temper [sanity]. I would not be mad" (I, v, 50–51). It's interesting to note in the context of madness: Hamlet feigned madness; Othello was driven mad; but Lear drives himself mad.

We are not given the impression his madness is caused by the ingratitude of Goneril and Regan, two chips off the old block in virulence and pride. What is emphasized is his pride, his vanity, his "hideous rashness," his bowing to flattery, his being a fool, his "stupid internal insensibility," his intolerance, his temper, his virulence. All of this is supported by a larger-than-life suggestion that, when it comes to ingratitude, comparatively speaking, Lear has no complaints, not only because he brought his situation on himself, but because of the obvious facts. There's a well known biblical precedence Shakespeare would not have missed concerning the ingratitude of sons and daughters toward their parents, one that renders Lear's rage absurd: the Absalom/David story. King David says: "Behold, my son, which came forth of my bowels, seeketh my life" (II Sam.16:11). When David's army went out to defend David against the attack by Absalom and his army, David said to his captains: "Deal gently for my sake with the young man, even with Absalom." When David is told his son is killed in battle, David "went up to the chamber over the gate and wept; and as he went, thus he said, 'O my son Absalom, my son, my son Absalom: would to God I Had died for thee, O Absalom, my son, my son.'" But David's mourning for his son is considered ingratitude:

> And Joab came into the house to the king, and said, Thou hast shamed this day the faces of all thy servants, which this day have saved thy life.... For thou hast declared this day, that thou regardest neither princes nor servants: for this day I perceive, that if Absalom had lived, and all we had died this day, then it had pleased thee well... [II Sam. 19:5–19:6].

It goes without saying, there is no comparison between patricide and a daughter's disrespect, even if you include the dismissal of fifty knights. David loved his son, grieved for him, would have died for him, even though his son set out to kill him and take over his kingdom. Lear cursed his daughter because she disrespected him and also dismissed fifty of his knights, which "shook his manhood." Ironically, if we think of King David, Lear's excessive selfishness (speaking of himself as: "So kind a father!") is even more outrageous considering David's selflessness responding to the ultimate filial ingratitude.

The King David/Absalom story is not the only example of filial ingratitude that renders King Lear's complaints and rage absurd by comparison. Lear unwittingly prefigures another example when he curses his daughter for the second time after discovering she has ordered fifty of his followers to depart within a fortnight. Lear cries, saying:

Old fond eyes,
Beweep this cause again, I'll pluck ye out
And cast you with the waters that you lose
To temper clay [I, iv, 323–325].

Act II opens with Edmund hatching his second manifestation of filial ingratitude, which culminates in the plucking out of his father's eyes. Edmund stabs himself, then cries out, "Father, Father!" When Gloucester enters, Edmund tells him that Edgar stabbed him when he tried to dissuade Edgar from patricide:

I told him the revenging gods
'Gainst parricides did all their thunders bend,
Spoke with how manifold and strong a bond
The child was bound to the father. Sir, in fine,
Seeing how loathly opposite I stood
To his unnatural purpose, in fell motion
With his prepared sword he charges home
My unprovided body, lanced my arm [II, i, 47–54].

Consequently, good Edgar is now on the lam because of lies told by his evil brother, Edmund, who has also succeeded in turning their father unnaturally against son Edgar. But this is again the case that honest Gloucester has no defense against the superior cunning of evil Edmund. So, believing him, Gloucester declares, regarding Edgar:

Let him fly far.
Not in this land shall he remain uncaught,
And found — dispatch. The noble Duke my master,
My worthy arch and patron, comes tonight.
By his authority I will proclaim it,
That he which finds him shall deserve our thanks,
Bringing the murderous caitiff to the stake.
He that conceals him, death [II, i, 58–65].

Mark Gloucester's homage to the duke exemplified by "noble," "master," "worthy arch and patron," homage that will soon turn to horror. But I see more than plot in this. I see Shakespeare breaking down barriers and structures of reason lived in, especially those from the top down, courtesy of Aristotle.

Shakespeare is way ahead of his time, as far ahead as the "millennial generation (1982–2003)."[18] He is against hierarchical systems, they lend themselves to bigotry. Just because Gloucester is an earl, a subordinate or lower rank, Shakespeare mocks the system by having Gloucester refer to the Duke of Cornwall as "my master," when the duke is so far below the human level of Gloucester as to be on the monster level, below human and below animal. The millennial generation doesn't accept things from the top down, nor does Shakespeare in this play, making Lear the top. We've seen where that gets us. It makes for a slave to duty, like Kent; and Lear, the king, isn't even worthy of Kent. Lear has the temperament of a bigot, and there is nothing "noble" or "worthy" about the duke. It's degenerate at the top. Classism is bigotry; it's also anti–Christ. "Change has to come from the bottom up," says Barack Obama, the unifier, which is one of the reasons he is so in tune with the millennial generation, as is Shakespeare.

So it's not just that Gloucester is proof that "honesty hath no fence against superior cunning,"[19] the cunning of Edgar, the duke, and Regan, for example, but also because of his place in the hierarchy which determines his attitude, deference, duty, and behavior toward the duke. Edmund, meanwhile, after being assured his father will "work the means to make him, Edmund, capable of becoming heir" in place of Edgar, is soon to betray his father to get more from the duke. He lies about Edgar being part of Lear's train, and then places himself in the service of the duke. He becomes *his* at the duke's request:

For you, Edmund,
Whose virtue and obedience doth this instant
So much commend itself, you shall be ours.
Natures of such deep trust we shall much need
You we first seize on [II, i, 114–118].

Another example of misjudgment at the top. Yet another misjudgment, officially inexcusable, callously made by the duke, leads to Lear's complete breakdown. It's more than his pride can bear. The duke knows the protocol and is reminded by Kent but to no avail. He is about to put Kent into the stocks and Kent pleads with him:

Call not your stocks for me. I serve the King,
On whose employment I was sent to you.
You shall do small respect, show too bold malice
Against the grace and person of my master,
Stocking his messenger [II, ii, 135–139].

G. B. Harrison's gloss supports Kent's plea: "As the King's representative, Kent is entitled to respectful treatment; to put him in the stocks is to offer an intolerable insult to the King."[20] To Lear it *is* intolerable, that's the point. Gloucester pleads as well, at his peril. His goodness and compassion will be his downfall. He begs the duke not to put Kent in the stocks:

Let me beseech your Grace not to do so.
His fault is much, and the good King his master

> Will check him for 't. Your purposed low correction
> Is such as basest and contemned'st wretches
> For pilfering and most common trespasses
> Are punished with. The King must take it ill
> That he, so slightly valued in his messenger,
> Should have him this restrained [II, ii, 147–154].

Kent is put in the stocks nevertheless. He takes it philosophically, saying: "A good man's fortune may grow at heels,"[21] meaning ("even a good man may suffer a shabby fate.") Is this another take on the "human condition" for which critics applaud this play? Or could it have been avoided? Though the statement is true on its face, does it really apply to Kent in his situation? Shakespeare has bad things happen only to the good people in the play, and fate has nothing to do with it. In the case of Kent, his mouth got him into trouble with the duke, the husband of Regan whom he knows well, especially well enough to know that the words of love she spoke to Lear were false; and that she is in league with Goneril, whose servant he, Kent, attacked. He knew the two sisters were conspiring against Lear, and that he was in the enemy camp and should have acquitted himself accordingly, instead of overreaching on behalf of Lear. Also, Kent should have surmised that the duke would be in league with his wife, Regan, and that even if he didn't know the word "Ajax" would anger the duke, he should have known by the very mention of "stocks," that the duke had no respect nor concern for Lear, nor regard for him as the king and couldn't care less about how he would feel about his man being in the stocks. So that to a great extent he brought the stocks on himself. There is also the matter of seeing his duty to Lear as his whole purpose in living, his very being, his life, his identity. I don't think Shakespeare is promoting such an existence. I think he satirizes it as part of his satire of the "divine right of kings" concept, by allusion to the Apostle Paul's saying: "For to me to live is Christ, and to die is gain" (Phil. 1:21). Kent had said to Lear in the very beginning:

> Royal Lear,
> Whom I have ever honored as my King,
> Loved as my father, as my master followed,
> As my great patron thought on in my prayers...
> My life I never held but as a pawn
> To wage against thy enemies, nor fear to lose it,
> Thy safety being the motive [I, i, 142–145, 157–159].

In essence, Kent is saying: "To me to live is Lear, and to die is gain." But this is a sacrifice to be made only for Christ.

Lear's reaction upon first seeing Kent in the stocks emphasizes the gravity of the insult. He cannot believe his daughter and son-in-law have put

Kent, his messenger, in the stocks. Five times he says, "No," to Kent when told, and "No, no, they would not." Then:

> They durst not do 't.
> They could not, would not do 't. 'Tis worse than murder
> To do upon respect such violent outrage [II, iv, 22–24].

(He doesn't know what "violent outrage" is. "Violent outrage" best describes what Gloucester is soon to suffer.)

The enormity of Lear's pride, of his sense of self as king, that he would hold disrespect as worse than murder, is the violent outrage. His priorities are inordinately all out of proportion to the issues of life, to the heart, wherein are the issues of life. "Hearken to Solomon; hearken to the wise man, thou fool. Keep thy heart," he says, "with all diligence; let all thy senses be alert for keeping that out of which are the issues of life."[22] This is from Bernard's First Step of Pride, Curiosity, which Shakespeare uses to attack Aristotle. It is especially an attack on seeing people scientifically, as things or specimens, separating subject from object, the Aristotelian way, not the Christ way, in which we are all one, and we see through the heart.

Lear's Fool steps in for a moment to call him "thou fool" (from above). But Lear seems not to hear him. He is too distressed to hear:

> O how this mother swells up toward my heart!
> "Hysterica passio," down, thou climbing sorrow,
> Thy element's below! [II, iv, 56–58].

The gloss on this, is as follows:

> The "mother," called also "hysterica passio," was an overwhelming feeling of physical distress and suffocation. Lear's mental suffering is now beginning to cause a physical breakdown. This sensation, and the violent throbbing of his heart until it finally ceases, can be traced in Lear's speeches.[23]

This is not exactly an effort to "Keep thy heart with all diligence," as advised by the wise man Solomon, as previously quoted, to whom Lear does not hearken. For, he is soon to say: "Oh, me, my heart, my rising heart! But down!" He is on a steady decline into madness due to pride of dignity he no longer possesses, dignity defined as "the state of being worthy, honored, or esteemed." Being bigoted, tyrannical, and arrogant, he is not "worthy." And, he is neither "honored" nor "esteemed" to say the least. After being chastised by his daughter, the "king" says: "On my knees I beg / That you'll vouchsafe me raiment, bed, and food." When Regan tells him to return to Goneril, saying he's wronged her, he answers: "Ask her forgiveness? / Do you but mark how this becomes the house" ("suits my dignity"[24] [Harrison]). Of course, Goneril and Regan are bigoted themselves in their age prejudice, represented in Regan's contempt for Lear:

> Oh, sir, you are old,
> Nature in you stands on the very verge
> Of her confine. You should be ruled and led
> By some discretion that discerns your state
> Better than you yourself [II, iv, 148–152].

To Gloucester, Edmund accuses Edgar of the same prejudice:

> This policy and reverence of age makes the world bitter to the best of our times, keeps our fortunes from us till our oldness cannot relish them. I begin to find an idle and fond bondage in the oppression of aged tyranny, who sways not as it hath power, but as it is suffered [I, ii, 47–52].

When Lear says to Regan: "I gave you all," she answers: "And in good time you gave it."

Goneril arrives and speaks to Lear in terms of his "dotage." Discovering that Goneril and Regan are in cahoots, even after his complaints to Regan of Goneril's mistreatment, Lear's decline deepens. He says: "O sides, you are too tough, / Will you yet hold?" And then to Goneril: "I prithee, Daughter, do not make me mad." Adding, "I can stay with Regan, / I and my hundred knights." But Regan declares:

> Not altogether so.
> I looked not for you yet, am not provided
> For your fit welcome.
> * * *
> If you will come to me,
> ... I entreat you
> To bring but five and twenty. To no more
> Will I give place or notice [II, iv, 234–236, 249–252].

Fifty being more than twenty-five, he switches back to Goneril. But the two sisters are obviously intent on jerking their father around. Goneril adds injury to insult by saying he doesn't even need *one*. Lear then utters those famous poignant words: "Oh, reason not the need." He cries out to "Heavens," but not to "Our Father who art in heaven." We know this because he mentions "gods" and "revenges," and God has said: "'Vengeance is mine,' saith the Lord, 'I will repay.'" Lear goes from prayer mode to a would-be indomitable mode he can't carry off, but succeeds well enough to reflect the very characteristics of a bigot, such as obstinacy, intolerance, and pride.

Touch me with noble anger,
And let not women's weapons, water drops,
Stain my man's cheeks! No, you unnatural hags,
I will have such revenges on you both
That all the world shall — will do such
things—
What they are, yet I know not, but they shall be
The terrors of the earth. You think I'll weep.
No, I'll not weep.
I have full cause of weeping, but this heart
Shall break into a hundred thousand flaws
Or ere I'll weep. O fool, I shall go mad! [II, iv, 279–289].

He leaves, along with Gloucester, Kent and Fool. A storm and tempest are forecast. As to Lear's two daughters, for the first time there is a hint of filial feeling in that quarter. Because of the storm, Regan says if it were just Lear personally she'd "receive him gladly. But not one followerer." But minutes after, at Gloucester's alarm, she changes her tune:

O, sir, to willful men
The injuries that they themselves procure
Must be their schoolmasters [II, iv, 305–307].

Actually, not considering the source, or, ironically considering the source, there is much truth in that statement, especially as it applies to willful Lear. One would be hard put to find a more willful person than Lear on the heath in the storm.

On the heath, Lear is in "high rage" and the storm is in "high rage." Doors have been shut to both. A bystander describes the scene. In answer to Kent's question, "Where's the King?" he says:

Contending with the fretful elements,
Bids the wind blow the earth into the sea,
Or swell the curled waters 'bove the main,
That things might change or cease; tears his white hair,
Which the impetuous blasts, with eyeless rage,
Catch in their fury, and make nothing of;
Strives in his little world of man to outscorn
The to-and-fro-conflicting wind and rain.
This night, wherein the cub-drawn bear would couch,
The lion and the belly-pinched wolf
Keep their fur dry, unbonneted he runs,
And bids what will take all [III, i, 4–14].

Just as "Hell hath no fury like a woman's scorn," this storm hath no fury like Lear's scorn. The storm contains "impetuous blasts with eyeless rage," but

Lear's impetuous blasts are not "eyeless rages" because, in his self-centeredness, he sees the storm only in terms of himself. Being egocentric, vain, proud, self-pitying, and selfish, he wants the storm to destroy everyone and the world because he can't have what he wants, the trappings of a king, an entourage of one hundred knights and other outward appearances of kingship for show. His dramatic tantrum ends in self-pity:

> Blow, winds, and crack your cheeks! Rage! Blow!
> You cataracts and hurricanes, spout
> Till you have drenched our steeples, drowned the cocks!
> You sulphurous and thought-executing fires,
> Vaunt-coutiers to oak-cleaving thunderbolts,
> Singe my white head! And thou, all-shaking thunder,
> Smite flat the thick rotundity o'the world!
> Crack nature's molds, all germens spill at once
> That make ingrateful man!
> Rumble thy bellyful! Spit, fire! Spout, rain!
> Nor rain, wind, thunder, fire, are my daughters.
> I tax not you, you elements, with unkindness.
> I never gave you kingdom, called you children,
> You owe me no subscription. Then let fall
> Your horrible pleasure. Here I stand, your slave,
> A poor, infirm, weak, and despised old man.
> But yet I call you servile ministers
> That have with two pernicious daughters joined
> Your high-engendered battles 'gainst a head
> So old and white as this. Oh, oh! 'Tis foul! [III, i, 4–24].

Although the storm rages in concert with Lear's outcries against filial ingratitude, it also ironically calls attention to something tantamount to frivolousness, especially as compared to the unimaginable and unspeakable filial ingratitude described in Act III. One of the last declarations Lear makes on the heath, is: "I am a man / More sinned against than sinning." This is not true! The man more sinned against than sinning is Gloucester. In fact, the Gloucester tragedy is a foil for the Lear tragedy to expose Lear's tragic flaws, and to set off his complaints of ingratitude as feeble, and his presumption of entitlements as audacious.

Act III has been called "perhaps the single most extraordinary act of any Shakespearean play."[25] It opens with Lear on the heath, as described above. He is persuaded by Kent to come out of the storm into a hovel. He says: "My wits begin to turn," and "I am cold myself.... Come, bring us to this hovel" (III, ii, 69, 78). Lear, the Fool, and Kent exit. In the meantime, a very brief scene 3 focuses on the goodness and compassion of Gloucester, and his betrayal by his son, Edmund. Speaking to Edmund regarding the duke, Regan, and Goneril, Gloucester says in his concerns about Lear:

> Alack, alack, Edmund, I like not this unnatural dealing. When I desired their leave that I might pity him, they took from me the use of mine own house, charged me, on pain of their perpetual displeasure, neither to speak of him, entreat for him, nor any way sustain him [III, iii, 1–6].

Deceiving his father in his response, Edmund says: "Most savage and unnatural!" (III, iii, 7). Having no reason to doubt Edmund's sincerity, or trustworthiness, Gloucester takes Edmund into his confidence regarding "a division betwixt the Dukes, and a worse matter than that." He tells Edmund of a letter received "this night" that was "dangerous to be spoken," and so was locked in his closet. He adds that powers are on their way to revenge the injuries done to the king; that he and Edmund "must incline to the King"; and that none of what he is telling Edmund must be told to the duke. As soon as Gloucester leaves, Edmund makes plans to tell the duke everything instantly, knowing he will deserve more from the duke by betraying his own father.

It therefore becomes more and more difficult to feel sorry for Lear when he complains of filial ingratitude, and of being shut out on such a night, he and one hundred knights without whom he would not go in. It also becomes difficult when he doesn't know himself, as indicated, for example when he says: "O Regan, Goneril! / Your old kind father, whose frank heart gave all—." Not once has Shakespeare portrayed Lear as an "old kind father." We are not moved to pity for Lear when Gloucester's portrayal comes to mind, when real filial ingratitude is projected, and the worst is yet to come.

Scene 4 takes place in a hovel. We begin to see a change in Lear. For the first time, he thinks of the needs of someone other than himself. What he realizes he's been ignorant of is the Second Step of Truth, Knowing Your Neighbor; that is, sympathizing with his ills. "He learns others' wants from his own. He learns from his own miseries how to commiserate with others who are miserable, judging the common wretchedness from his own."[26] Lear says:

> Poor naked wretches, wheresoe'er you are,
> That bide the pelting of this pitiless storm,
> How shall your houseless heads and unfed sides,
> Your looped and windowed raggedness, defend you
> From seasons such as these? Oh, I have ta'en
> Too little care of this! Take physic, pomp,
> Expose thyself to feel what wretches feel,
> That thou mayst shake the superflux to them
> And show the Heavens more just [III, iv, 28–36].

Hidden in the hovel is Edgar disguised as Poor Tom, the madman, naked, covered only with a blanket. Seeing him, Lear relapses into madness again.

He says to Poor Tom: "Hast thou given all to thy two daughters? / And art thou come to this?" And again, when Poor Tom starts talking gibberish:

> What, have his daughters brought him to this pass?
> Couldst thou save nothing? Didst thou give them all?

When Kent says: "He hath no daughters, sir." Lear responds violently:

> Death, traitor! Nothing could have subdued nature
> To such a lowness but his unkind daughters.
> Is it the fashion that discarded fathers
> Should have thus little mercy on their flesh?
> Judicious punishment! 'Twas this flesh begot
> Those pelican daughters [III, iv, 72–77].

These repeated references to these unkind, ungrateful, pelican daughters serve to emphasize how little Lear has to complain of in this vein compared to Gloucester.

Such a comparison affords another attack on Aristotle; Lear representing the Aristotelian focus on the external, the senses, the superficial, the trappings and accommodations of kingship; Gloucester representing the Bernardian focus on the internal, the heart, and "that within which passeth show." Even Lear as naked, as "unaccommodated man" makes the point. It's still outward show. He sees Poor Tom naked, the storm still blowing, and says:

> Why, thou wert better in thy grave than to answer with thy uncovered body this extremity of the skies. Is man no more than this? Consider him well. Thou owest the worm no silk, the beast no hide, the sheep no wool, the cat no perfume. Ha! Here's three on 's are sophisticated. Thou art the thing itself. Unaccommodated man is no more but such a poor, bare, forked animal as thou art. Off, off, you lendings! Come, unbutton here [Tearing off his clothes] [III, iii, 104–113].

In stark contrariety Gloucester enters clothed in compassion. He says to naked Lear:

> Go in with me. My duty cannot suffer
> To obey in all your daughters' hard commands.
> Though their injuctions be to bar my doors
> And let this tyrannous night take hold upon you,
> Yet have I ventured to come seek you out
> And bring you where both fire and food is ready [III, iv, 153–158].

Lear hesitates a while to talk with Poor Tom, whom Gloucester does not know is Edgar. Kent says to Gloucester: "Importune him once more to go, my lord. / His wits begin to unsettle." In response, Gloucester compares what he erroneously considers the similarity between the filial ingratitude he suffered and that suffered by Lear. The erroneousness of the similarity, however, ironically calls attention to the difference. For example, Gloucester says:

> Canst thou blame him?
> His daughters seek his death. Ah, that good Kent!
> He said it would be thus, poor banished man!
> Thou say'st the King grows mad. I'll tell thee, friend,
> I am almost mad myself. I had a son,
> Now outlawed from my blood. He sought my life
> But lately, very late. I loved him, friend,
> No father his son dearer. Truth to tell thee,
> The grief hath crazed my wits. What a night's this! [III, iv, 168–175].

From the way he feels, Gloucester may think he knows how Lear feels but he doesn't know because there are more differences than similarities in the two fathers and in their situations. To begin with, Lear has no knowledge of his daughters' seeking his death, so he is not feeling what Gloucester feels, nor can he be driven mad by knowledge he does not have. Lear's wits are crazed by his pride, his patriarchy, his self-aggrandizing kingship, and his bigotry. We never see any of these flaws in Gloucester. Nor have we ever seen in Lear the love of a father for his children that we see in Gloucester. Nor does Lear have Gloucester's compassion for others, for his neighbor, as we see him demonstrate in risking his life for Lear. So, compared to Gloucester, Lear doesn't even know what filial ingratitude is; nor does he know what ingratitude to *his* benefactor is. We are reminded of Lear's ingratitude to his benefactor when he mentions "Poor naked wretches," and "Oh, I have ta'en / Too little care of this," which is an allusion to Christ's description of the last judgment: "As ye do unto the least of these my brethren, ye do unto me." And:

> Inasmuch as ye did it not to one of the least of these, ye did it not to me. And these shall go away into everlasting punishment but the righteous into life eternal [Matt. 25:31–46].

In bringing Lear "to where fire and food is ready," Gloucester takes along "the least of these," Poor Tom, whom he does not know to be his beloved son, Edgar, whom Gloucester was betrayed into believing betrayed him; the culprit being his beloved son, Edmund. Scene iv ends with Lear and Poor Tom being succored by Gloucester, who is soon to be in worse need of succor, which emphasizes again how much Lear's complaints of filial ingratitude pale by comparison to Gloucester's.

Scene v exists only to expose the Duke of Cornwall and Gloucester's son, Edmund, plotting the conspiracy against Gloucester. Edmund is more like Iago than ever. In betraying his father by showing Gloucester's secret letter to the duke, he says: "How malicious is my fortune, that I must repent to be just." His fortune *is* malicious, ill-gotten by betrayal of his loving father under the pretext of loyalty to his duke, to whom, not to appear callous, he feigns repentance for betraying his father although the "just" cause is not the loyalty itself but what Edmund gains by it: Earl of Gloucester, land, etc., of which he does not repent. An additional gain is not a gain at all, for, the replacement is far inferior to the original: "thou shalt find a dearer father in my love," says the duke to Edmund. And this after ordering Edmund to participate in the arrest of his real father: "Seek out where thy father is, that he may be ready for our apprehension." Edmund's response is ominous. In an aside, he says: "If I find him comforting the King, it will stuff his suspicion more fully" (III, v, 21).

In the preceding, Edmund makes a connection that takes Gloucester's role as foil to a new level and dimension. Lear is set off to such a disadvantage as to be seen as costing Gloucester his eyes. First of all, if we compare Lear's injured pride of dignity to thoughts of patricide, it's possible to see the irony in the one needing succoring the most, succoring, even to the risk of his life, the one who needs it the least. If it had not been for Lear's pride, hideous rashness, bigotry, and egomania, he would not have driven himself mad, and would not have needed rescuing by Gloucester, and therefore Gloucester would not have been in the wrong place at the wrong time rescuing Lear, and consequently "stuff[ing] his suspicion more fully," which leads to the putting out of his eyes.

Act III, scene vi, Gloucester re-enters the farmhouse where he has taken Lear, Kent, Edgar, and the Fool. He is told Lear's wits are gone. He says to Kent:

> Good friend, I prithee take him in thy arms.
> I have o'erheard a plot of death upon him.
> There is a litter ready, lay him in 't,
> And drive toward Dover, friend, where thou shalt meet
> Both welcome and protection. Take up thy master.
> If thou shouldst dally half an hour, his life,
> With thine and all that offer to defend him,
> Stand in assured loss. Take up, take up,
> And follow me, that will to some provision
> Give thee quick conduct [III, vi, 95–104].

Act III, scene vii, the scene of horror, takes place in Gloucester's castle, where Gloucester's house guests— Edmund, now Earl of Gloucester (unbeknownst to his father, Earl of Gloucester); Cornwall, Regan, and Goneril— accost him with "the traitor Gloucester" and declare, in front of his beloved son, Edmund: "Hang him instantly." "Pluck out his eyes." Cornwall adds:

> Leave him to my displeasure. Edmund, keep you our sister company. The revenges we are bound to take upon your traitorous father are not fit for your beholding [III, vii, 6–8].

He gives the order: "Go seek the traitor Gloucester. / Pinion him like a thief, bring him before us." Giving a phoney and hypocritical deference to *noblesse oblige*, he adds:

> Though well we may not pass upon his life
> Without the form of justice, yet our power
> Shall do a courtesy to our wrath, which men
> May blame but not control [III, vii, 24–27].

In other words, "yet because we are all-powerful we will give way to our wrath,"[27] that is, we will give way to bigotry. And these are "our betters," which is an irony Shakespeare attacks in Edgar's observation at the end of Scene vi, as he watches Gloucester, truly one of "our betters," engineer Lear's escape:

> When we our betters see bearing our woes,
> We scarcely think our miseries our foes [III, vi, 109–110].

In Scene vii, Shakespeare makes a dramatic ironic distinction between those who really are "our betters," and those who by *noblesse oblige* are supposed to be and expected to be, but fail miserably to be. But Shakespeare is also attacking the whole culture of hierarchy and class as fertile ground for bigotry. Kent, for example, is truly one of "our betters," but lives the life of a slave, and is abused by the highest of our so-called "betters," King Lear, who is a bigot.

When Gloucester is pinioned and brought in by order of his "betters," he makes an understatement that exposes the absurdity of the whole concept. He says:

> What mean your Graces? Good my friends, consider
> You are my guests... [III, vii, 30–31].

When Cornwall puts out one of Gloucester's eyes, Regan says: "One side will mock another, the other too," one of the "lower" class, a servant, proves himself to be truly one of "our betters" as he says to the duke:

> Hold your hand, my lord.
> I have served you ever since I was a child,
> But better service have I never done you
> Than now to bid you hold [III, vii, 71–74].

He and Cornwall draw swords and fight, Cornwall is wounded. Regan grabs a sword and runs at the servant from behind, killing him. Cornwall puts out

Gloucester's other eye. Gloucester cries out for Edmund. It is then that he learns the truth, from Regan, about Edmund. He says: "Oh, my follies! Then Edgar was abused. / Kind gods, forgive me that, and prosper him!" [III, vii, 91–2].

The scene draws to a close, giving us a life-size portrait of "our betters":

> 2. SERVANT: I'll never care what wickedness I do if this man [Cornwall] comes to good.
> 3. SERVANT: If she live long [Regan],
> And in the end meet the old course of death,
> Women will all turn monsters.
> 2. SERVANT: Let's follow the old Earl, and get the bedlam
> To lead him where he would. His roguish madness
> Allows itself to anything.
> 3. SERVANT: Go thou. I'll fetch some flax and whites of eggs
> To apply to his bleeding face. Now, Heaven help him!

Good Samaritans! This is also a good example of Bernard's Second Step of Truth, Knowing Your Neighbor, taken from "The Good Samaritan," a parable of Jesus:

> A certain man went down from Jerusalem to Jericho, and fell among thieves, which stripped him of his raiment, and wounded him, and departed, leaving him half dead. And by chance there came down a certain priest that way: and when he saw him, he passed by on the other side. And likewise a Levite, when he was at the place, came and looked on him, and passed by on the other side. But a certain Samaritan, as he journeyed, came where he was: and when he saw him, he had compassion on him. And went to him, and bound up his wounds, pouring in oil and wine, and set him on his own beast, and brought him to an inn, and took care of him. And on the morrow when he departed, he took out two pence, and gave them to the host, and said unto him, Take care of him; and whatsoever thou spendest more, when I come again, I will repay thee. Which now of these three, thinkest thou, has neighbour unto him that fell among the thieves? asked Jesus. And the lawyer said, He that shewed mercy on him [Luke 10:29–37].

With the putting out of Gloucester's eyes, and the talk of eyes and seeing, seeing takes center stage again, and most significantly as a way of feeling. Blind Gloucester says it most succinctly, when he says: "Ah, dear Son Edgar.... Might I but live to see thee in my touch, / I'd say I had eyes again!" (IV, i, 23–26) and when he speaks of the man "that will not see / Because he doth not feel" (IV, i, 71–72). Ironically, Blind Gloucester can see better than anyone else. So it is not true what he says to the old man, who, wanting to lead him, says to him: "Alack, sir, you cannot see your way," and Gloucester says: "I have no way and therefore want no eyes, / I stumbled when I saw." He has the way, the truth, and the light of Christ. Gloucester is projected as one to whom it can be said: "Blessed are your eyes, for they see: and your ears, for they hear." Edmund, Goneril, Regan, Cornwall, and Lear are projected as those about whom it can be said:

> For this people's heart is waxed gross, and
> Their ears are dull of hearing, and their eyes
> They have closed; lest at any time they should
> See with their eyes, and hear with their eyes
> And understand with their heart, and should
> Be converted and I should heal them [Matt. 13:15].

Edgar echoes the words of Jesus to his disciples: "Blessed are your eyes, for they see." He says to Gloucester in an aside: "Bless thy sweet eyes, they bleed," but they see. Gloucester echoes the words of Jesus in describing the last judgment. Jesus says: "As ye do unto the least of these my brethren, ye do unto me." In giving Poor Tom his purse, and asking Heaven to more equally distribute the wealth among rich and poor "so distribution should undo excess / And each man have enough," Gloucester is doing unto Christ. There also could be an allusion to the last judgment in Gloucester's charity to Poor Tom when he says: "Here, take this purse, thou whom the Heavens' plagues / Have humbled to all strokes" (so humble that you can endure anything); Jesus said, "He that shall endure to the end shall be saved." We can tie this in with Edgar's opening statement: "The lowest and most dejected thing of fortune, / Stands still in esperance [hope], lives not in fear" (IV, i, 3–4). "Christ in you the hope of glory" (Col. 1:27).

A Scriptural message is alluded to as well in Edgar's take on the world. He cries out when, for the first time, he sees his father blind, and being led by an old man:

> My father, poorly led? World, world, O world!
> But that thy strange mutations make us hate thee,
> Life would not yield to age [IV, i, 10–11].

But Scripture tells us:

> Love not the world, neither the things that are in the world. If any man love the world, the love of the Father is not in him. For all that is in the world, the lust of the flesh, and the lust of the eyes, and the pride of life, is not of the Father, but is of the world [John 15:16].

In Act IV, Scene ii, we're presented good examples of those who love the world and the things that are in the world, the love of the Father not being in them; good examples in Goneril, and Edmund, who, having disposed of his brother and father, now, through Goneril, looks to possess her half of Lear's kingdom. That's love of the world! So is the lust of the flesh demonstrated by Goneril toward Edmund:

Ere long you are like to hear,
If you dare venture in your own behalf,
A mistress's command. Wear this. Spare speech (Gives a favor).
Decline your head. This kiss, if it durst speak,
Would stretch thy spirits up into the air.
Conceive, and fare thee well [IV, ii, 19–23].

Edmund exits and Albany, Goneril's husband, enters. Shakespeare has Albany define the worthlessness of Goneril in terms of her unnatural lack of feeling for her father, to demonstrate, by allusion to Scripture, that the love of the Father is not in her. Albany says:

O Goneril!
You are not worth the dust which the rude wind
Blows in your face. I fear your disposition.
That nature which contemns its origin
Cannot be bordered certain in itself.
She that herself will sliver and disbranch
From her material sap, perforce must wither
And come to deadly use [IV, ii, 29–36].

In this, Shakespeare alludes to Scripture. Jesus says:

> I am the vine, ye are the branches: He that abideth in me, and I in him, the same bringeth forth much fruit: for without me ye can do nothing. If a man abide not in me, he is cast forth as a branch, and is withered: and men gather them, and cast them into the fire, and they are burned [John 15:5–6].

This text from the Bible is ironically ridiculed by Goneril. She answers Albany back, saying: "No more, the text is foolish." The irony is "The wisdom of the world," which is her wisdom, "is foolishness with God," not that God's wisdom is foolish, as she implies. Albany bears this out, as he continues:

Wisdom and goodness to the vile seem vile.
Filths savor but themselves. What have you done?
Tigers, not daughters, what have you performed?
A father, and a gracious aged man
Whose reverence even the head-lugged bear would lick,
Most barbarous, most degenerate, have you madded!
Could my good brother suffer you to do it?
A man, a prince, by him so benefitted!
If that the Heavens do not their visible spirits
Send quickly down to tame these vile offenses,
It will come.

> Humanity must perforce prey on itself,
> Like monsters of the deep [IV, ii, 38–49].

Humanity was already preying on itself via the African slave trade when those lines were written.

Albany continues his condemnation of Goneril for a reason, which we shall soon see, not that everything he says isn't true, for it is:

> See thyself, devil!
> Proper deformity seems not in the fiend
> So horrid as in woman....
> Thou changed and self-covered thing, for shame
> Bemonster not thy feature. Were 't my fitness
> To let these hands obey my blood,
> They are apt enough to dislocate and tear
> Thy flesh and bones. Howe'er thou art a fiend,
> A woman's shape doth shield thee [IV, ii, 59–67].

At the beginning of the very next scene we're presented a vividly dramatic contrast, or foil, that sets off Goneril to the enormously gross disadvantage intended by Albany's descriptive condemnation of her. Pivotal is the difference in humanness, in the capacity for feeling, for compassion, for sensitiveness in Cordelia, a Christ image compared to Goneril, a devil image. This difference represents the controlling theme of the play, and upon which it turns.

Kent asks a gentleman in the French camp near Dover: "Did your letters pierce the Queen to any demonstration of grief?" The gentleman answers:

> GENTLEMAN: Aye, sir. She took them, read them in my presence,
> And now and then an ample tear thrilled down
> Her delicate cheek. It seemed she was a queen
> Over her passion, who most rebel-like
> Sought to be king over her.
> KENT: Oh, then it moved her.
> GENTLEMAN: Not to a rage. Patience and Sorrow strove
> Who should express her goodliest. You have seen
> Sunshine and rain at once. Her smiles and tears
> Were like a better way. Those happy smilets
> That played on her ripe lip seemed not to know
> What guests were in her eyes, which parted thence
> As pearls from diamonds dropped. In brief,
> Sorrow would be a rarity most beloved
> If all could so become it.
> KENT: Made she no verbal question?
> GENTLEMAN: Faith, once or twice she heaved the name of "Father"
> Panting forth, as if it pressed her heart,

Cried "Sisters! Sisters! Shame of ladies! Sisters!
Kent! Father! Sisters! What, I' the storm? I' the night?
Let pity not be believed!" There she shook
The holy water from her heavenly eyes,
And clamor-moistened. Then away she started
To deal with grief alone [IV, iii, 12–33].

Kent tells the gentleman that Lear "by no means / Will yield to see Cordelia." When the gentleman asks: "Why, good sir?" Kent answers:

A sovereign shame so elbows him. His own unkindness
That stripped her from his benediction, turned her
To foreign casualties, gave her dear rights
To his doghearted daughters. These things sting
His mind so venomously that burning shame
Detains him from Cordelia [IV, iii, 43–49].

There is saving grace for Lear in this description, in that, according to Scripture: "A broken and a contrite heart, O God, thou wilt not despise" (Ps. 51:17). And in her anguished concern for her mad father, "As mad as the vexed sea," who disbranched her, Cordelia proves again she "loves not the world, neither the things that are in the world," for "the love of the Father is in her." For example, she desperately seeks to know "What can man's wisdom / In the restoring of his bereaved sense? / He that helps him take all my outward worth." And "No blown ambition doth our arms incite, / But love, dear love, and our aged father's right. Soon may I hear and see him!" (IV, iv, 2, 8–9, 27–29).

Scene v zooms in on the alarming contrast to Cordelia in the character of Regan. One of the first things Regan says is "It was great ignorance, Gloucester's eyes being out, / To let him live" (IV, v, 7–8). Another example she is of the world, that the love of the Father is not in her, is her lust of the flesh of Edmund. She says to Goneril's man, as she tries to intercept Goneril's letter to Edmund: "My lord is dead, Edmund and I have talked, / And more convenient is he for my hand / Than for your lady's." She adds: "If you do chance to hear of that blind traitor, / Preferment falls on him that cuts him off" (IV, v, 30–31, 37–38).

That will not be necessary if blind Gloucester has his way. All he wants is to die by falling off the high cliffs of Dover, to which he has offered to pay Poor Tom to lead him for that purpose. By and by they reach the place. Edgar as Poor Tom makes Gloucester believe he has reached the top of one of the cliffs of Dover. Edgar describes things below as they would look to someone at a great height: "The fishermen that walk upon the beach / Appear like mice," for example. Gloucester asks to stand where Edgar stands, gives him another purse, this one containing a precious jewel, and tells him: "Go thou further off. / Bid me farewell, and let me hear thee going." Edgar answers: "Now fare you well, good sir." He says to us: "Why I do trifle thus with his despair / Is done to cure it" (IV, vi, 33). Shakespeare is saying with Bernard that "Ignorance of God leads to despair, the greatest evil of all." And that "all those who lack knowledge of God are those who refuse to turn to him."[28] Edgar makes blind Gloucester think he has fallen off the cliff and survived, and tells him: "Thy life's a miracle," so to be grateful to God, his benefactor, the author of miracles. Gloucester is not sure if he has fallen or not. Edgar tells him to look up to where he has fallen from, but Gloucester reminds him: "Alack, I have no eyes." Edgar tells him:

> Think that the clearest gods, who make them honors
> Of men's impossibilities, have preserved thee [IV, vi, 73–74].

Gloucester says:

> I do remember now. Henceforth I'll bear
> Affliction till it do cry out itself
> "Enough, enough," and die.

Thus Edgar cures Gloucester of despair, and suicide at least temporarily.

In the fields near Dover they come upon Lear "fantastically dressed in wild flowers," but with his pride intact. Gloucester hears him rant, and says: "The trick of that voice / I do well remember, / Is 't not the King?" Lear proclaims: "Aye, every inch a king. / When I do stare, see how the subject quakes." He sets himself up as the king of kings, Jesus Christ, pardoning adultery, like Christ forgave the woman taken in adultery, telling her: "Go, and sin no more" (John 8:31). But ironically, unlike Christ, Lear does not consider adultery or lust of the flesh a sin. He says, for example:

> I pardon that man's life. What was thy cause?
> Adultery?
> Thou shalt not die. Die for adultery! No.
> The wren goes to 't, and the small gilded fly
> Does lecher in my sight.
> Let copulation thrive, for Gloucester's bastard son
> Was kinder to his father than my daughters
> Got 'tween the lawful sheets.
> To 't luxury [lust], pell mell!
> Behold yond simpering dame,
> Whose face between her forks [legs] presages snow,
> That minces virtue and shake the head
> To hear of pleasure's name.
> The fitchew, nor the soiled horse, goes to 't
> With a more riotous appetite.
> Down from the waist they are Centaurs,
> Though women all above [IV, vi, 110–127].

Lear thus demonstrates he is of the world, that the love of the Father is not in him (in more ways than one). He even declares succinctly: "I'll not love" (IV, vi, 141). His mention of Centaurs is significant in the end, as I will explain. In the above the relevance has to with lechery. The Centaurs were invited to a wedding feast and tried to carry off the bride and other women. His erroneous comparison of his daughters' treatment of him, with Edmund's treatment of Gloucester, is ironic in that it emphasizes his blind, egocentric, self-pity, and all the more so because he has no knowledge of Edmund's treatment of Gloucester, or that there was ever "a plot of death upon [he] himself" from which Gloucester rescued him.

Still in his divine-right-of-kings mode, when Gloucester pays homage with: "Oh, let me kiss that hand"—Lear obliges immortality with: "Let me wipe it first, it smells of mortality." Eyes take center stage again, and again with regard to "the superfluous and lust-dieted man that will not see / Because he doth not feel" (IV, i, 70–72). Gloucester asks Lear: "Dost thou know me?" Lust-dieted Lear answers: "I remember thine eyes well enough. Dost thou squiny at me ["look sideways like a prostitute"[29]]? No, do thy worst blind Cupid, I'll not love ["blind Cupid": the usual sign hung over a brothel.[29] Lear goes on to say: "Read thou this challenge, mark but the penning on 't." Gloucester's answer takes its ironic meaning from Bernard: "Were all the letters suns, I could not see one." Bernard says:

> When you are enlightened you can see even now the Sun of Justice that "enlightens every man who comes into this world," according to the degree of the light he gives, by which you are made somehow like him; but see him as he is you cannot, because not yet perfectly like him. That is why the Psalmist says: "Come to him and be enlightened, and your faces shall never be ashamed." That is very true, provided we are enlightened as much as we need, so that "with our unveiled faces contemplating the glory of God, all grow brighter and brighter as we are turned into the same image, as by the spirit of the Lord."[30]

Gloucester's answer is ironic because it isn't true, in that he is enlightened and can see even now, though blind, the Sun of Justice. He is enlightened, because he sees how this world goes feelingly. When Lear says, speaking as a man of the world, not enlightened, not of the Father, not spiritually:

> No eyes in your head, nor no money in your purse? Your eyes are in a heavy case, your purse in a light. Yet you see how this world goes [IV, vi, 149–151].

Gloucester answers: "I see it feelingly," which means he can see because he can feel, because he loves.

Lear's response, though ironic coming from him, is pivotal:

> What, art mad? A man may see how this world goes with no eyes. Look with thine ears. See how yond Justice rails upon yond simple thief. Hark, in thine ear. Change places and, handy-dandy, which is the Justice, which is the thief? [IV, vi, 153–158].

It's an allusion to Bernard developed from the centurion, who, when he stood facing the Crucified, saw that he thus cried out and breathed his last, he said: "Truly this man was the Son of God!" It was the sound of his voice that inspired his belief, it was by the voice that he recognized the Son of God, and not by the face. Perhaps he was one of those sheep of whom Christ said: "My sheep hear my voice (John 10:27)."[31] So when Lear says: "A man may see how this world goes with no eyes. Look with thine ears," Shakespeare is saying: "A man may walk by faith, not by sight" (II Cor. 5:7); and "faith comes from hearing"[32]; "the hearing succeeded where the sight failed. Appearances deceived the eye, but truth poured itself into the ear"; and "faith is the state of being ultimately concerned."[33]

As Lear goes on to hold forth on the wisdom of the world, Shakespeare, using Bernard, attacks Aristotle's system of knowledge, which is the wisdom of the world, especially of the Renaissance world, and based on the bodily senses, which explains the play's pivotal focus on "seeing" Lear's real tragedy is he doesn't "see better." The following by Bernard contains Shakespeare's meaning, the basis of his attack on Aristotle and the Renaissance in defense of "real" Christianity, his "ultimate concern" and corrective.

> The eye is not dependable either for truth or wisdom, for Isaiah says: "Woe to you who are wise in your own eyes." Can wisdom which is accursed be good? It is of the world, and for that reason is folly in God's sight. The wisdom that is good and true ... "is drawn out of secret places." Why then seek it from without, in your bodily senses? Taste resides in the palate, but wisdom in the heart. Do not look for wisdom with your eyes of flesh, because flesh and blood will not reveal it to you, but the spirit. Do not look for it in what the mouth tastes, for it is not found in the land of those who live for pleasure.... The woman whose wisdom was still carnal was rightly forbidden to touch the risen flesh of the Word, because she depended more on what she saw than on what she heard, that is, on her bodily senses rather than on God's word. She did not believe that he whom she saw dead would rise again, though he himself had made this promise. Hence her eye did not rest till her sight was satisfied, because for her there was no consolation from the faith, even God's promise was not sure.... And yet she, who refused to be consoled by the word of the Lord, ceased her crying when she saw him, because she valued experience above faith. But experience is deceptive. She is impelled, therefore, to seek the surer knowledge of faith, which discerns truths unknown to the senses, beyond the range of experience.... With the power to understand invisible truths, faith does not know the poverty of the senses; it transcends even the limits of human reason, the capacity of

> nature, the bounds of experience. Why do you ask the eye to do what it is not equipped to do? And why does the hand endeavor to examine things beyond its reach? What you may learn from these senses is of limited value.[34]

Lear tells Gloucester to "Get thee glass eyes / And like a scurvy politician, seem / To see the things thou dost not." It's telling Gloucester's eyes to do what they are not equipped to do in more ways that one. Gloucester is blind physically but not spiritually. He cannot *seem* to see the things he does not see because he is neither a liar nor a hypocrite, nor a bigot, nor of the world. Lear also poses: "If thou wilt weep my fortunes, take my eyes" (IV, vi, 180). But Lear's eyes are not dependable either for truth or wisdom, and he is wise in his own eyes. His wisdom is of the world and for that reason is folly with God. The eyes are only the windows of the soul. Gloucester doesn't need Lear's eyes to weep Lear's fortune, if he had them he wouldn't weep. Lear does not weep. Gloucester weeps for Lear without eyes because the love of the Father is in him. Lear goes on to say: "I am even / The natural fool of Fortune." Not so. He is fortune's fool, not by birth, but because he chooses to be, like Dante the pilgrim chooses *not* to be. Lear is fortune's fool because he chooses the wisdom of the world, which is foolishness with God, over the wisdom of the Father.

When Lear awakes to find Cordelia standing over him, he makes statements that complete the context for his previous mention of "Centaurs": "There's Hell, there's darkness, there's the sulphurous pit, / Burning, scalding, stench, consumption." He says to Cordelia:

> You do me wrong to take me out of the grave.
> Thou art a soul in bliss, but I am bound
> Upon a wheel of fire that mine own tears
> Do scald like molten lead [IV, vii, 45–48].

We are reminded of Ixion, the father of the Centaurs, begotten by his embrace of a false god, and who, for ingratitude to his benefactor, Zeus, who had purified Ixion for earlier crimes, is punished by being bound on a wheel that turned forever in Hell. In choosing Aristotle's system of knowledge, the wisdom of the world, over Christ, Lear embraced a false god out of ingratitude to his benefactor, Jesus Christ, who pardoned his sins by nailing them to the cross (to paraphrase Bernard). For ingratitude to the same benefactor, Satan, Judas, Brutus, and Cassius—the latter three "champed" in the mouth of Satan—are woeful in the pit of Dante's *Inferno*. "The soul up there that has the greatest punishment is Judas Iscariot, who has his head within and plies his legs outside."[35]

"Fool" has a double meaning: the meaning the Fool uses; and the meaning implied by "the wisdom of the world is foolishness with God." The Fool's meaning also includes Lear's treatment of Cordelia. A third meaning could well have to do with the First Step of Truth, Knowing Yourself. He says to Cordelia, for example: "I am a very foolish fond old man"; and "Pray you now, forget and forgive; I am old and foolish." He never seems to fully appreciate the loyalty, goodness, and wisdom of Kent, but Cordelia makes up for it:

> O thou good Kent, how shall I live and work,
> To match thy goodness? My life will be too short,
> And every measure fail me [IV, vii, 1–3].

The theme of "eyes" is brought full circle by Kent and Lear. Lear doesn't recognize Kent at first. He says: "Who are you? / Mine eyes are not o' the best...." Kent knows that. He's the one who told Lear in the beginning: "See better, Lear."

Perhaps Albany's assessment is fitting:

> All friends shall taste
> The wages of their virtue, and all foes
> The cup of their deservings [V, iii, 302–304].

With Goneril and Regan, one poisons the other then kills herself. These two monsters taste the wages of their deservings. So too does Cornwall and the monster of monsters, Edmund. "Wages" applies more to "all foes" than to "All friends," in keeping with the old saw: "The wages of sin is death." The "cup" applies more to "All friends" than it does to "all foes" because it calls to mind the cup Christ mentions in his prayer, saying: "O my Father, if it be possible, let this cup pass from me: nevertheless not as I will, but as thou wilt" (Matt. 26:39). The "virtue" of "All friends," as well as the "cup," identifies Gloucester, Edgar, Kent, Cordelia, Cornwall's servants, and Albany with Christ. So, too, does Cordelia's observation:

> We are not the first
> Who with best meaning have incurred the worst [V, iii, 4–5].

Certainly there is no better symbol of that observation than Christ on the cross. Moreover, Cordelia is identifiable with Christ in her forgiveness and compassion for her father, as well as in suggesting the representation of Christ in the Pieta, when Lear carries her dead body in his arms. In this is suggested a victory over death, the resurrection. Christ and eternal life are called to mind in Kent's last words: "I have a journey, sir, shortly to go. / My master calls me, I must not say no." Christ said: "My sheep hear my voice, and I know them, and they follow me: and I give unto them eternal life" (John 10:27–28).

Good men, Edgar and Albany, will restore order, and Edgar will become king. So that Shakespeare did not intend that *King Lear* be seen as projecting "immense pessimism" as critics have said. Similar to Greek tragedy, triumph is even to be seen in Lear's "anagnorisis," his self-realization. As a Classics scholar explains:

> It is the "hamartia," the human frailty or failure, the "metabole," the reversal, and the "anagnorisis," the realization, that provide the succession of tragic events.... But tragedy is not pessimistic, as some would maintain, or gloomy, for the concentration is not on the "metabole," but on the glorious, hard-won, hard-to-hold "anagnorisis." It is this act of unblinking clarity that justified man to himself, and always shall, in a world of puny gods and senseless fate.[36]

But "God," to Shakespeare, is no "puny god," and Christ rescues man from "senseless fate." And Lear achieves that hard-won anagnorisis.

MACBETH

"The powerful shall be powerfully tormented."[1]

In keeping with the theme of bigotry, culminating in this discussion, to say the lust for power is the root cause of bigotry is to center the theme. The play opens with thunder and lightning and three witches. As we enter these portals, it wouldn't be too farfetched to imagine the inscription: "Abandon every hope, you who enter."[2] Moreover, we get a telling clue remembering what Marcellus said when the ghost of Hamlet's father "faded on the crowing of the cock"[3]:

> Some say that ever 'gainst that season comes
> Wherein Our Saviour's birth is celebrated,
> The bird of dawning singeth all night long.
> And then, they say, no spirit dare stir abroad,
> The nights are wholesome, then no planets strike,
> No fairy takes nor witch hath power to charm,
> So hallowed and so gracious is the time.[4]

When *Macbeth* opens, and throughout, witches do have power to charm. Our Saviour is never celebrated, spirits stir abroad, the nights are not wholesome, and the time is neither hallowed nor gracious. So, "abandon every hope" is appropriate.

Macbeth is the story primarily of the gradual effects of the lust for power on the soul of a man and his wife. The witches, and Lady Macbeth, represent supernaturally evil spirits, one of the sources from which thoughts arise in Macbeth. According to Bernard, "The soul, which is made in the image of God, consists of three faculties: memory, will, and reason."[5] The opening focus of the play is the memory, so we'll start there:

> The "memory" is the thinking faculty. It is the most essential faculty, for without it the soul would not only fail to be a human soul, but would fail to be a soul at all. In the state of spiritual death the memory is devoted to thoughts which are not thoughts of truth; ... impure and evil thoughts of various sorts....[6]

"There are three functions of the soul: thought, emotion, and intention; residing respectively in the memory, the will, and the reason."

> "Thoughts" arise from three sources: they originate in our own souls, or they are inspired in us by evil spirits, or they are inspired in us by God.

> We "speak," as it were, the thoughts which originate in us; that is, we are the cause of them. But we "hear" the thoughts which are inspired in us, for something external is the cause of them, and we are merely receptive.[7]

The witches "Hover through the fog and filthy air" "to meet with Macbeth" to inspire in him ambitious thoughts of power:

> 1. WITCH: All hail, Macbeth! Hail to thee,
> Thane of Glamis!
> 2. WITCH: All hail, Macbeth! Hail to thee,
> Thane of Cawdor!
> 3. WITCH: All hail, Macbeth! Hail to thee,
> King hereafter! [I, iii, 48–50].

That these "evil spirits" succeed is indicated by Macbeth's reaction to what he has "heard," which is a manifestation of inspiration. We have it on the authority of a witness. Banquo says to Macbeth and to the witches:

> Good sir, why do you start, and then seem to fear
> Things that do sound so fair? I' the name of truth,
> Are ye fantastical, or that indeed
> Which outwardly ye show? My noble partner
> ... seems rapt withal [I, iii, 51–57].

This would indicate the "evil spirits" made a not unwelcome impression not unlike inspiration. For, Macbeth says in an aside: "Glamis, and Thane of Cawdor. / The greatest is behind." We can tell by his added thoughts, to which we are privy by "asides," that his thinking has been inspired by evil thoughts that, in turn, have given rise to thoughts that originate in his own soul. For example, he says to himself: "Two truths are told / As happy prologues to the swelling act / Of the imperial theme." ("The first two truths are like the prologue to a powerful scene which will lead me to the crown.")[8] Macbeth goes on to say to himself:

> This supernatural soliciting
> Cannot be ill, cannot be good. If ill,
> Why hath it given me earnest of success,
> Commencing in a truth? I am Thane of Cawdor [I, iii, 130–133].

As he continues, we note a switch from thoughts inspired by evil spirits, to thoughts originating in his own soul. He says, for example:

> If good, why do I yield to that suggestion
> Whose horrid image doth unfix my hair
> And make my seated heart knock at my ribs,
> Against the use of nature? Present fears
> Are less than horrible imaginings.
> My thought, whose murder yet is but fantastical,

Shakes so my single state of man that function
Is smothered in surmise, and nothing is
But what is not [I, iii, 130–142].

The "suggestion" (murder) he "speaks" of, that he now "yields" to, he did not "hear" from "evil spirits," the witches. ("We speak the thoughts which originate in us....") He gets off the murder thought and says to himself: "If chance will have me King, why, chance may crown me, / Without my stir." And, "Come what may, / Time and the hour runs through the roughest day." But when the king, Duncan, announces, "Our eldest, Malcolm, whom we name hereafter / The Prince of Cumberland," the thought of murder grows in Macbeth. He says to himself:

The Prince of Cumberland! That is a step
On which I must fall down or else o'erleap,
For in my way it lies. Stars, hide your fires,
Let not light see my black and deep desires.
The eye wink at the hand, yet let that be
Which the eye fears, when it is done, to see [I, iv, 48–53].

When he speaks here of his "black and deep desires," he speaks of the "will" of his soul. But before we leave the sources of our thoughts, it's important to note the following by Bernard, which may be a clue to Macbeth's tragic flaw:

> It is of little consequence to us to know the source of evil within us, provided we know it is there; no matter what its source we must watch and pray that we may not consent to it.[9]

But getting back to Macbeth's "dark and deep desires," his "will":

> The "will" is the emotional faculty. Willing is a matter of feeling, not of mere thinking or mere choosing. There is no problem of free will, because the will is free by definition. Freedom is opposed to necessity; to act "freely" is defined as meaning to act "willingly." Lust of the flesh, lust of the eyes, and worldly ambition drive the will into delight for things of the earth; and this is spiritual death.[10]

"Dark and deep desires" is not our first clue Macbeth "is not forced to be evil by some other cause, but simply chooses to be so at the behest of his own will."[11] He does not desire good, and Bernard tells us: "When we desire good, then our will is good; when evil, evil." We know by "dark and deep desires" Macbeth's will is not good. And that "It is our own will that enslaves us to the devil, not his power."[12] This is underscored by the fact Macbeth's thoughts never arise from the third source, thoughts "inspired in us by God."

Scene v opens with Lady Macbeth reading a letter from Macbeth concerning his encounter with the witches and their "Hail, King that shall be." The witches and Lady Macbeth remind us of *Titus Andronicus* and what a basic humanistic education in *Metamorphosis* can produce. Speaking of Lady Macbeth, Marvin Rosenberg states: "Here was the figure of Medusa, the Amazon, Omphale, and Medea"; Medusa had "the petrifying power to turn to stone anything that met its gaze."[13] Lady Macbeth also resembles the Amazons, women warriors. "The name means 'breastless,' and it is said that they removed their right breasts in order to better handle the bow. Heracles was sold as a slave to Omphale, queen of Lydia. There he was set to women's work, while Omphale assumed his lion's skin and club."[14] Medea was a witch, whose "magic arts" helped Jason and the Argonauts recover the golden fleece. She murdered and cut in pieces her younger brother Absyrtus and scattered the fragments. She took vengeance on Pelias for the wrong done by him to Jason's family. First she restored Aeson to youth by boiling him in a cauldron with magic herbs, and then persuaded the daughters of Pelias to submit their father to the same process. But on this occasion the right herbs were omitted, and the experiment resulted in Pelias's death. Jason and Medea fled to Corinth, where Jason, ambitious and weary of his barbarian Medea, arranged to marry the daughter of Creon, king of Corinth. The desertion and ingratitude of the man she loved roused the savage in Medea, and her rage was outspoken. She contrived the deaths of Jason's bride and of her father. Then she killed her own children to revenge herself on Jason, having found where he was most vulnerable. In this combination of Greek myths we have the role models for Lady Macbeth. And we are reminded of something the Duke of Albany said to his wife Goneril, which may well be said of Lady Macbeth:

> See thyself, devil!
> Proper deformity seems not in the fiend
> So horrid as in woman.[15]

As soon as she finishes the letter we begin to see the supernaturally evil role models in Lady Macbeth.

Right away we notice the difference between the source of her first thoughts and the source of Macbeth's first thoughts. His are first inspired in him by evil spirits; hers originate in her own soul. She speaks the thoughts which originate in her; that is, she is the cause of them. She is so supernaturally evil she fears Macbeth isn't evil enough (for murder) and she hates human feeling, the lack of which Shakespeare satirizes in all of his major plays. She says, for example, regarding Macbeth's becoming king:

> Yet I do fear thy nature.
> It is too full o' the milk of human kindness
> To catch the nearest way. Thou wouldst be great,
> Art not without ambition, but without
> The illness should attend it. What thou wouldst highly,
> That wouldst thou holily — wouldst not play false,

And yet wouldst wrongly win. Thou'dst have, great Glamis,
That which cries "Thus thou must do, if thou have it,
And that which rather thou does fear to do
Than wishest should be undone" [I, v, 17–26].

She then speaks of becoming (like the witches) the evil spirit inspiring thoughts in Macbeth, so that he "hears" the thoughts she inspires in him, she being the something external that is the cause of them, and he being merely receptive. She says:

Hie thee higher,
That I may pour my spirits in thine ear,
And chastise with the valor of my tongue
All that impedes thee from the golden round
Which fate and metaphysical aid doth seem
To have crowned withal [I, v, 26–31].

The word she uses for wickedness—"illness"—is profound. It emphasizes her knowledge of her own wickedness. She wastes no time getting on with it. The king isn't even there yet and she's got plans for him, holding forth in the style of the masters she's learned from: Medusa, the Amazon, Omphale, and Medea:

The raven himself is hoarse
That croaks the fatal entrance of Duncan
Under my battlements. Come, you spirits
That tend on mortal thoughts, unsex me here,
And fill me, from the crown to the toe, topfull
Of direst cruelty! Make thick my blood,
Stop up the access and passage to remorse,
That no compunctious visitings of nature
Shake my fell purpose, nor keep peace between
The effect and it! Come to my woman's breasts,
And take my milk for gall, you murdering ministers,
Wherever in your sightless substances
You wait on nature's mischief! Come, thick night,
And pall thee in the dunnest smoke of Hell,
That my keen knife see not the wound it makes,
Nor Heaven peep through the blanket of the dark
To cry "Hold, hold!" [I, v, 39–54].

It seems that the obvious result of the Renaissance humanist basic education in Ovid is the transformation of humanness. "The classical myths were well known through readings of Ovid—a basic text in grammar school education."[16] Lady Macbeth is a good example of "things that change, new being / Out of old,"[17] a transformation of the human into the monster. She is determined to transform her husband, who "is too full o' the milk of human kindness," from human to monster, a new being out of the old. But first she herself wants to be transformed. Just as Ovid calls on the gods he says created miraculous changes, Lady Macbeth calls on "you spirits," which must be evil spirits because she later calls them "you murdering ministers" ("spirits of murder" [Harrison]). She commands them to "unsex" her; fill her full of "direst cruelty," thicken her blood: stop up any human feeling of remorse or pity: turn her milk into gall, and make it possible for her to murder with her knife without being seen because of "the dark, thick night" covering with the "dunnest smoke of Hell," so that even "Heaven can't peep through the blanket of the dark." She is violently unabashed, vehemently blatant, uncompromisingly ruthless, and unequivocally direct and granite in her desire for transformation from womankind and humankind to augment and intensify her savage lust for power even through murder. She'd be willing to cut off her breast like the Amazons, adopt the lion skin and club of Heracles, like Omphale, and butcher and murder as viciously as Medea. She has the kind of outrageous pride and lust for power that Satan had in trying to overthrow God and rule Heaven. Can anyone imagine a healthier contrast to Lady Macbeth than Mary, whose "soul doth magnify the Lord?" (Luke 1:46). Lady Macbeth is the mother of all bigotry. When Macbeth arrives home he announces the arrival of Duncan that very night. When asked, "When goes he hence?" Macbeth answers: "Tomorrow, as he purposes." Lady Macbeth responds:

Oh, never
Shall sun that morrow see!
Your face, my Thane, is as a book where men
May read strange matters. To beguile the time,
Look like the time, bear welcome in your eye,
Your hand, your tongue. Look like the innocent flower
But be the serpent under 't. He that's coming
Must be provided for. And you shall put
This night's great business into my dispatch,
Which shall to all our nights and days to come
Give solely sovereign sway and masterdom [I, v, 62–71].

By "sovereign sway" is meant "royal, absolute power" (Harrison), which is what it's all about. Although the thought of murder has occurred to him, has originated in his own soul, now that he's brought right down to it, he is not so sure. He says: "We will speak further." He's really not sure he wants to murder the king, whether he has the will. He is not as wicked as his wife, by her own admission. She says he's not without ambition, "but without / The illness [wickedness] should attend it." The memory, will, and reason of her soul are all in sync, but such is not the case with Macbeth.

With the arrival of Duncan, the whole atmosphere dramatically changes outside Macbeth's castle. Not only is there a drastic contrast, the outside being ominous in its tranquility, but its aura is suggestive of "that season / Wherein

Our Saviour's birth is celebrated, / The bird of dawning singeth all night long / ...The nights are wholesome.... No witch hath power to charm, / So hallowed and so gracious is the time."[18] Duncan makes the time "hallowed and gracious." The implication certainly is that "real" Christianity is a far more wholesome basic grammar school education than *Metamorphoses*. This is hinted at with "temple," in "The temple-haunting martlet" outside the castle. Also, "the heaven's breath." No bird could survive the toxic air inside. Nor could such a scene as seen by Duncan and Banquo be seen by such as Lady Macbeth. Her soul is too wicked for her eyes to see beauty. Shakespeare has Duncan and Banquo say with outrageous irony:

> This castle hath a pleasant seat, the air
> Nimbly and sweetly recommends itself
> Unto our gentle senses.
> (Banquo) This guest of summer
> The temple-haunting martlet, does approve
> By his loved mansionry that the heaven's breath
> Smells wooingly here. No jutty, frieze,
> Buttress, nor coign of vantage but this bird
> Hath made his pendent bed and procreant cradle.
> Where they most breed and haunt, I have observed
> The air is delicate [I, vi, 1–9].

It's all spoiled when Lady Macbeth enters. The air is no longer sweet, nor recommends itself to gentle senses, nor smells like heaven's breath, nor is delicate. She pollutes it with her presence.

As the next scene opens we are privy to Macbeth's thoughts through the workings of the reason of his soul as defined by Bernard:

> The "reason" is the choosing faculty. It distinguishes good and bad ... expedient and inexpedient ... true and false. It does so infallibly so long as it is illuminated by the light which created it. But when it has lost that light it makes errors. Being thus fallible, it cannot restore itself by its own power, but must be aided by faith, which infallibly makes those distinctions which corrupt reason is no longer able to make.
>
> The will and the reason are distinct faculties because their functions are distinct, but they always act together. Willing implies choosing that which is willed; and choosing implies willing that which is chosen. The joint action of will and reason is consent. The consenting faculty, that is, the joint faculty of will and reason, is called free choice; the word "free" means willing, and the word "choice" means the action of the reason in its inflexible judgment.[19]

It's possible to trace Macbeth's thoughts using these definitional guidelines, in addition to the function of the reason, which is intention.

> "Intention" is of three kinds: the reason may be intent on the expedient, the good, or the true. We usually choose what appears to be expedient.

> In order to choose what is really expedient, two things are necessary, love and wisdom. Without love, we deliberately choose as expedient that which we correctly know to be wrong. Without wisdom, we ignorantly choose as expedient that which we incorrectly believe to be right.[20]

In the beginning, Macbeth's reason seems to be intent on the expedient in the context of evil thoughts originating in his own soul in the state of spiritual death. He says:

> If it were done when 'tis done, then 'twere well
> It were done quickly. If the assassination
> Could trammel up the consequence, and catch,
> With his surcease, success, that but this blow
> Might be the be-all and the end-all here,
> But here, upon this bank and shoal of time,
> We'd jump [risk] the life to come. But in these cases
> We still have judgment here, that we but teach
> Bloody instructions, which being taught return
> To plague the inventor [I, vii, 1–10].

He wants to be able to murder the king and have the consequences die with the king. In other words, he wants to get away with murder, which indicates he has an ill will. "Now, it is only right," says Bernard, "that people who have done things deserving of punishment should be punished. If they are quite unwilling to be punished, it means they do not will what is right. And the more discordant it is with righteousness, the more is the will unrighteous, and consequently evil."[21] This is even more the case with Macbeth because he considers the consequences: risking the life to come and reaping what he has sewn. But, as Bernard states: "Wisdom will not enter an ill-willed soul."[22] Macbeth thus goes on to say:

> This even-handed justice
> Commends the ingredients of our poisoned chalice
> To our own lips [I, vii, 10–12].

He begins to reconsider committing the murder, and the focus is "consideration." "Intention on the true is called 'consideration.'"[23] Macbeth considers the true aspects of his situation. Focusing on the King, even on his Christ-like attributes, Macbeth says:

> He's here in double trust.
> First, as I am his kinsman and his subject,
> Strong both against the deed. Then as his host
> Who should against his murder shut the door.
> Not bear the knife myself [I, vii, 12–16].

His reason has obviously lost the light which created it, or he wouldn't even be going through this kind of consideration for the purpose of such an intention, or even having murder as an intention to begin with, and his next consideration should have been a clue, but instead he proves his loss by unwittingly alluding to that light via the Christ-like attributes of Duncan:

> Besides, this Duncan
> Hath born his faculties so meek, hath been
> So clear [innocent] in his great office, that his virtues
> Will plead like angels trumpet-tongued against
> The deep damnation of his taking-off.
> And pity, like a naked newborn babe,
> Striding the blast, or Heaven's cherubin horsed
> Upon the sightless couriers of the air,
> Shall blow the horrid deed in every eye,
> That tears shall drown the wind [I, vii, 16–28].

What unspeakably beautiful language and images! Although it's ironic to place such incredible language into the mouth of the damned, it does serve to emphasize by contrast the depths of the wickedness of the speaker. He is forced to conclude, all things considered, that he hasn't sufficient motivation, will, or reason (intent) to murder the king:

> I have no spur
> To prick the sides of my intent, but only
> Vaulting ambition, which o'erleaps itself
> And falls on the other [I, vii, 25–28].

He relates this decision to Lady Macbeth:

> We will proceed no further in this business.
> He hath honored me of late, and I have bought
> Golden opinions from all sorts of people,
> Which would be worn now in their newest gloss,
> Not cast aside so soon [I, vii, 31–34].

Lady Macbeth responds with the rage of one of her role models: Medea. She is again the external, evil spirit source of thoughts by which Macbeth is inspired. Her argument is logical, however, as well as Scriptural: Jesus said, "As a man thinketh in his heart, so is he." She first exposes his hypocrisy. The outrageousness of "murder" never occurs to her:

> Was the hope drunk
> Wherein you dressed yourself? Hath it slept since?
> And wakes it now, to look so green and pale
> At what it did so freely? From this time
> Such I account thy love. Art thou afeard
> To be the same in thine own act and valor
> As thou art in desire? Wouldst thou have that
> Which thou esteem'st the ornament of life
> And live a coward in thine own esteem,

Letting "I dare not" wait upon "I would,"
Like the poor cat i' the adage? [I, vii, 35–44].

("The proverb is common and runs 'The cat would eat fish but would not wet her feet."[24])

"As thou art in desire" refers to the "will." Desire is of the will, the emotional faculty of the soul. As Jesus says: "For out of the heart proceed evil thoughts, murders, adulteries, fornications, thefts, false witness, blasphemies (Matt. 15:19). Lady Macbeth knows Macbeth has murder in his heart and she wants him to be who he is and not a hypocrite. She next emasculates him or at least challenges his manhood. He tells her: "I dare do all that may become a man. / Who dares do more is none," which is a significant answer, considering she's no woman and proves it. She says, for example, in answer to his "Who dares do more is [no man]":

What beast was't then
That made you break this enterprise to me?
When you durst do it, then you were a man,
And to be more than you were, you would
Be so much more the man.... I have given suck, and know
How tender 'tis to love the babe that milks me.
I would, while it was smiling in my face,
Have plucked my nipple from his boneless gums
And dashed the brains out, had I so sworn as you
Have done to this [I, vii, 47–58].

How could any woman, let alone a mother, even imagine dashing her baby's brains out, even say the words? Unless she's Medea, who is not a real woman but a monster, which is the point. Lady Macbeth is not a real woman, but a monster.

Macbeth worries: "If we should fail?" His wife answers: "We fail! / But screw your courage to the sticking-place / And we'll not fail." Not only are they oblivious to "Thou shalt not kill," and to the outrageousness of the act itself, they don't even take into consideration the gravity of the act of killing a king:

The single and peculiar life is bound
With all the strength and armor of the mind
To keep itself from noyance, but much more
That spirit upon whose weal depends and rests
The lives of many. The cease of majesty
Dies not alone, but like a gulf doth draw
What's near it with it. It is a massy wheel
Fixed on the summit of the highest mount
To whose huge spokes ten thousand lesser things
Are mortised and adjoined; which, when it falls,
Each small annexment, petty consequence,

> Attends the boisterous ruin. Never alone
> Did the King sigh but with a general groan.[25]

Duncan is not one of the least of these brethren, but, it is suggested that as the Macbeths do unto him, they do unto Christ. In addition to his Christ-likeness, as described, the reason of Duncan's soul is "illumined by the light which created it."[26] The function of reason being "intention," the function of his reason is intention on the good, which is called "religion." He fits Bernard's highest distinction:

> 1. Although all men seek the expedient, all men do not seek the good.
> 2. Only men of upright will prefer what appears to be the good.
> 3. Only men of upright and strong will perform what appears to be the good, instead of the evil preferred by the flesh.
> 4. Only men of upright and strong will and enlightened understanding perform what is in fact the good.[27]

This is Duncan. Further, "The fundamental requirements of true religion are love and wisdom, that is, good will and enlightened understanding."[28] As Bernard goes on to explain, we sense more deeply how good Shakespeare intended Duncan to be seen and how devastating his murder is meant to leave us:

> The understanding is enlightened by the Word of God, and the will is purified by the Spirit of God. But without love we do not will to perform the good which we know. And without understanding the stronger our good will the more we err.[29]

And we're left all the more devastated by how far the contrary opposite Duncan is from Macbeth and Lady Macbeth.

Once Lady Macbeth explains in detail to Macbeth just how the murder of Duncan is to be carried out, he says to her, with ironic significance:

> Bring forth men children only,
> For thy undaunted mettle should compose
> Nothing but males [I, vii, 72–74].

For it would be unnatural in females. But Lady Macbeth wins him over. Perhaps, like Medusa, Lady Macbeth has "the petrifying power to turn to stone anything that met its gaze."[30] Be that as it may, Macbeth gives his consent. He says:

> I am settled, and bend up
> Each corporal agent to this terrible feat.
> Away, and mock the time with fairest show.
> False face must hide what the false heart doth know [I, vii, 79–82].

With his consent, Macbeth's soul dies, as depicted according to Bernard's explanation of how the soul dies:

> If a sin is suggested to the memory by thought, that is a blemish in the soul, although not a disease. But if the will is moved to the sin by an emotional desire for it, then the soul is diseased, although not fatally. But if the reason also is incline to the sin by intention, so that the sin is consented to, then the soul dies."[31]

Of equal significance, although never seen in this play is the idea that "to consent is to be saved."[32]

We have seen the sin of murder suggested to the memory of Macbeth's soul by thought originating in his own soul: "My thought, whose murder yet is but fantastical" (I, iii, 139) ("in which murder is as yet only imagined" [Harrison gloss]). We have seen the will of Macbeth's soul "moved to the sin by an emotional desire for it":

> The Prince of Cumberland! That is a step
> On which I must fall down or else o'erleap,
> For in my way it lies. Stars, hide your fires,
> Let not light see my black and deep desires [I, iv, 48–51].

And, we have seen the reason of Macbeth's soul "inclined to the sin of murder by intention, so that the sin is consented to." What remains to be seen is the effect all of this will have on Macbeth.

The first effect is immediate. Macbeth sees a dagger before him in a vision:

> Is this a dagger which I see before me,
> The handle toward my hand? Come, let me clutch thee.
> I have thee not, and yet I see thee still.
> Art thou not, fatal vision, sensible
> To feeling as to sight? Or art thou but
> A dagger of the mind, a false creation,
> Proceeding from the heat-oppressed brain?
> I see thee yet, in form as palpable
> As this which I now draw.
> Thou marshal'st me the way that I was going,
> And such an instrument I was to use.
> Mine eyes are made the fools o' the other senses,
> Or else worth all the rest. I see thee still,
> And on thy blade and dudgeon gouts of blood,
> Which was not there before. There's no such thing.
> It is the bloody business which informs
> Thus to mine eyes [II, i, 33–49].

Macbeth is quite right, "it is the bloody business which informs / Thus to mine eyes" that bloody business being his intention to murder the king, for, "it is sin only which troubles and dims the sight." Also, "For as our corporeal sight is hindered either by some interior humour, or by the injection of some exterior dust: so also the spiritual sight is sometimes troubled by the allurement of ... ambition."[33]

As Macbeth continues, we are reminded that when Christ is celebrated, "the nights are wholesome, no spirits dare stir abroad, no fairy takes nor witch hath power to charm, / So hallowed and so gracious is the time."[34] And the air surrounding Christ-like Duncan is sweet and delicate, and then "Heaven's breath / Smells wooingly." So we know by significant contrast that the night Macbeth beholds reflects the wickedness in the beholder. In his prelude to murder, he says:

> Now o'er the one half-world
> Nature seems dead, and wicked dreams abuse
> The curtained sleep. Witchcraft celebrates
> Pale Hecate's offerings, and withered murder,
> Alarumed by his sentinel, the wolf,
> Whose howl 's his watch, thus with his stealthy pace,
> With Tarquin's ravishing strides, toward his design
> Moves like a ghost [II, i, 49–56].

We are primed for evil by such a description. In transit to the abomination his concern is to move by stealth:

> Thou sure and firm-set earth,
> Hear not my steps, which way they walk, for fear
> Thy very stones prate of my whereabout,
> And take the present horror from the time,
> Which now suits with it. Whiles I threat, he lives
> Words to the heat of deeds too cold breath gives.
> I go, and it is done. The bell invites me.
> Hear it not, Duncan, for it is a knell
> That summons thee to Heaven, or to Hell [II, i, 56–64].

When next we meet Macbeth he will have done the deed. We will notice the effect this has on him and on Lady Macbeth.

As Scene ii opens, Lady Macbeth is talking to herself and is nervously alarmed at the shrieking of an owl: "Hark! Peace!" She hears Macbeth's voice within cry: "Who's there? What ho!" and she starts:

> Alack, I am afraid they have awaked
> And 'tis not done. The attempt and not the deed
> Confounds us. Hard! I laid their daggers ready,
> He could not miss 'em. Had he not resembled
> My father as he slept, I had done 't [II, ii, 10–14].

This is the first crack in her armor. Macbeth enters and says: "I have done the deed." Looking at his hands, he says: "This is a sorry sight." She responds: "A foolish thought, to say a sorry sight," which is true. It's like straining at a gnat and swallowing a camel. He demonstrates a "stupid internal insensibility." It's as if it had never occurred to him that the heinous crimes he committed would have an effect on him as long as he did not get caught. But he proceeds to recite the dying prayers of the grooms he has murdered, and then wonders why he could not say "Amen" / "When they did say 'God bless us!'" Lady Macbeth interjects: "Consider it not so deeply," which is telling if we think of consider as in consideration, and deeply as in soul. But Macbeth is not assuaged: he asks:

> But wherefore could not I pronounce "Amen"?
> I had most need of blessing, and "Amen"
> Stuck in my throat [II, ii, 31–33].

Lady Macbeth answers with a most telling irony:

> These deeds must not be thought
> After these ways. So, it will make us mad [II, ii, 34–35].

Not only is she herself the first victim of her own prophecy, but, in addition to the effect the consent to and commission of sin is having on Macbeth's body, his eyes and hand, sin is obviously having an effect on his mind any time he expects God to bless him for murder. From these moments on we are confronted with a preponderance of evidence of his madness. Hamlet feigns madness; Othello is driven mad; Lear drives himself mad; the lust for power drives Macbeth mad.

He hears a voice call out repeatedly: "Macbeth shall sleep no more"— "Sleep ... the Balm of hurt minds." Lady Macbeth reprimands him. A bit obtuse in her use of the word "brainsickly," she says:

> Who was it that thus cried? Why, worthy Thane,
> You do unbend your noble strength to think
> So brainsickly of things. Go get some water
> And wash this filthy witness from your hand.
> Why did you bring these daggers from the place?
> They must lie there. Go carry them, and smear
> The sleepy grooms with blood [II, ii, 44–49].

But Macbeth cannot obey those orders: "I'll go no more. / I am afraid to think what I have done, / Look on 't again I dare not." His wife retorts:

> Infirm of purpose!
> Give me the daggers. The sleeping and the dead
> Are but as pictures. 'Tis the eye of childhood
> That fears a painted devil. If he do bleed,
> I'll gild the faces of the grooms withal,
> For it must seem their guilt [II, ii, 52–57].

This bravado and pride on her part are soon to go before a fall. After she's gone, madness comes down on Macbeth again as he hears knocking again and wonders why every noise appalls him. Looking at his hands again, he says:

What hands are here? Ha! They pluck out mine eyes!
Will all great Neptune's ocean wash this blood
Clean from my band? No, this my hand will rather
The multitudinous seas incarnadine,
Making the green one red [II, ii, 59–63].

His murder-committing hands pluck out his eyes because "it is sin only which troubles and dims the sight."[35] Lady Macbeth returns, and says:

My hands are of your color, but I shame
To wear a heart so white [II, ii, 64–65].

She will soon have cause to eat those words.

What we are seeing in Macbeth and are soon to see in Lady Macbeth is a dramatization of one of Bernard's sermons in which the love of wickedness is shown to indicate hatred of one's own soul and body, which can explain why murder has such an effect on Macbeth and Lady Macbeth:

> This hatred as well of the Body as of the Soul, is rather in effect than affection. So the phrenetick man hates his own flesh, when he endeavours to mischief himself; the deliberation of Reason being asleep in him. But can there be a worse phrensie than impenitency of heart, and an obstinate resolution to go on in sin? For such an one lays violent hands upon himself; nor does he tear and gnaw his flesh, but his mind. If thou hast seen a man fret, scratch his hands til they bleed again, thou hast in such an one a clear and lively pourtraicture of a Soul when it sins.... So we tear and wound our unhappy Souls with our own hands; but with this difference, that we wound them so much the more grievously, by how much a spiritual Creature is more excellent, and more hardly cured. We do this out of a stupid internal insensibility. For the Soul being poured out abroad, it has no sense of its internal dammages; because it is not within itself, but [in its lust for power (Macbeth)].... "Where thy treasure is," says our Lord, "there also is thy heart."[36]

While his wife is ashamed to wear a heart so white, and planning their cover, Macbeth is becoming penitent. He says: "To know my deed, 'twere best not know myself." And upon hearing the knocking again, he says: "Wake Duncan with thy knocking! I would thou couldst!" What he and his wife have done is beyond the capacity of a spiritual creature to endure sanguinely. The effect of murder upon their mind has been a tearing and gnawing devastation with more to come.

Our first clue there's more to come is the suggestion of a similarity between nature's reaction to the outrageous murder of Duncan and nature's reaction to the outrageous murder of Christ. The reaction to the Crucifixion began about the sixth hour:

> and there was a darkness over all the earth until the ninth hour. And the sun was darkened, and behold, the veil of the temple was rent in twain

> from the top to the bottom, and the earth did quake, and the rocks rent; And the graves were opened; and many bodies of the saints which slept arose. And came out of the graves ... and went into the holy city, and appeared unto many [Matt. 27:51–53].

Right before the discovery of Duncan's body, Lennox tells Macbeth about the night before, which is the very night Macbeth murdered Duncan. Lennox says:

> Where we lay,
> Our chimneys were blown down, and, as they say,
> Lamentings heard in the air, strange screams of death
> And prophesying with accents terrible
> Of dire combustion and confused events
> New-hatched to the woeful time. The obscure bird
> Clamored the livelong night. Some say the earth
> Was feverous and did shake [II, iii, 59–66].

Macbeth's response: "'Twas a rough night." Truer words were never spoken, although he and Lennox don't mean the same thing by "rough." But there is the suggestion that to murder Duncan is to crucify Christ again. Both were loving, innocent, good, and just men in whom no evil can be found. The reverent reaction of Macduff, who discovered the murdered Duncan, adds even more substance to the similarities. He says:

> Confusion now hath made his masterpiece.
> Most sacrilegious murder hath broke open
> The Lord's anointed temple, and stole thence
> The life o' the building [II, iii, 71–74].

As he continues he recalls the saints coming out of their opened graves and appearing unto many after the Resurrection:

> Awake, awake!
> Ring the alarum bell. Murder and treason!
> Banquo and Donalbain! Macolm! Awake!
> Shake off this downy sleep, death's counterfeit,
> And look on death itself! Up, up, and see
> The great doom's image! Malcolm! Banquo!
> As from your graves rise up, and walk like sprites
> To countenance this horror. Ring the bell [II, iii, 78–85].

There is profound irony in Macbeth's response to Macduff's alarm. The statement is true of him as the murderer, and at the same time fitting as a cover–up for his being the murderer. And he is in full knowledge of what he is saying and why in both instances:

> Had I but died an hour before this chance,
> I had lived a blessed time, for from this instant
> There's nothing serious in mortality.

> All is but toys. Renown and grace is dead,
> The wine of life is drawn, and the mere lees
> Is left this vault to brag of [II, iii, 96–101].

He's saying if he had died an hour before killing Duncan, he would have lived a blessed time. There's no chance for blessedness now. Neither his life nor human life itself is worth living, not because Duncan is dead, but because he killed him. "Renown and grace is dead," not only because Duncan is dead but because the chance of renown and grace for Macbeth is dead because of what killing Duncan has done to his soul. Nothing but the dregs of life is left. Macbeth has reached a state of deep depression, and the fact that his words above quoted also serve as a cover–up for the benefit of those around him is indicative of "an obstinate resolution to go on in sin," which recalls the question: "But can there be a worse phrensie than impenitency of heart, and an obstinate resolution to go on in sin?"[37] We shall see, for Macbeth seems to have reached the state of final impenitence, "the greatest crime of all, an unforgivable blasphemy":

> In his agitation he is either swallowed up by excessive sadness and lost in a deep depression from which he will never have the consolation of emerging, in accord with Scripture's saying that the wicked man shows only contempt when caught in the midst of evils; or he will dissimulate, flatter himself with false reasonings and, as far as in him lies, surrender irrevocably to the world, to find his pleasure and delight in what advantages it offers. But just when he believes that he has peace and security, misfortunes of all kinds will overwhelm him and he will not escape. Thus despair, the greatest evil of all, follows on ignorance of God.[38]

The next example, after the above quoted, is Macbeth's despair before having Banquo murdered. Speaking to Lady Macbeth, he says:

> But the frame of things disjoint, both the worlds suffer
> Ere we will eat our meal in fear and sleep
> In the affliction of these terrible dreams
> That shake us nightly. Better be with the dead,
> Whom we, to gain our peace, have sent to peace,
> Than on the torture of the mind to lie
> In restless ecstasy [madness]. Duncan is in his grave,
> After life's fitful fever he sleeps well.
> Treason has done his worst. Nor steel, nor poison,
> Malice domestic, foreign levy, nothing,
> Can touch him further [III, ii, 16–26].

So here he exudes despair and admits madness ("restless ecstasy") that "worse phrensie": "impenitency of heart."

In Macbeth's obstinate resolution to go on in sin, Bernard's teaching: "It is our own will that enslaves us to the devil, not his power,"[39] is clearly acknowledged in Macbeth's Machiavellian resolution to kill Banquo. He says in a soliloquy:

To be thus is nothing,
But to be safely thus. Our fears in Banquo
Stick deep, and in his royalty of nature
Reigns that which would be feared. 'Tis much he dares
And to that dauntless temper of his mind,
He hath a wisdom that doth guide his valor
To act in safety. There is none but he
Whose being do I fear. And under him
My Genius is rebuked, as it is said
Mark Antony's was by Caesar. He chid the sisters
When they first put the name of King upon me,
And bade them speak to him. Then prophetlike
They hailed him father to a line of kings.
Upon my head they placed a fruitless crown
And put a barren scepter in my grip,
Thence to be wrenched with an unlineal hand,
No son of mine succeeding. If 't be so,
For Banquo's issue have I filed [defiled] my mind,
For them the gracious Duncan have I murdered,
Put rancors in the vessel of my peace
Only for them, and mine eternal jewel [immortal soul]
Given to the common enemy of man [the Devil]
To make them kings—the seed of Banquo kings!
Rather than so, come, Fate, into the list,
And champion me to the utterance!
["á l'outrance," to the uttermost, a term in chivalry for a combat to the death[38] [III, i, 48–72].[40]

He succeeds in having Banquo murdered, but between his despair and his madness, a connection is revealed when he is told Banquo's son, Fleance, escaped. Banquo's murderer tells Macbeth: "Fleance is 'scaped." Macbeth responds in an aside:

Then comes my fit again. I had else been perfect,
Whole as the marble, founded as the rock,
As broad and general as the casing air.
But now I am cabined, cribbed, confined, bound in
To saucy doubts and fears.—But Banquo's safe? [In his grave] [III, iv, 21–25].

Apparently, the "fit" he speaks of is hallucinosis, for, moments following this conversation with the cutthroat, and right in front of the seated guests at the banquet table, he alone sees the ghost of Banquo seated in the king's chair, and he does literally have a fit. With conduct most unbecoming a king and a host, to say the least, he blames his guest for the existence of the ghost, he unwittingly exposes his own guilt, and in shouts he threatens and challenges the ghost until the queen dismisses the guests, who conclude the king is unwell.

In Machiavellian style, Macbeth feels he has to kill everyone who might have a legitimate claim to his throne. It's what one does if one wants to stay in power. It's only to be expected, as Machiavelli puts it in *The Prince* (*Il Principe*). Besides, as Macbeth says:

> I am in blood
> Stepped in so far that should I wade no more,
> Returning were as tedious as go o'er [III, iv, 136–138].

If we recall Bernard's definition of the faculties and functions of the Soul, we can tell by Macbeth's next statement that he plans to put the deliberation of reason to sleep in him, so that "if a sin is suggested to the Memory by thought, and the Will is moved to the sin by an emotional desire for it,"[41] he's going to commit the sin. He says: "Strange things I have in head that will to hand, / Which must be acted ere they may be scanned." This also means Macbeth has reached Bernard's "The Twelfth Step of Pride, Habitual Sinning":

> But when by the terrible judgment of God impunity follows the first lapses, the tasted pleasure is repeated freely, and found sweet. As lust awakes, reason is lulled to sleep, and the habit becomes binding. The wretch is drawn into the depths of sin, the captive is given over to the tyranny of vice, so that, swallowed up by a whirlpool of carnal desires and forgetting both his own reason and the fear of God, "the fool saith in his heart, There is no God." He now allows himself to do whatever he pleases, he no longer keeps his mind, hands, or feet from improper thoughts, deeds, or explorations; but whatever comes to his heart, lips, or hand he ponders maliciously, prattles boastfully, or performs viciously. In the same way that the good man who has gone up all these steps finally flies toward life with eager heart and without exertion because of his good habits, so the wicked man who has gone down the same hastens toward death without trepidation because of his evil ways, not restraining himself by reason, not refraining from aught through fear. It is those midway who grow weary and are distressed, now tormented by the fear of hell, now held back by old habits as they strive to go up or down. Only the highest and the lowest fly without hindrance or exertion. The former eager for life, the latter prone to death, they hasten along. Love makes the one eager, lust makes the other prone; sympathy feels no exertion in the one, apathy in the other. In the former "perfect love," in the latter consummate wickedness, "casteth out fear." Truth makes one secure, blindness the other. The twelfth step, therefore, may be called the habitual sinning by which the fear of God is lost and contempt of God incurred.[42]

Therefore, Macbeth even says to Lady Macbeth:

> My strange and self-abuse
> Is the initiate fear a novice's fear that wants hard use.
> We are yet but young in deed [III, iv, 141–143].

In other words, "when I have more experience in murder I shall not be troubled with apparitions."[43]

Experience is next gained via his suspicions concerning Macduff's absence from the banquet, which had already been aroused, prompting his dispatch of a servant spy to the kitchen of Macduff. But before we go there: Macbeth has stated his plan to go again to the witches. He says: "More shall they speak, for now I am bent to know, / By the worst means, the worst." And it's interesting to note how closely Hecate, the goddess of witchcraft, echoes the Twelfth Step of Pride, in saying Macbeth "shall spurn fate, scorn death, and bear / His hopes 'bove wisdom, grace, and fear." Macbeth does in fact learn the worst by the worst means. What he perceives to be the good news is really the bad news, as it turns out. He is told to "Beware Macduff," but then he's told:

> Be bloody, bold, and resolute, laugh to scorn
> The power of man, for none of woman born
> Shall harm Macbeth [IV, i, 79–81].

He says: "Then live Macduff. What need I fear of thee?" But he will kill Macduff nonetheless, "just to make assurance double sure, / And take a bond of fate." More good news/bad news comes in the dubious assurance that:

> Macbeth shall never vanquished be until
> Great Birnam Wood to high Dunsinane Hill
> Shall come against him [IV, i, 92–94].

"That will never be," says Macbeth. "Who can impress the forest, bid the tree / Unfix his earthbound root?" (IV, i, 94–96). In answer to his question "Shall Banquo's issue ever / Reign in this kingdom?" the witches present a show of eight kings, all in the Banquo line, with Banquo at the end, smiling at Macbeth. The witches then vanish and Macbeth curses them.

He is soon approached by messengers who bring him word that Macduff has fled to England. He states again his decision to put the deliberation of reason to sleep in him and do whatever comes to his heart, reflecting again the twelfth step of pride. He says in an aside, from thoughts originating in his own soul:

> Time, thou anticipatest my dread exploits.
> The flighty purpose never is o'ertook
> Unless the deed go with it. From this moment
> The very firstlings of my heart shall be
> The firstlings of my hand. And even now,
> To crown my thoughts with acts, be it thought and done.
> The castle of Macduff I will surprise,
> Seize upon Fife, give to the edge o' the sword
> His wife, his babes, and all unfortunate souls

> That trace him in his line. No boasting like a fool,
> This deed I'll do before this purpose cool [IV, i, 144–154].

Macduff is told in England by Ross, the horror:

> Your castle is surprised, your wife and babes
> Savagely slaughtered [IV, iii, 204–205].

This really is the nadir, the depths of sin. Having taken the twelfth step of pride, as indicated above, "whatever comes to his heart, lips, or hand he ponders maliciously, prattles boastfully, and performs viciously,"[44] (as Lady Macbeth wanted him to do).

Act V fulfills the prophecy: "The powerful shall be powerfully tormented" (Wis. 6:6). It opens with a doctor and a gentlewoman discussing Lady Macbeth's sleepwalking. We are told she keeps a light by her at all times; her eyes are open but their sense is shut; and she is constantly rubbing her hands as if washing them, saying:

> Out, damned spot! Out, I say!... What, will these hands never be clean? [V, i, 39, 46].

She finds "A little water will [not] clear her of this deed." "But it is the heart that is to be cleansed, that God may be seen,"[45] says Bernard. Based on this same sermon, a connection is suggested linking "her eyes are open but their sense is shut," the "damned spot," and the light she keeps by her at all times although her reason has lost the light which created it. Bernard states:

> Detestable spot, which takes away from us the beatifying vision, for it is sin only which troubles and dims the sight: nor does anything else seem to separate betwixt the Eye and Light, betwixt God and Man.[46]

The "damned spot," the "detestable spot," has a further significance as well, which explains the truth of her agonizing complaint:

> Here's the smell of the blood still. All the perfumes of Arabia will not sweeten this little hand. Oh, oh, oh!

It's that the "damned spot" represents the memory of past sins:

> Sins exist in the memory even when past; and the memory of past sins is what constitutes the torment of hell, which is everlasting because the sins cannot be eradicated from the memory. Even the miraculous forgiveness of sins cannot delete them from the memory, for that would be to destroy the memory.[47]

And Lady Macbeth suggests this when she says: "Out, damned spot! Out, I say!... Hell is murky." In other words, she suffers "the torments of hell." Her complete statement reveals that "sins exist in the memory even when past,"[48] as her memory takes her back over "past sins":

> Out, damned spot! Out, I say! One, two—why, then 'tis time to do 't. Hell is murky. Fie, my lord, fie! A soldier, and afeard? What need we fear who knows it, when none can call our power to account? Yet who would have thought the old man to have so much blood in him? [V, i, 39–45].

And again:

> Wash your hands, put on your nightgown, look not so pale. I tell you yet again, Banquo's buried, he cannot come out on 's grave.
>
> To bed, to bed, there's knocking at the gate. Come, come, come, come, give me your hand. What's done cannot be undone. To bed, to bed, to bed.

She is obviously mad. And she personifies the description of such a person, previously quoted:

> For such an one lays violent hands upon herself; nor does she tear and gnaw her flesh, but her mind.... So we tear and wound our unhappy souls with our own hands; but with this difference, that we wound them so much the more grievously, by how much a spiritual Creature is more excellent and more hardly cured.[49]

Macbeth knows the cause, and asks the impossible of the doctor, according to Shakespeare's use of Bernard:

> Cure her...
> Canst thou not minister to a mind diseased,
> Pluck from the memory a rooted sorrow,
> Raze out the written troubles of the brain,
> And with some sweet oblivious antidote
> Cleanse the stuffed bosom of that perilous stuff
> Which weighs upon the heart? [V, iii, 39–44].

The next we hear of her, it's "The Queen, my lord, is dead." And as Bernard described: "For such an one lays violent hands upon herself"[50]; we are told that Macbeth's "fiendlike Queen, by self and violent hands / Took her own life" (V, viii, 69–71).

When Macbeth is told his wife his dead, his response reveals something Bernard teaches about the soul: "A soul which lacks knowledge of truth cannot be said to be alive, but is so far dead in itself; likewise one which does not possess love is without sensitivity. The life of the soul, therefore, is truth; its sensitivity, love."[51] The truth Bernard speaks of is Christ. And the knowledge that is life, Bernard reveals as: "Truth bears witness, saying: 'This is life eternal, that they might know thee the true God, and Jesus Christ, whom thou hast sent.'"[52] Macbeth's response exposes a lack of love and sensitivity towards his wife. It also exposes the deep depression and hopeless despair characteristic of the final impenitence; and exposes the apathy characteristic of the twelfth step of pride. Macbeth can only offer the pessimistic view of life of one who does not know Christ:

She should have died hereafter;
There would have been a time for such a word.
Tomorrow, and tomorrow, and tomorrow
Creeps in this petty pace from day to day,
To the last syllable of recorded time,
And all our yesterdays have lighted fools
The way to dusty death. Out, out, brief candle!
Life's but a walking shadow, a poor player
That struts and frets his hour upon the stage
And then is heard no more. It is a tale
Told by an idiot, full of sound and fury,
Signifying nothing [V, vi, 17–28].

One is forced to pause after such language, such poetry.

A statement Macbeth makes earlier reflects this same mood which indicates the same cause:

I have lived long enough. My way of life
Is fall'n into the sear [withered], the yellow leaf,
And that which should accompany old age,
As honor, love, obedience, troops of friends,
I must not look to have, but in their stead
Curses, not loud but deep, mouth-honor, breath,
Which the poor heart would fain deny, and dare not [V, iii, 22–28].

His life is "withered," because, as Christ states: "If a man abide not in me, he is cast forth as a branch, and is withered; and men gather them, and cast them into the fire, and they are burned" (John 15:6).

All the while the army led by Malcolm and Macduff is marching toward Macbeth and his army. At Birnam Wood Malcolm tells his soldiers:

Let every soldier hew him down a bough,
And bear 't before him. Thereby shall we shadow [conceal]
The numbers of our host, and make discovery
Err in report of us [V, iv, 4–7].

A messenger tells Macbeth:

As I did stand my watch upon the hill,
I looked toward Birnam, and anon methought
The wood began to move [V, vi, 32–34].

Macbeth's answer exposes here on out his twelfth-step-of-pride attitude: "The wicked man who has gone down these steps hastens toward death without trepidation because of his evil ways, not restraining himself by reason, not refraining from aught through fear ... consummate wickedness, "casteth out fear."[53] Macbeth says to the messenger:

If thou speak'st false,
Upon the next tree shalt thou hang alive

Till famine cling thee. If thy speech be sooth,
I care not if thou dost for me as much,
I pull in resolution, and begin
To doubt the equivocation of the fiend
That lies like truth. "Fear not, till Birnam Wood
Do come to Dunsinane." And now a wood
Comes toward Dunsinane. Arm, arm, and out!
If this which he avouches does appear.
There is nor flying hence nor tarrying here.
I 'gin to be aweary of the sun,
And wish the estate o' the world were now undone.
Ring the alarum bell! Blow, wind! Come, wrack!
At least we'll die with harness [armor] on our back [V, v, 38–52].

Even when he says, confronting Macduff: "I bear a charmed life, which must not yield / To one of woman born," and Macduff tells him:

Despair thy charm,
And let the angel whom thou still hast served
Tell thee Macduff was from his mother's womb
Untimely ripped [V, viii, 13–15].

Macbeth is fearless: "Lay on, Macduff, / And damned be him that first cries "Hold, enough!" (V, viii, 33–34). ("Consummate wickedness 'casteth out fear.'")[54] That first to cry is already damned!

At the end, Macduff enters with Macbeth's head, crying: "Hail, King! (to Malcolm). For so thou art. Behold where stands / The usurper's cursed head. The time is free ... Hail, King of Scotland!" King Malcolm gives perhaps the quintessential message of the play, in promising:

...what needful else
That calls upon us, by the grace of grace
We will perform in measure, time, and place [full measure] [V, viii, 71–73].

The "grace of grace" pulls the whole play together in terms of Bernard's explanation:

> In order that our willing, derived from our free choice may be perfect, we need the two-fold gift of grace: namely, true wisdom, which means the turning of the will to good, and full power, which means its confirmation in good.[55]

CHAPTER NOTES

Preface

1. Irenaeus, *Against Heresies*, in the Ante-Nicene Fathers, Vol. 1 (Buffalo, Christian Literature Publishing, 1885).

2. Kim Hall, *Things of Darkness: Economies of Race and Gender in Early Modern England* (Ithaca and London: Cornell University Press, 1995).

3. From the book jacket of Harold Bloom, *Shakespeare: The Invention of the Human* (New York: Riverhead Books, 1998).

4. Bloom, *Invention of the Human*, 493.

5. Ibid., 506.

6. Ibid.

7. Marjorie Garber, *Shakespeare After All* (New York: Anchor Books, 2004), 661.

8. Ibid., 660.

9. Ibid., 661.

10. Ibid.

Introduction

1. Daniel P. Mannix, *Black Cargoes: A History of the Atlantic Slave Trade, 1518–1865* (New York: Viking Press, 1968), xiii.

2. Paul Tillich, *The New Being*, "Our Ultimate Concern," Chapter 20, (New York: Scribner's, 1955), 152–160.

3. Ibid.

4. Ibid.

5. Jonathan Swift, "A Sermon on the Trinity," *The Works of the Rev. Jonathan Swift, D.D. Dean of St. Patrick's, Dublin, Arranged by Thomas Sheridan* (London: J. Johnson, et al., 1801), 25–26.

6. William Rose Benét, *The Reader's Encyclopedia*, 2nd ed. (New York: Thomas Y. Crowell, 1965), 485.

7. Marjorie Garber, *Shakespeare After All* (New York: Anchor Books, 2004), 73.

8. Marvin Rosenberg, *Macbeth*, in *A Norton Critical Edition*, edited by Edward Pechter (New York and London: W. W. Norton, 2004), 285.

9. Sir Paul Harvey, ed. and com., *The Oxford Companion to Classical Literature* (Oxford: at the Clarendon Press, 1955), 263–264.

10. Bernard of Clairvaux, "Sermon 30," *Sermons on the Song of Songs* (Kalamazoo: Cistercian Publications, 1980), 121.

11. Michael Woods, writer and presenter, *In Search of Shakespeare*, PBS Video, 2003.

12. Garber, *Shakespeare After All*, 3.

13. Ibid., 7.

14. Ibid., 74.

15. Mannix, *Black Cargoes*, 32.

16. Ibid.

17. Hugh Thomas, *The Slave Trade: The Story of the Atlantic Slave Trade, 1440–1870* (New York: Simon and Schuster, 1997), 115.

18. Stephen Greenblatt, *Will in the World: How Shakespeare Became Shakespeare* (New York: W. W. Norton, 2004), 90–91.

19. Ibid., 91.

20. Ibid.

21. Ibid., 97–98.

22. Ibid., 115–116.

23. Ibid.

24. Ibid., 173.

25. Philip Schaff, ed., *A Dictionary of the Bible*, 4th ed. (Philadelphia: American Sunday-School Union, 1880 and 1885), 9.

26. Schaff, *Dictionary*, 406.

27. Garber, *Shakespeare After All*, 73.

Titus Andronicus

1. Sir Paul Harvey, ed. *The Oxford Companion to Classical Literature* (Oxford: Clarendon Press, 1955), 220–221.

2. Bernard of Clairvaux, *The Steps of Humility*, trans. George Bosworth Burch (Cambridge: Harvard University Press, 1950), 153.

3. Harvey, *Classical Literature*, 220–221.

4. Ibid.

5. Bernard, *Steps of Humility*, 153.

6. Harvey, *Classical Literature*, 197.

7. Ibid., 171.

8. William Rose Benét, *The Reader's Encyclopedia*, 2nd ed. (New York: Thomas Y. Crowell, 1965), 327.

9. Swift, "On the Testimony of Conscience," in *Works*, vol. 10.

10. Harvey, *Classical Literature*, 16.

11. Ibid., 739–740.

12. Ibid., 348.

13. Ibid., 396.

14. Benét, *The Reader's Encyclopedia*, 505.

15. Harvey, *Classical Literature*, 143.

16. Benét, *The Reader's Encyclopedia*, 6.
17. Ibid., 201.
18. Bernard, *Steps of Humility*, 39.
19. Bernard of Clairvaux, *On Grace and Free Choice*, trans. Daniel O'Donovan (Kalamazoo: Cistercian Publications, 1980), 54–55.
20. Harvey, *Classical Literature*, 324.
21. Benét, *The Reader's Encyclopedia*, 485.
22. Bernard, *On Grace*, 58.
23. Bernard, *Steps of Humility*, 153.
24. Garber, *Shakespeare After All*, 82.
25. Bernard, "Sermon 31," *Song of Songs*, 126.
26. Bernard, "Sermon 32," *Song of Songs*, 126.
27. Garber, *Shakespeare After All*, 83.
28. Bernard *On Grace*, 74.
29. Bernard, *Steps of Humility*, 30.
30. Robert Grosseteste, quoted in David L. Jeffrey, *The Early English Lyric & Franciscan Spirituality* (Lincoln: University of Nebraska Press, 1975), 93.
31. Harvey, *Classical Literature*, 441.
32. Garber, *Shakespeare After All*, 87.
33. Bernard, *On Grace*, 74.
34. Ibid., 59.
35. Shakespeare, *The Tempest* (I, ii, 363–364).
36. Nolan B. Harmon, ed., *The Interpreter's Bible: The Holy Scriptures in the King James and Revised Standard Versions with General Articles and Introduction, Exegesis, Exposition for Each Book of the Bible, in Twelve Volumes* (Nashville: Abingdon, repr. 1978), 62.

The Merchant of Venice

1. Kim F. Hall, *Things of Darkness: Economies of Race and Gender in Early Modern England* (Ithaca and London: Cornell University Press, 1995), 85, 165, 166, 207.

Kim F. Hall, "Guess Who's Coming to Dinner? Colonization and Miscegenation in *The Merchant of Venice*," in *A Norton Critical Edition of The Merchant of Venice*, edited by Leah S. Marcus, ed. (New York: W. W. Norton, 2006), 290–291.

2. Leah S. Marcus, "Preface," *A Norton Critical Edition of The Merchant of Venice*, edited by Leah S. Marcus, ed. (New York: W. W. Norton, 2006), ix.
3. Daniel P. Mannix, *Black Cargoes: A History of the Atlantic Slave Trade, 1518–1865* (New York: Viking Press, 1968), 21–22.
4. Hall, *Norton*, 291.
5. William Rose Benét, *The Reader's Encyclopedia*, 2nd ed. (New York: Thomas Y. Crowell, 1965), 345.
6. Stephen Greenblatt, *Will in the World: How Shakespeare Became Shakespeare* (New York: W. W. Norton, 2004), 258.
7. Mannix, *Black Cargoes*, xiii.
8. Hugh Thomas, *The Slave Trade: The Story of the Atlantic Slave Trade, 1440–1870* (New York: Simon and Schuster, 1997), 115.
9. Woods, *In Search of Shakespeare.*
10. Thomas, *The Slave Trade*, 42.
11. Ibid., 72.
12. Ibid.
13. Ibid., 113.
14. Garry Wills, *Venice: Lion City, The Religion of Empire* (New York: Simon and Schuster, 2001), 19.
15. Ibid., 13.
16. Ibid., 73–74.
17. Ibid., 112.
18. Ibid., 124.
19. Hall, *Things of Darkness*, 85.
20. Greenblatt, *Will in the World*, 261.
21. Bernard of Clairvaux, *The Steps of Humility*, trans. George Bosworth Burch (Cambridge: Harvard University Press, 1950), 39.
22. St. Augustine, *The City of God* (London: Everyman, 1945), 98.
23. Bernard, *Steps of Humility*, 60.
24. Ibid., 12–13.
25. Ibid., 61.
26. Nolan B. Harmon, ed., *The Interpreter's Bible: The Holy Scriptures in the King James and Revised Standard Versions with General Articles and Introduction, Exegesis, Exposition for Each Book of the Bible, in Twelve Volumes* (Nashville: Abingdon, repr. 1978), exegesis on Genesis 30:27–43.
27. Ibid., 709.
28. Mannix, *Black Cargoes*, 33.
29. Greenblatt, *Will in the World*, 265.
30. St. Augustine, *City of God*, 98.
31. Shakespeare, *Titus Andronicus* (II, iii, 38–39).
32. Bernard of Clairvaux, *On Grace and Free Choice*, trans. Daniel O'Donovan (Kalamazoo: Cistercian Publications, 1980), 74.
33. Shakespeare, *The Merchant of Venice*, footnote 91, p56.
34. Shakespeare, *Titus Andronicus* (IV, ii, 77).
35. Ibid., V, i, 40.
36. Shakespeare, Titus Andronicus, V, iii, 183–189.
37. Bernard, *On Grace*, 59.
38. Lewis Allan, "Strange Fruit" (Marks Music/BMI, 1937).
39. Irenaeus, *Against Heresies*, in *The Anti-Nicene Fathers, Vol. 1: The Apostlic Fathers, Justin Martry-Irenaeus* (Buffalo: Christian Literature Publishing, 1885), 309, 315.
40. Ibid., 310.
41. Ibid., 309.

42. Bernard, *Steps of Humility*, 149.
43. Ibid., 39.
44. Bernard of Clairvaux, "Sermon 23," *Sermons on the Song of Songs* (Kalamazoo: Cistercian Publications, 1980), 25.
45. Bernard, *Steps of Humility*, 74.
46. Leah S. Marcus, *A Norton Critical Edition of The Merchant of Venice* (New York: W. W. Norton, 2006), ix.
47. Greenblatt, *Will in the World*, 253.
48. Alan Sinfield, "How to Read *The Merchant of Venice* Without Being Heterosexist," in Marcus, *A Norton Critical Edition*, 270.
49. Bernard, *Steps of Humility*, 72.
50. Ibid., 72–73.
51. Ibid., 74.
52. Ibid., 149.

Hamlet

1. Elaine L. Robinson, *Gulliver as Slave Trader: Racism Reviled by Jonathan Swift* (Jefferson, North Carolina, and London: McFarland, 2006), 37, 42.
2. Bernard, *Steps of Humility*, 23.
3. Ibid., 34.
4. Ibid., 12.
5. Ibid., 23.
6. Nolan B. Harmon, ed., *The Interpreter's Bible: The Holy Scriptures in the King James and Revised Standard Versions with General Articles and Introduction, Exegesis, Exposition for Each Book of the Bible, in Twelve Volumes* (Nashville: Abingdon, repr. 1978), exegesis on Genesis 38:8.
7. Shakespeare, *King Lear* (IV, ii, 32–36).
8. Bernard of Clairvaux, *On Grace and Free Choice*, trans. Daniel O'Donovan (Kalamazoo: Cistercian Publications, 1980), 62.
9. Harmon, *Interpreter's Bible*, exegesis on Psalm 8.
10. Bernard, "Sermon 36," *Sermons on the Song of Songs* (Kalamazoo: Cistercian Publications, 1980), 178.
11. Ibid., 179.
12. Ibid., 178.
13. Ibid.
14. Bernard, *On Grace*, 74.
15. Ibid.
16. Bernard, "Sermon 38," *Song of Songs*, 187.
17. Shakespeare, *Macbeth* (IV, i, 146–149).
18. Bernard, "Sermon 26," *Song of Songs*, 71.
19. Bernard of Clairvaux, *A Mirror that Flatters Not* (London, 1677), Chap II.
20. Bernard, "Sermon 24," *Song of Songs*, Heb. 11:6.
21. Ibid., 48–49.
22. Ibid.
23. Ibid., 44–45.
24. Bernard, *Steps of Humility*, 12.
25. Harmon, *Interpreter's Bible*, exegesis on Matthew 10:28–32.
26. *Interpreter's Bible*, exegesis on Matthew 10:28–32.
27. Bernard, *On Grace*, 74.
28. Anonymous, *Everyman*, in David Bevington, *Medieval Drama* (Boston: Houghton Mifflin, 1975), 941, lines 22–35, 56–59.
29. Ibid., lines 894–901.
30. Ibid., lines 912–915.

Othello

1. Stephen Greenblatt, *Will in the World: How Shakespeare Became Shakespeare* (New York: W. W. Norton, 2004), 325.
2. *Merriam-Webster's Collegiate Dictionary, Tenth Edition* (Springfield: Merriam-Webster, 2001).
3. Martin Orkin, *Shakespeare Against Apartheid* (Craighall, South Africa: Ad. Donker, 1987), 76.
4. Toni Morrison, *Beloved* (New York: Alfred A. Knopf, 1987), 151.
5. Jonathan Swift, *Gulliver's Travels*, in *Gulliver's Travels and Other Writings by Jonathan Swift*, edited by Louis Landa (Boston: Houghton Mifflin, 1960), 47.
6. Orkin, *Shakespeare Against Apartheid*, 288.
7. Michael Neill, "Unproper Beds: Race, Adultery, and the Hideous in *Othello*," in William Shakespeare, *Othello*, edited by Edward Pechter, *A Norton Critical Edition* (New York, London: W. W. Norton, 2004), 313.
8. Neill, "Unproper Beds," 328.
9. Orkin, *Shakespeare Against Apartheid*, 313.
10. Neill, "Unproper Beds," 328.
11. Shakespeare, *The Merchant of Venice* (III, ii, 77–82).
12. Neill, "Unproper Beds," 325.
13. Hugh Thomas, *The Slave Trade: The Story of the Atlantic Slave Trade: 1440–1870* (New York: Simon and Schuster, 1997), 28.
14. Aristotle, *The Politics* (London: Penguin, 1981), 64–69.
15. Ibid., Introduction.
16. Thomas Rymer, "A Bloody Farce," in *A Norton Critical Edition on Othello*, edited by Edward Pechter (New York: W. W. Norton, 2004), 202.
17. Ibid., 210.
18. Ibid., 202.
19. Charles Gilden, "Comments on Rymer's Othello," in Pechter, *Othello*, 231.

20. Ibid., 212.
21. Samuel Taylor Coleridge, "Comments on *Othello*," in Pechter, *Othello*, 232.
22. Ibid.
23. A. C. Bradley, "The Most Painfully Exciting and the Most Terrible of Shakespeare's Tragedies," in *A Norton Critical Edition of Othello* (New York, London: W. W. Norton, 2004), 242.
24. Charles Lamb, "Othello's Color: Theatrical versus Literary Representation," in Pechter, *Othello*, 221.
25. Ibid.
26. Ibid.
27. Ibid.
28. Bradley, "Painfully Exciting," 242.
29. Ibid.
30. Ibid., 243.
31. Daniel P. Mannix, *Black Cargoes: A History of the Atlantic Slave Trade, 1518–1865* (New York: Viking Press, 1962), 32.
32. G. B. Harrison, ed., *Shakespeare: Major Plays and the Sonnets* (New York: Harcourt, Brace, 1948), 704.
33. Shakespeare, *Hamlet* (I, i, 76–86).
34. Swift, "Thoughts on Various Subjects," in Thomas Sheridan, ed., *The Works of Rev. Jonathan Swift in Nineteen Volumes* (London: J. Johnson, J. Nichols, et al., 1801), 461.
35. Harrison, *Shakespeare*, footnote, 706.
36. Jonathan Swift, *Gulliver's Travels*, in *Gulliver's Travels and Other Writings by Jonathan Swift*, edited by Louis Landa (Boston: Houghton Mifflin, 1960), 47.
37. Marjorie Garber, *Shakespeare After All* (New York: Anchor Books/Random House, 2004), 596.
38. Robert Graves, *The Reader Over Your Shoulder* (New York: Vintage Books, 1979), 4.
39. Harrison, *Shakespeare, Othello*, footnote (I, iii, 90).
40. Bernard of Clairvaux, "Sermon 31," *Sermons on the Song of Songs* (Kalamazoo: Cistercian Publications, 1980), 125.
41. Swift, *Gulliver's Travels*, 47.
42. Bernard, "Sermon 28," *Song of Songs*, 92.
43. Harrison, *Shakespeare*, 710.
44. Bernard of Clairvaux, *The Steps of Humility*, trans. George Bosworth Burch (Cambridge: Harvard University Press, 1950), 23.
45. Roger Rosenblatt, *Black Fiction* (Cambridge: Harvard University Press, 1974), 9–10.
46. J. A. Cuddon, *The Penguin Dictionary of Literary Terms and Literary Theory*, 4th ed. (London: Penguin, 1999), 928.
47. Harrison, *Shakespeare, Othello*, footnote (III, iii, 90–92).
48. Oxford English Dictionary.
49. "Thoughts arise from three sources: they originate in our own souls, or they are inspired in us by evil spirits, or they are inspired in us by God." Bernard, *Steps of Humility*, 23.
50. *Merriam-Webster's Collegiate Dictionary*, 10th ed.
51. Bernard, *Steps of Humility*, 28.
52. Cuddon, *Penguin Dictionary*.
53. Bernard quoting Jer.4:22 in Bernard of Clairvaux, *On Grace and Free Choice*, trans. Daniel O'Donovan (Kalamazoo: Cistercian Publications, 1980), 76.
54. Shakespeare, *Othello* (III, iii, 359–367).
55. Bernard, "Sermon 24," *Song of Songs*, 42.
56. Ibid., 3–4.
57. Ibid, 48.
58. Swift, *Gulliver's Travels*, 47.
59. Harrison, *Shakespeare, Othello* (IV, I, 35–44).
60. Bernard, *Steps of Humility*, 13.
61. Ibid.
62. Bernard, *On Grace*, 58.
63. Ibid., 55.
64. Bernard, "Sermon 35," *Song of Songs*, 165.
65. Bernard, *On Grace*, 59–60.
66. Bernard, *Steps of Humility*, 13.
67. Ibid., 9.
68. Bernard, "Sermon 38," *Song of Songs*, 187.
69. Ibid.

King Lear

1. Marjorie Garber, *Shakespeare After All* (New York: Anchor Books/Random House, 2004), 649.
2. Stanley Wells and Gary Taylor, ed., *The Oxford Shakespeare: The Complete Works*, 2nd ed. (Oxford: Clarendon Press, 2005), 909.
3. G. B. Harrison, ed., *Shakespeare: Major Plays and the Sonnets* (New York: Harcourt, Brace, 1948), 780.
4. Paul Tillich, *A History of Christian Thought: From its Judaic and Hellenistic Origins to Existentialism*, edited by Carl E. Braaten (New York: Simon and Schuster, 1968), 197.
5. Bernard, *The Steps of Humility*, trans. George Bosworth Burch (Cambridge: Harvard University Press, 1950), 181.
6. Bernard, "Sermon 28," *Sermons on the Song of Songs* (Kalamazoo: Cistercian Publications, 1980), 94–95.
7. Thomas Sheridan, ed., *The Works of Rev. Jonathan Swift in Nineteen Volumes*, vol. 10

(London: J. Johnson, J. Nichols, et al., 1801), 166.

8. Bernard, "Sermon 36," *Song of Songs*, 177–178.

9. Harrison, *Shakespeare*, *Hamlet* (I, i, 75–86).

10. Stephen G. Nichols, Jr., *Romanesque Signs*, (New Haven and London: Yale University Press, 1983), 6.

11. Swift, "Thoughts on Various Subjects," in Sheridan, *The Works of Rev. Jonathan Swift*, 452.

12. Bernard, *On Grace and Free Choice*, trans. Daniel O'Donovan (Kalamazoo: Cistercian Publications, 1977), 62, 74.

13. Stephen Greenblatt, *Will in the World: How Shakespeare Became Shakespeare* (New York: W. W. Norton, 2004), 37.

14. G.B. Harrison, *Shakespeare*, 794.

15. Bernard, "Sermon 23," *Song of Songs*, 30.

16. Bernard, *A Mirror That Flatters Not* (London, 1677), Chap. IV.

17. Bernard, *Mirror*, 6.

18. Morley Winograd and Michael D. Hais, *Millennial Makeover: My Space, YouTube, and the Future of American Politics* (New Brunswick, NJ: Rutgers University Press, 2008), 1.

19. Jonathan Swift, *Gulliver's Travels*, in *Introduction to Jonathan Swift, Gulliver's Travels and Other Writings*, edited by Louis Landa (Boston: Houghton Mifflin, 1960), 47.

20. Harrison, *Shakespeare*, 799.

21. Shakespeare, *King Lear* (II, ii, 164).

22. Bernard, *Steps of Humility*, 181.

23. Harrison, *Shakespeare*, 801 footnote.

24. Ibid.

25. Garber, *Shakespeare After All*, 667.

26. Bernard, *Steps of Humility*, 153.

27. Harrison, *Shakespeare*, 811.

28. Bernard, "Sermon 38," *Song of Songs*, 188.

29. Harrison, *Shakespeare*, 819.

30. Bernard, "Sermon 31," *Song of Songs*,126.

31. Bernard, "Sermon 28," *Song of Songs*, 91–93.

32. Ibid., 94–96.

33. Tillich, *History of Christian Thought*, 152.

34. Bernard, "Sermon 28," *Song of Songs*, 88.

35. Dante Alghieri, *The Inferno*, in *The Divine Comedy*, trans. with a commentary by Charles S. Singleton (Princeton: Princeton University Press, 1970), Canto XXXIV, 61–63.

36. Charles Rowan Beye, *Ancient Greek Literature and Society* (New York: Doubleday, 1975), 262.

37. Bernard, "Sermon 28," *Song of Songs*, 94–96.

Macbeth

1. The Book of Wisdom 6:6, translated by Bernard of Clairvaux from the Latin Vulgate.

2. Dante, *The Inferno*, in *The Divine Comedy*, trans. with a commentary by Charles S. Singleton (Princeton: Princeton University Press, 1970), Canto III, 9.

3. Shakespeare, *Hamlet* (I, i, 158–164).

4. *Hamlet* (I, i, 158–164).

5. Bernard, *Steps of Humility*, trans. George Bosworth Burch (Cambridge: Harvard University Press, 1950), 10.

6. Ibid., 12.

7. Ibid., 23.

8. Harrison, *Shakespeare*, 836.

9. Bernard in Birch, 12.

10. Bernard, *On Grace*, 65.

11. Ibid., 74.

12. Ibid.

13. Marvin Rosenberg, "Culture, Character, and Conscience in Shakespeare," in *A Norton Critical Edition of Macbeth* (New York: W.W. Norton, 2004), 285.

14. Sir Paul Harvey, ed. *The Oxford Companion to Classical Literature* (Oxford: Clarendon Press, 1955), 263.

15. Shakespeare, *King Lear* (IV, ii, 59–61).

16. Garber, 73.

17. Ovid, *The Metamorphosis*, trans. Horace Gregory (New York: Penguin Books, 2001), 31.

18. *Hamlet* (I, i, 158–164).

19. Bernard, *Steps of Humility*, 13.

20. Ibid., 26–27.

21. Bernard, *On Grace*, 87.

22. Ibid.

23. Bernard, *Steps of Humility*, 28.

24. Harrison, *Shakespeare*, 839.

25. *Hamlet* (III, iii, 11–23).

26. Bernard, *Steps of Humility*, 13.

27. Ibid., 27.

28. Ibid.

29. Ibid.

30. Harvey, *Classical Literature*, 189.

31. Bernard, *Steps of Humility*, 34.

32. Bernard, *On Grace*, 55.

33. Bernard, *A Mirror That Flatters Not*, 32.

34. *Hamlet* (I, i, 158–164).

35. Bernard, *A Mirror That Flatters Not*, 32.

36. Bernard, Ibid., 6.

37. Ibid.

38. Bernard, *On Grace*, 74.

39. Bernard, "Sermon 38," 187.

40. Harrison, *Shakespeare*, 845.

41. Bernard in Burch, 34.

42. Bernard, *Steps of Humility*, 225.

43. Harrison, *Shakespeare*, 849.

44. Bernard, *Steps of Humility*, 225.
45. Bernard, *Mirror*, 32.
46. Ibid.
47. Bernard, *Steps of Humility*, 12.
48. Ibid.
49. Bernard, *Mirror*, 6.
50. Ibid.
51. Bernard, *Steps of Humility*, 7.
52. Ibid., 8.
53. Ibid., 225.
54. Ibid.
55. Bernard, *On Grace*, 75.

Bibliography

Allan, Lewis. "Strange Fruit." Marks Music/BMI, 1937.

Aristotle. *The Politics*. London: Penguin, 1981.

Augustine, St. *The City of God*. London: Everyman edition, 1945.

Benét, William Rose. *The Reader's Encyclopedia*, 2nd ed. New York: Thomas Y. Crowell, 1965.

Bernard of Clairvaux, *Sermons on the Song of Songs*. Kalamazoo: Cistercian Publications, 1980.

_____. *A Mirror that Flatters Not*. London, 1677.

_____. *On Grace and Free Choice*, trans. Daniel O'Donovan. Kalamazoo: Cistercian Publications, 1980.

_____. *The Steps of Humility*, trans. George Bosworth Burch. Cambridge: Harvard University Press, 1950.

Beye, Charles Rowan. *Ancient Greek Literature and Society*. New York: Doubleday, 1975.

Bradley, A. C. "The Most Painfully Exciting and the Most Terrible of Shakespeare's Tragedies." In *A Norton Critical Edition on Othello*. New York: W. W. Norton, 2004.

Coleridge, Samuel Taylor. "Comments on *Othello*." In *A Norton Critical Edition on Othello*. New York: W. W. Norton, 2004.

Cuddon, J. A., ed. *The Penguin Dictionary of Literary Terms and Literary Theory*, 4th ed. London: Penguin, 1999.

Dante, Alighieri. *The Divine Comedy*. Trans. Charles S. Singleton. Princeton: Princeton University Press, 1970.

_____. *Everyman*. In David Bevington, *Medieval Drama*. Boston: Houghton Mifflin, 1975.

Garber, Marjorie. *Shakespeare After All*. New York: Anchor Books/Random House, 2004.

Gilden, Charles. "Comments on Rymer's *Othello*." In *A Norton Critical Edition on Othello*. New York: W. W. Norton, 2004.

Graves, Robert. *The Reader Over Your Shoulder*. New York: Vintage Books, 1979.

Greenblatt, Stephen. *Will in the World: How Shakespeare Became Shakespeare*. New York: W. W. Norton, 2004.

"Guess Who's Coming to Dinner? Colonization and Miscegenation in *The Merchant of Venice*." In *A Norton Critical Edition on The Merchant of Venice*, ed. Leah S. Marcus. New York: W. W. Norton, 2006.

Hall, Kim F. *Things of Darkness: Economies of Race and Gender in Early Modern England*. Ithaca and London: Cornell University Press, 1995.

Harmon, Nolan B., ed. *The Interpreter's Bible: The Holy Scriptures in the King James and Revised Standard Versions with General Articles and Introduction, Exegesis, Exposition for Each Book of the Bible, in Twelve Volumes*. Nashville: Abingdon, repr. 1978.

Harrison, G. B., ed. *Shakespeare: Major Plays and the Sonnets*. New York: Harcourt, Brace, 1948.

Harvey, Sir Paul, ed. *The Oxford Companion to Classical Literature*. Oxford: Clarendon Press, 1955.

Irenaeus. *Against Heresies*. In *The Ante-Nicene Fathers, Vol. 1: The Apostlic Fathers, Justin Martry-Irenaeus*. Buffalo: Christian Literature Publishing, 1885.

Jeffrey, David L. *The Early English Lyric & Franciscan Spirituality*. Lincoln: University of Nebraska Press, 1975.

Lamb, Charles. "Othello's Color: Theatrical versus Literary Representation." In *A Norton Critical Edition of Othello*. New York: W. W. Norton, 2004.

Mannix, Daniel P. *Black Cargoes: A History of the Atlantic Slave Trade, 1518–1865*. New York: Viking Press, 1968.

Marcus, Leah S., ed. *A Norton Critical Edition of Merchant of Venice*. New York: W. W. Norton, 2006.

Morrison, Toni. *Beloved*. New York: Alfred A. Knopf, 1987.

Neill, Michael. "Unproper Beds: Race, Adultery, and the Hideous in *Othello*." In *A Norton Critical Edition of Othello*, ed. Edward Pechter. New York and London: W. W. Norton, 2004.

Nichols, Stephen G. *Romanesque Signs*. New Haven and London: Yale University Press, 1983.

Orkin, Martin. *Shakespeare Against Apartheid*. Craighall, South Africa: Ad. Donker, 1987.

Ovid. *The Metamorphosis*. trans. Horace Gregory. New York: Penguin Books, 2001.

Riding, Alan. "Britain Confronts Legacy of Slave Trade." *New York Times* (20 March 2007). **PAGES?**

Robinson, Elaine L. *Gulliver as Slave Trader: Racism Reviled by Jonathan Swift*. Jefferson, NC: McFarland, 2006.

Rosenberg, Marvin. "Culture, Character, and Conscience in Shakespeare." In *A Norton Critical Edition on Macbeth*. New York: W. W. Norton, 2004.

Rosenblatt, Roger. *Black Fiction*. Cambridge: Harvard University Press, 1974.

Rymer, Thomas. "A Bloody Farce." In *A Norton Critical Edition on Othello*, ed. Edward Pechter. New York: W. W. Norton, 2004.

Schaff, Philip, ed. *A Dictionary of the Bible*. 4th ed. Philadelphia: American Sunday-School Union, 1880–1885.

Sinfield, Alan. "How to Read *The Merchant of Venice* Without Being Heterosexist." In a Norton Critical Edition, 2006.

Swift, Jonathan. *Gulliver's Travels*. In *Gulliver's Travels and Other Writings by Jonathan Swift*, ed. Louis Landa. Boston: Houghton Mifflin, 1960.

_____. *The Works of Rev. Jonathan Swift in Nineteen Volumes*. Thomas Sheridan, ed. London: J. Johnson, J. Nichols, et al., 1801.

Thomas, Hugh. *The Slave Trade: The Story of the Atlantic Slave Trade, 1440–1870*. New York: Simon and Schuster, 1997.

Tillich, Paul. *A History of Christian Thought: From its Judaic and Hellenistic Origins to Existentialism*, ed. Carl E. Braaten. New York: Simon and Schuster, 1968.

_____. *The New Being*. New York: Scribner's, 1995.

Wells, Stanley, and Gary Taylor, eds. *The Oxford Shakespeare: The Complete Works*. 2nd ed. Oxford: Clarendon Press, 2005.

Wills, Garry. *Venice: Lion City, The Religion of Empire*. New York: Simon and Schuster, 2001.

Winograd, Morley, and Michael D. Hais. *Millennial Makeover: My Space, YouTube, and the Future of American Politics*. New Brunswick, NJ: Rutgers University Press, 2008.

Woods, Michael. *In Search of Shakespeare*. PBS Video, 2003.

INDEX